Word-by-Word Translations of Songs and Arias

Part II — Italian

A companion to
The Singer's Repertoire

by
Arthur Schoep
and
Daniel Harris

The Scarecrow Press, Inc.
Lanham, Md., & London   1972

SCARECROW PRESS, INC.

Published in the United States of America
by Scarecrow Press, Inc.
A wholly owned subsidiary of
The Rowman & Littlefield Publishing Group, Inc.
4501 Forbes Boulevard, Suite 200, Lanham, Maryland 20706
www.scarecrowpress.com

PO Box 317
Oxford
OX2 9RU, UK

ISBN 0-8108-0463-8

Library of Congress Catalog Card Number 66-13746

Contents

Preface

Word-by-Word Translations of Songs and Arias, Part II: Italian of The Singer's Repertoire Series, has been awaited since Part I - German and French was published in 1966. A book of translations of the Italian repertoire seems to be particularly relevant because the monodic revolution of the Camerata triggered the birth of most of this early repertoire, the significant part of which was that the words were of great importance. Therefore, it is still essential that the words of the early repertoire be understood.

The same is true of the classical period. Since Mozart is very well represented in this volume, it might be well to quote from his letter to Aloysia Weber concerning the interpretation of the Andromeda scene, "Ah, lo previdi," which he wrote for her. "I advise you to watch the expression marks--to think carefully of the meaning and force of the words--to put yourself in all seriousness into Andromeda's situation and passion!--and to imagine that you really are that very person."* Surely the "meaning and force of the words" are as valuable to interpretation today as in the time of Mozart.

Too frequently the key to the interpretation of an Italian song is missing because a word-for-word translation is not known or is misunderstood. When the meaning of the words is superimposed on the human voice as a musical instrument, singing becomes a most colorful and communicative art. The authors hope their efforts will enable singers and teachers of singing to make significant progress in attaining this high goal.

The Singer's Repertoire Series (Scarecrow Press) began in 1956 with multiple listings for coloratura soprano, lyric soprano, dramatic soprano, mezzo soprano, contralto, lyric tenor, dramatic tenor, baritone and bass. The second

---

*Mozart's Letters, edited by Eric Blom, translated by Emily Anderson, Baltimore, Penguin Books, 1956, p. 124.

edition of The Singer's Repertoire was enlarged and includes over 1,000 lists published in four volumes: Volume I, Soprano; Volume II, Mezzo Soprano and Contralto; Volume III, Lyric Tenor and Dramatic Tenor; and Volume IV, Baritone and Bass. Volume V, Program Notes for The Singer's Repertoire (Coffin & Singer, Scarecrow Press) listed over 1,000 program notes that could be used in concert and recital programs. Volume VI, Phonetic Readings of Songs and Arias (Coffin, Errolle, Singer, & Delattre, Pruett Press, Boulder, Colorado), on pronunciation of repertoire, gives the classical pronunciation of songs in Italian, German, and French. Word-by-Word Translations, Part I - German and French, is Volume VII of The Singer's Repertoire, and Word-by-Word Translations, Part II - Italian, by Schoep and Harris, is Volume VIII.

As the creator of The Singer's Repertoire, I have invited Arthur Schoep and Daniel Harris to be the authors of this volume of Italian translations. Both are widely known to singers and teachers of singing and have eminent qualifications for writing this volume. Mr. Schoep has concentrated on the Italian opera repertoire, and Mr. Harris has concentrated on the Italian song repertoire.

Arthur Schoep is professor of music at North Texas State University, Denton, Texas. He received his musical training at the University of South Dakota, the Eastman School of Music, the New England Conservatory of Music, and the University of Colorado. As a Fulbright scholar, he studied at the University of Amsterdam, the Royal University at Utrecht, and the Amsterdam Conservatory of Music in The Netherlands. He was formerly artistic director of Denver Lyric Theatre. He is internationally known as an opera educator, having headed the opera departments of several universities, and having founded, directed, or taught in more than 40 summer opera workshops in the United States and Canada. He was for six years a member of the opera department faculty at the Berkshire Music Center at Tanglewood. He is the co-author with Boris Goldovsky of Bringing Arias to Life (G. Schirmer, New York). He has written a number of articles for the Bulletin of the National Association of Teachers of Singing, Opera Canada, and the Journal of the National Opera Association, of which he is president.

Daniel Harris is acting head of the Voice Department at the University of Miami, Coral Gables, Florida. He received his musical training at Otterbein Conservatory of

Music, in private study in New York, and during eight years of advanced study and professional activity in Italy, France, and Belgium. In the United States he has appeared with the Chicago City Opera, the Metropolitan Opera Company, the Boston Symphony Orchestra, and the New York Philharmonic Orchestra. After a year as assistant to Pasquale Amato at Louisiana State University, Mr. Harris became a member of the faculty of Oberlin College Conservatory, where he taught voice for 29 years, introduced the production of opera, and taught the conservatory Italian and French courses. He was one of the founders of the National Opera Association and later served as its president. In 1966, Mr. Harris served as language coach for the Metropolitan Opera National Company; in 1967 he served in the same capacity with the American National Opera Company. He is the author of an English translation of Monteverdi's <u>Il Combattimento di Tancredi e Clorinda.</u>

We are grateful to G. Ricordi & Co. for permission to use Italian texts of songs by Donaudy and arias from <u>Gianni Schicchi</u>, <u>Suor Angelica</u>, and <u>Turandot</u> by Puccini; we are grateful also to G. Schirmer, Inc. for permission to use their copyrighted translations in this volume.

Berton Coffin, Professor and
Head, Division of Voice
University of Colorado
Boulder, Colorado

January, 1971

Procedures
For Using These Translations

In making these word-by-word translations, it has been found necessary to add or delete words for clarification of meaning. The rule for use is as follows: in the literal English translation in line 2, read the words in parentheses ( ) and omit the words in brackets [ ].

Frequently the Italian language resists word-by-word translation. The word order may differ so radically from English that the translation of each word may not produce an intelligible meaning. The frequent inversion of subject and object may lead to an unsuspected incorrect interpretation. A characteristic difference between Italian and English is the use of the pronoun. In Italian, the verb alone may imply the pronoun (e. g., the verb "sento" is translated "I feel," even if "Io," the pronoun for "I," is not present). When the pronoun is missing in the Italian text, it is supplied with the translation of the verb and connected to it with a hyphen: "I-feel." It is common in Italian to attach both direct and indirect objects to verbs (e. g., "dammelo" is translated "give-it-to-me"). Whenever an Italian word is translated by the use of several English words, the translation is linked together with hyphens. The hyphen is also used when there is an elision in the Italian text (e. g., "un' alma" becomes "a-soul").

In Italian the article "the" is used in many cases where it is omitted in English. One may find both "la gioia mia" ("the joy my") and "la mia gioia" ("the my joy"). It is to be understood that although the inverted word order is not changed into fluent English, the translation of both "la gioia mia" and "la mia gioia" is "my joy." In poetic usage, especially, various spellings are possible for the same word. The word "heart," for instance, can be spelled "cuore," "core," "cuor," and "cor" in Italian.

In many cases, words that are meaningless or redundant, especially reflexive pronouns, should be omitted when reading word-by-word translations. These words appear in brackets. In some cases, words not found in the Italian text must be added for understanding or fluency. These words appear in parentheses. When the word-by-word translation is obscure, an explanatory third line has been added. It is used as sparingly as possible, however; when the meaning seems clear, even though the word order differs considerably from fluent English, the third line will not be utilized. In a few cases, the paraphrase of an entire text has been added below the word-by-word translation.

In some instances, where operatic arias have occasional interpolated lines sung by other characters, the interpolated lines have been omitted. Translations of arias from some operas composed to a text other than Italian, but now often sung in Italian (e. g. , Dinorah, La Fille du Regiment), are not included in this volume.

Index

The texts in this volume are listed alphabetically by composer. Arias from the same opera are listed alphabetically under the opera. Compositions by Mozart are listed in the following order: concert arias, opera arias, and songs. An index of titles and first lines appears in the back of the book. When an aria has a recitative preceding it, and a well-known title (other than the first line of text) as well, it is listed three times in the index. Nedda's aria from Pagliacci, for instance, is listed as "Ballatella," its common title; as "Qual fiamma avea nel guardo," the first line of the recitative; and as "Stridono lassù," the first line of the aria.

Collections

In addition to many selections published separately, material from the following collections has been used.

Title	Editor	Publisher
Belcanto (10 arie antiche italiane)	Tomelleri	G. Ricordi
Alte Meister des Bel canto, Vols. I-III	Landshoff	C. F. Peters Corp.
24 Italian Songs and Arias		G. Schirmer & Co.
Arie Antiche, Vols. I-III	Parisotti	G. Ricordi
Mozart, 21 Concert Arias for Soprano, Vols. I-II		G. Schirmer & Co.

Handel, 6 Italienische Arien, Vols. I-II	Hans Gal	Hinrichsen
12 Arie Italiane dei Secoli XVII & XVIII	Zanon	G. Ricordi
Alessandro Scarlatti, Five Songs	Moriarty	Boston Music Co.
A. Scarlatti, Ten arias for high voice	Robinson	G. Schirmer & Co.
A. Scarlatti, 4 Cantate	Tintori	G. Ricordi
Antonio Vivaldi, 5 arias	Edmunds	Boston Music Co.
A. Vivaldi, 6 arie	Gentili	G. Ricordi
Classic Italian Songs, Vols. I-III	Glenn and Taylor	Ditson
Haydn, Arie dalle opere	Vecsey	Boosey & Hawkes
Schubert, Gesaenge, Vol. VI		C. F. Peters Corp.
Arie Scelte, Vols. I-IV		G. Ricordi
Arie di Stile Antico	Donaudy	G. Ricordi

Di stella infesta l'aspra inclemenza
Of (a) star hostile the-bitter enmity
(The bitter enmity of a hostile star)

tutto m'invola;
everything from-me-takes-away;
(takes everything away from me;)

mio cor, pazienza!
my heart, (have) patience!

Il più mi resta,
The most (important) to-me remains,
(The greatest thing remaining,)

che, se ben sola,
which, if [well] (the) only,
(although the only one,)

è l'innocenza.
is [the] (my) innocence.
(is my innocence.)

Ah, che non ho più lagrime
Ah, that not have-I more tears
(Alas, that I have no more tears)

per disfogar l'affanno
to vent the-anguish

che mi consuma il cor.
which [to-me] consumes [the] (my) heart.

E pure a tante lagrime
And yet to so-many tears

ti mostri più tiranno
yourself you-show more (a) tyrant

con me, crudele amor.
with me, cruel love.

Anonymous   AMOR, FAMMI GODER

Amor, fammi goder!
Love, make-me [rejoice] (happy)!

Fammi baciar quel labbro,
Make-me kiss [that lip] (those lips),

asperso di cinabro,
sprinkled with vermilion,

che serve d'arco a te,
which serve[s] as-(a)-bow to you,

bendato arcier!
blind-folded archer!

Anonymous   O LEGGIADRI OCCHI BELLI

O leggiadri occhi belli, occhi miei cari
O charming eyes beautiful, eyes my dear,

vivi raggi del ciel sereni e chiari.
vivid rays of-the sky serene and clear.

Poichè tanto bramate di vedermi languire,
Since so-much you-desire to see-me languish,

di vedermi morire, occhi belli che adoro,
to see-me die, eyes beautiful that I-adore,

deh mirate ch'io moro.
then see that-I [die] (am dying).

O serene mie luci, o luci amate,
O serene my eyes, o eyes beloved,

tanto crude al mio amor quanto spietate,
as cruel to-[the] my love as pitiless,

poichè tanto godete della fiamma ch'io sento,
since so-much you-are-happy with-the flame which-I feel,

del mio grave tormento,
with-[the] my heavy torment,

deh miratemi un poco e gioite al mio foco.
then look-at-me a little and be-happy with-[the] my fire.

4

Bach, J. S.   AMORE TRADITORE

Aria:
Amore traditore, tu non m'inganni più,
Love traitor, you (do) not me-deceive longer,

non voglio più catene,
not I-want more chains,
(I want no more chains,)

non voglio affanni, pene, cordoglio e servitù.
not I-want anxieties, pains, grief and slavery.

Recit. :
Voglio provar, se posso sanar l'anima mia
I-want to-try, if I-can to-heal [the]-soul my

dalla piaga fatale,
from-the wound fatal,

e viver si può senza il tuo strale;
and to-live one can without [the] your arrow;

non sia più la speranza lusinga del dolore,
not let-be more [the] hope allurement of-[the] sorrow,
(let hope no longer be the bait for sorrow,)

e la gioia nel mio core,
and the joy in-[the] my heart,

più tuo scherzo sarà nella mia costanza.
(no) longer your sport will-be in-[the] my constancy.

Aria:
Chi in amore ha nemica la sorte,
He-who in love has (as an) enemy [the] fate,

è follia se non lascia d'amar.
it-is folly, if not he-stops from-loving.

Sprezzi l'alma le crude ritorte,
Let-despise the-soul the cruel bonds,

se non trova mercede al penar.
if not it-finds reward [to-the] (for its) suffering.

Dormi, bella, dormi tu?
Are-you-sleeping, beautiful-one, are-you sleeping?

Se dormi sognati d'esser men cruda,
If you-sleep, dream [yourself] of-being less cruel,

se vegli porgimi qualche pietà.
if you-wake, offer-me some pity.

Sospiri profondi tramando dal cor
Sighs deep I-send-forth from-the heart

e tu non rispondi, ahi barbaro amor.
and you (do) not reply, ah, cruel love.

Bei lumi rubelli
Beautiful [lights] (eyes) rebellious,

chi mai, chi v'apriva?
who ever, who you-opened?
(who opened you?)

E tu non favelli: ahi barbaro amor.
And you (do) not speak: ah, cruel love.

Bassani   POSATE, DORMITE
                          (Ah, se tu dormi ancora)

Ah, se tu dormi ancora, e se dormendo
Ah, if you sleep yet, and if sleeping

tante pene mi dai,
so-many pains to-me you-give,

non destarti giammai,
(do) not awaken [yourself] ever,

che non saria bastante
for not would-be enough

a soffrirti svegliata un core amante.
to endure-you awakened a heart loving.
(for a loving heart could not endure you awakened.)

Posate, dormite, pupille gradite;
Rest, slumber, eyes [welcome] (lovely);

e il vostro rigore
and (may) [the] your severity

lasci ancora posare un stanco core.
let still rest a tired heart.
(and may a tired heart let your severity rest.)

Dormite, posate, pupille adorate;
Sleep, rest, eyes adored;

e in placido obblio
and in quiet oblivion

dorma il vostro furor, ch'io parto. Addio.
let-sleep [the] your anger, for-I leave. Goodbye.

Beethoven   AH, PERFIDO!

Recit.:
Ah, perfido, spergiuro,
Ah, perfidious-one, perjured-one,

barbaro traditor, tu parti?
cruel traitor, you depart?

e son questi gl'ultimi tuoi congedi?
and are these [the]-last your farewells?

Ove s'intese tirannia più crudel?
Where itself-has-heard tyranny more cruel?
(Where has one heard of more cruel tyranny?)

Va, scellerato! Va, pur fuggi da me,
Go, scoundrel! Go, then flee from me,

l'ira de'Numi non fuggirai!
the-wrath of-the-Gods not you-will-escape!
(you will not escape the wrath of the gods!)

Se v'è giustizia in Ciel, se v'è pietà,
If there-is justice in heaven, if there-is pity,

congiureranno a gara tutti a punirti!
they-will-conspire in contest all to punish-you!
(they will compete with each other to punish you!)

Ombra seguace,
(A) spectre following,
(A spectre, following you,)

presente, ovunque vai, vedrò le mie vendette;
present, wherever you-go, I-will-see [the] my vengeance[s];

io già le godo immaginando;
I already them enjoy imagining;
(I already enjoy it in my imagination;)

i fulmini ti veggo già balenar d'intorno.
the lightning[s] [to]-you I-see already flash around.
(I already see the lightning flash around you.)

Ah no, ah no, fermate, vindici Dei,
Ah no, ah no, stop, avenging gods,

risparmiate quel cor, ferite il mio!
spare that heart, wound [the] mine!

S'ei non è più qual era son'io qual fui;
If-he not is longer what he-was, am-I what I-was;
(Though he is no longer what he was, I am still what I was;)

per lui vivea, voglio morir per lui!
for him I-lived, I-want to-die for him!

Aria:
Per pietà, non dirmi addio,
In pity, (do) not say-to-me goodbye,

di te priva che farò?
of you deprived, what shall-I-do?

Tu lo sai, bell'idol mio,
You it know, beautiful-idol mine,

io d'affanno morirò.
I of-anguish will-die.

Ah crudel! tu vuoi ch'io mora!
Ah cruel-one! you want that-I die!
            (you want me to die!)

Tu non hai pietà di me?
You have not pity for me?
(Have you no pity for me?)

Perchè rendi a chi t'adora
Why (do)-you-render to the-one-who you-adores

così barbara mercè?
such barbarous reward?

Dite voi, se in tanto affanno
Tell-me [you] if in so-much anxiety

non son degna di pietà?
not I-am worthy of compassion?

IN QUESTA TOMBA OSCURA

In questa tomba oscura lasciami riposar;
In this tomb dark let-me rest;

quando vivevo, ingrato,
when I-was-alive, ungrateful-one,

dovevi a me pensar.
you-had-to of me think.
(you should have thought of me.)

Lascia che l'ombre ignude
Let [that] the-spirits naked

godansi pace almen,
enjoy-[for-themselves] peace at-least,

e non bagnar mie ceneri d'inutile velen.
and (do) not bathe my ashes with-useless poison.

Bellini   CASTA DIVA
                          (Norma)

Casta Diva, che inargenti
Chaste goddess, who bathes-in-silver

queste sacre antiche piante,
these sacred old trees,

A noi volgi il bel sembiante,
To us turn [the] (your) beautiful face,

senza nube e senza vel.
without cloud and without veil.

Tempra tu de' cori ardenti
Temper [you of]-the hearts burning,

tempra ancora lo zel audace,
temper still the zeal bold,

Spargi in terra quella pace
Scatter [in] (on) earth that peace

che regnar tu fai nel ciel.
that to-reign you make in-[the] heaven.

Fine al rito,
End [to]-the rite,

e il sacro bosco sia disgombro dai profani.
and the sacred grove be disencumbered of-the profane-ones.
(and let the profane ones leave the sacred grove.)

Quando il Nume irato e fosco
When the God, angry and dark,

chiegga il sangue dei Romani,
asks the blood of-the Romans,

Dal druidico delubro la mia voce tuonerà.
From-the druid temple [the] my voice will-thunder-forth.

Cadrà...punirlo io posso...
He-will-fall...to-punish-him I can...

(Ma punirlo il cor non sa.
(But to-punish-him the heart not knows-how.

11

Ah! Bello a me ritorna del fido amor primiero,
Ah, beautiful to me return of-the faithful love first,
(Ah, return to me the beauty of our first love,)

E contro il mondo intiero difesa a te sarò.
And against the world entire defense to you I-will-be.
           (entire world)

Ah! Bello a me ritorna del raggio tuo sereno,
Ah, beautiful to me return of-the ray your serene,
(Ah, return to me your serene ray,)

E vita nel tuo seno, e patria
And life in-[the] your bosom, and fatherland

e ciel avrò.
and heaven I-will-have.

Ah! riedi ancora qual eri allor quando,
Ah, return again as you-were then, when,

ah quando il cor ti diedi.
ah, when [the] (my) heart to-you I-gave.

Bellini   AH! NON CREDEA MIRARTI
                                        (La Sonnambula)

Recit. :
L'anello mio.. l'anello...ei me l'ha tolto...
[The]-ring my...the-ring...he from-me it-has taken-away...
                    (he took it away from me...)

Ma non può rapirmi l'immagin sua.
But not is-he-able to-snatch-away-from-me [the]-image his.
                                        (his image.)

Sculta ella è qui...nel petto.
Carved it is here..in-[the] (my) breast.

Nè te, d'eterno affetto tenero pegno, o fior...
Nor you, of-eternal passion (the) tender pledge, O flower...

Nè te perdei. Ancor ti bacio, ma inaridito sei.
Nor you did-I-lose. Again you I-kiss, but dried-up you-are.

Aria:
Ah! non credea mirarti
Ah, not did-I-believe to-behold-you

si presto estinto, o fiore;
so speedily dead, O flower;

passasti al par d'amor, che un giorno sol durò.
you-passed [to]-the same of-love, that one day only lasted.
(you faded as quickly as love that lasted only one day.)

Potria novel vigore il pianto mio recarti...
Could new vigor [the] weeping my bring-you...

Ma ravvivar l'amore il pianto mio, ah, no, non può!
But to-revive [the]-love [the] weeping my, ah, no, not it-can!
(But my weeping cannot bring back love!)

Bellini

AH! NON GIUNGE
(La Sonnambula)

Ah! non giunge uman pensiero
Ah, not arrives human thought

al contento ond'io son piena:
at-the happiness of-which I-am full:

a miei sensi io credo appena;
[to] my feelings, I believe scarcely;

tu m'affida, o mio tesor!
[you] me-trust, O my treasure!
(trust me,)

Ah! mi abbraccia, e sempre insieme,
Ah, me embrace, and always together,
    (embrace me,)

sempre uniti in una speme,
always united in one hope,

della terra in cui viviamo,
[of]-(on)-the earth in which we-live,

ci formiamo un ciel d'amor.
here let-us-fashion a heaven of-love.

Oh gioia!   Oh qual gioia!
Oh, joy!   Oh, what joy!

Tanto sospirerò,
So-much I-shall-sigh,

tanto mi lagnerò,
so-much [myself] I-shall-grieve,

che intender le farò
that understand to-her I-shall-make
(that I shall make her understand)

che per lei moro!
that for her I-die!

Pur l'alma le dirà:
But the-soul to-her will-say:

cara t'adoro!
dear-one, you-I-adore!

Boito   L'ALTRA NOTTE
                         (Mefistofele)

L'altra notte in fondo al mare
The-other night into (the) bottom [to] (of)-the sea

il mio bimbo hanno gittato;
[the] my baby they-have thrown;

Or per farmi delirare dicon
Now to make-me rave-in-madness they-say

ch'io l'abbia affogato.
that-I it-have drowned.

L'aura è fredda, il carcer fosco,
The-air is cold, the prison dark,

e la mesta anima mia come il passero del bosco
and [the] sad spirit my, like the sparrow of-the forest

vola, vola, vola via...
flies, flies, flies away...

Ah! di me pietà!
Ah, [of] (on) me (have) pity!

In letargico sopore è mia madre addormentata,
In lethargic drowsiness is my mother gone-to-sleep,

e per colmo dell'orrore
and for (the) height of-[the]-horror,

dicon ch'io l'abbia attoscata.
they-say that-I her-have poisoned.

Bononcini, G. B.   L'ESPERTO NOCCHIERO

L'esperto nocchiero perchè torna al lido
The-expert sailor why returns-he to-the shore

appena partî?
as-soon-as he-departed?

Del vento cangiato, del flutto turbato
[Of]-the wind changed, [of]-the wave disturbed

s'accorse e fuggî!
[himself]-he-perceived and fled!

Se il mar lusinghiero sapea ch'era infido
If the sea flattering he-knew that-[it]-was deceptive
(If he knew that the sea was deceptive)

perchè mai salpò?
why ever did-he-sail?

Salpò ma ingannato al lido lasciato
He-sailed, but deceived (by the sea) to-the shore left-behind

in breve tornò.
in brief-time he-returned.

Bononcini, G. B.   PER LA GLORIA D'ADORARVI

Per la gloria d'adorarvi
For the glory of-adoring-you

voglio amarvi o luci care.
I-want to-love-you, O eyes dear.

Amando penerò;
Loving I-will-suffer;

ma sempre v'amerò, sì sì nel mio penare.
but always you-I-will-love, yes yes in-[the] my suffering.

Senza speme di diletto vano affetto è sospirare;
Without hope of pleasure vain affection it-is to-sigh;

ma i vostro dolci rai
but [the] your sweet [rays] (glances)

chi vagheggiar può mai e non v'amare?
who admire can ever, and not you-love?
(but who can admire your glances and not love you?)

Più non ti voglio credere,
More not you do-I-wish to-believe,
(No longer do I wish to believe you,)

penosa gelosia!
painful jealousy!

Tu vuoi con freddo gelo
You want with cold chill

estinguere il mio foco;
to-extinguish [the] my fire;

ma per l'ardor, ch'io celo,
but for the-ardor, which-I conceal,

questo tuo gelo è poco.
[this] your chill is little.

Nè mai gli saprà cedere
Nor ever to-it will-know-how to-yield

la bella fiamma mia.
[the] beautiful flame my.
(nor will my flame know how to yield to your chill.)

Bononcini, G.M.   CARA, SI, TU MI CONSUMI

Cara, sì, tu mi consumi,
Dear-one, yes, you me consume,
                    (you make me pine away,)

mi fai penar e il cor t'adora!
me you-make suffer and [the] (my) heart you-adores!
(you make me suffer and my heart adores you!)

Sanno i tuoi lumi innamorar
Know-how [the] your eyes to-inflame-with-love
(Your eyes know how to kindle love)

le selve e i fiumi e i sassi ancora.
the woods and the streams and the stones even.
(in woods, streams, and even stones.)

Deh più a me non v'ascondete,
Then longer [to] (from) me (do) not yourself hide,

luci vaghe del mio sol.
eyes lovely of-[the] my sun.

Con svelarvi, se voi siete,
[With] (by) revealing-yourself, if you are (there),

voi potete far quest'alma fuor di duol.
you can make this-soul out of pain.
(you can end my suffering.)

Caccini   AMARILLI

Amarilli, mia bella,
Amaryllis, my beautiful-one,

non credi, O del mio cor dolce desio,
not do-you-believe, O of-[the] my heart sweet desire,
(O my heart's sweet desire, do you not believe)

d'esser tu l'amor mio?
to-be you the-love my?
(that you are my beloved?)

Credilo pur: e se timor t'assale,
Believe-it nevertheless, and if fear you-assails,

dubitar non ti vale.*
to-doubt not you avails.
(to doubt it does not avail you.)

Aprimi il petto,
Open-to-me the bosom,
(Open my bosom,)

e vedrai scritto in core,
and you-will-see written upon (my) heart,

Amarilli è'il mio amore.
Amaryllis is-[the] my love.

*The original text for this line was:
prendi questo mio strale.
take this my arrow.

Amor, che attendi?
Love, what do-you-wait-for?

Su: che non prendi gli strali omai?
Up: that not you-take [the] arrows now?
(Why do you not take your arrows now?)

Amor, vendetta.
Love, revenge.

Amor, saetta
Love, strike (with your arrow)

quel cor che altero sdegna il tuo impero.
that heart which proud disdains [the] your power.

Dall'alto cielo fulmina Giove,
From-[the]-high heaven strikes-lightning Jove,
(From high heaven, Jove strikes with lightning,)

l'arcier di Delo saette piove,
the-archer of Delos arrows rains,

ma lo stral d'oro s'orni d'alloro;
but the arrow of-gold (let)-itself-decorate with-laurel;
(but let the golden arrow of Cupid win the laurels;)

che di possanza ogni altro avanza.
which [of] (for) power every other surpasses.
(for it surpasses all others in power.)

Odi, Euterpe, il dolce canto
Hear, Euterpe, the sweet song

che a lo stil Amor m'impetra
which to the pen Love from-me-entreats
(love entreats me to write)

ed accorda al dolce canto
and accords to-the sweet song

l'aureo suon della mia cetra,
the-golden sound of-[the] my lyre,

che a dir quel ch'ei mi ragiona
for to say that which-he to-me discourses
(what he tells me to say)

troppo dolce amor mi sprona.
too sweet (a) love me spurs-on.

Di notturno e casto velo
With (a) nocturnal and chaste veil

la mia Lidia il sen copria;
[the] my Lidia [the] her bosom covered;

ma la luna in mezzo il ciel
but the moon in-(the) midst (of)-the heaven

dolcemente il sen m'apria;
gently the bosom to-me-opened;

ch'a mirar si bel tesoro
so-that-to behold such (a) beautiful treasure

lampeggiò di fiamme d'oro.
it-flashed with flames of-gold.

E vedea soave e pura
And I-saw sweet and pure

la sua neve il petto aprire;
[the] its snow the bosom [open] (reveal);

e sentia di dolce cure
and I-felt with gentle care

nel mio petto il cor languire;
in-[the] my bosom the heart languish;

e salir veloce e leve il mio cor tra neve e neve
and rise swift and light [the] my heart between snow and snow

e da quei soavi albori sfavillava un dolce foco;
and from those pleasant dawns sparkled a gentle fire;

e le grazie con gli amori
and the graces with the cupids

avean quivi un dolce loco;
had there a sweet place;

e se quivi il cor giungea,
and if there the heart arrived,

su la neve il cor m'ardea.
upon the snow the heart to-me-burned.

Tu ch'hai le penne, Amore,
You who-have [the] wings, love,

e sai spiegarle a volo,
and know-how to-spread-them in flight,

deh muove ratto un volo
then move quickly [a] (in) flight

fin là dov'è il mio core.
to there where-is [the] my heart.

E, se non sai la via,
And, if not you-know the road,

coi miei sospir t'invia.
with-[the] my sighs yourself-send.

Va pur: che'l troverai
Go then, for-[it] you-will-find (my heart)

tra'l velo e'l bianco seno,
between-the veil and-the white bosom,

o tra'l dolce e'l sereno
or between-the sweetness and-the serenity

de'luminosi rai,
of-the-luminous rays,

o tra'bei nodi d'oro
or among-the-beautiful knots of-gold

del mio dolce tesoro.
of-[the] my sweet treasure.

Alma del core, spirto dell'alma,
Soul of-[the] (my) heart, spirit of-[the]-(my)-soul,

sempre costante t'adorerò.
always constant you-I-will-adore.

Sarò contento nel mio tormento
I-shall-be happy in-[the] my torment

se quel bel labbro baciar potrò.
if [that] (those) beautiful lip(s) kiss I-can.
(if I shall be able to kiss those beautiful lips.)

Come raggio di sol, mite e sereno,
As (a) ray of (the) sun, mild and serene,

sovra placidi flutti si riposa
upon (the) placid waves itself rests

mentre del mare nel profondo seno
while of-the sea in-the profound bosom
(while in the profound bosom of the sea)

sta la tempesta ascosa,
remains the tempest hidden,
(the tempest remains hidden,)

così riso talor gaio e pacato
so laughter sometimes gay and peaceful

di contento, di gioia un labbro infiora,
with contentment, with joy a lip touches,

mentre nel suo segreto il cor piagato
while in-[the] its secret (depths) the heart wounded

s'angoscia e si martora.
itself-anguishes and itself tortures.
(suffers anguish and martyrdom.)

SEBBEN CRUDELE

Sebben, crudele mi fai languir,
Although, cruel-one, me you-make languish,

sempre fedele ti voglio amar.
always faithful you I-want to-love.

Con la lunghezza del mio servir
With the length of-[the] my servitude

la tua fierezza saprò stancar
[the] your pride I-will-know-how to-wear-down.

Selve amiche, ombrose piante,
Woods friendly, shady trees,

fido albergo del mio core,
faithful refuge of-[the] my heart,

chiede a voi quest'alma amante
asks of you this-soul loving
(this loving soul asks of you)

qualche pace al suo dolore.
some peace for-[the] its sorrow.
(peace for its sorrow.)

Vaghe luci, è troppo crudo
Lovely eyes, is too cruel
          (too cruel is)

il destino del mio core,
the destiny of-[the] my heart,

che languendo al vostro ardore
which languishing at-[the] your ardor

dee la fiamma in sen celar.
must the flame in (its) bosom conceal.

Si tiranna è la mia sorte,
So harsh is [the] my fate,

che soffrir dovrò la morte,
for suffer I-shall-have-to [the] death,
          (I shall have to die,)

pria che al mio fatale amore
before [that] to-[the] my fatal love
(before, for my fatal love,)

premio un dì possa sperar.
(a) reward one day I-may hope-for.
(I may hope for a reward.)

Carissimi   COSI VOLETE

Così volete, così sarà,
Thus you-want (it), thus it-will-be,

bella tiranna, che cinta siete di crudeltà!
beautiful tyrant, who girded are with cruelty!

Se dal fonte del tuo core
If from-the fountain of-[the] your heart

ne distillano i martiri,
[from-there] distill the tortures,
(tortures are distilled)

tuo rigore nel dolore
your severity in-[the] pain

faccia pago i miei sospiri!
let-make satisfied [the] my sighs!
(let my sighs satisfy your severity!)

Se godete a miei tormenti,
If you-rejoice at my torments,

il penar mi sarà gioco;
[the] suffering to-me will-be play;

il mio letto sia ricetto
[the] my bed let-it-be shelter

d'un infermo, e sarà poco!
of-an infirm-one, and it-will-be (of)-little-(consequence)!

Se ver me sempre severa
If toward me always stern
(If always toward me)

d'esser cruda alfin ti vanti,
of-being cruel at-last yourself you-vaunt,
(you pride yourself in being cruel,)

tra catene dian le pene
among chains let-give the pains
(let chains and suffering be)

sol rimedio ai tristi pianti!
only remedy to-[the] (my) sad weeping[s]!
(the only remedy for my weeping!)

32

Deh, deh, contentatevi ch'io mi lamenti,
Well then, satisfy-yourself that-I [myself] lament,

ch'esser tacito più non si può!
for-to-be silent longer not one can!

Atro nembo allor che tuona,
(A) black storm now that thunders,

par che insegni a chieder aita
it-appears that it-advises to call-for help
(seems to advise calling for help)

e la bocca della ferita
and the mouth of-the wound

benchè muta pietà risuona!
although mute, (for) pity [sounds] (calls-out)!

Carissimi   FILLI, NON T'AMO PIU

Filli, non t'amo più,
Phyllis, not you-I-love more,
(Phyllis, I love you no longer,)

e se nol credi a me,
and if not [it] you-believe [to] me,

vedi, che ho sciolto il piè
see, [that] I-have unshackled [the] (my) foot

dalla tua servitù.
from-[the] your slavery.

Negato ogni ristoro del mio fedel servire,
Denied every compensation [of-the] (for) my faithful serving,

il tuo volto crudel più non adoro.
[the] your face cruel more not I-adore.
(I no longer adore your cruel face.)

La mia fede altrui giurata,
[The] my faith to-another sworn,

alla fuga ognor m'affretta;
to-[the] flight always me-urges;

ma la diva, che m'alletta,
but the goddess, who me-charms,

tiene l'alma incatenata.
holds [the] (my)-soul enchained.

In un dubbio si molesto,
In an uncertainty so annoying,

infelice, che farò!
unhappy-me, what shall-I-do!

Sono infido se qui resto,
I-am unfaithful, if here I-remain,

son crudel, se me ne vo.
I-am cruel, if [myself] from-here I-go.

Se da te, bella, m'involo,
If from you, beautiful-one, myself-I-take-away,

d'un Teseo son più tiranno;
than-a Theseus I-am more tyrannical;

se mi fermo in questo suolo,
if [myself] I-stop in this soil,

troppo, ohimè, Florinda inganno!
too-much, alas, Florinda I-deceive!

Faccia io pure o quel o questo,
Do I however either that or this,

sempre reo mi chiamerò:
always guilty myself I-will-call:

sono infido, se qui resto,
I-am unfaithful, if here I-remain,

son crudel, se me ne vo.
I-am cruel, if [myself] from-here I-go.

Carissimi

No, no, non si speri!
No, no, not one let-hope!
     (One must not hope!)

E morta la speme!
Is dead [the] hope!
(Hope is dead!)

Piangete, pensieri!
Weep, thoughts!

A bruno vestiti, nel vostro dolore,
In mourning dressed, in-[the] your sorrow,

desiri traditi, lasciate il mio core!
desires betrayed, leave [the] my heart!

Le gioie d'amore son lampi fugaci,
The joys of-love are flashes fleeting,

mendaci, leggieri!
lying, frivolous!

Non posso vivere senza il mio ben.
Not I-can live without [the] my beloved.

Amor pietoso, dammi le piume,
Love merciful, give-me [the feathers] (wings),

Del mio bel nume guidami in sen.
Of-[the] my beautiful deity guide-me into (the) bosom.
(Guide me into the bosom of my beloved.)

Piangete, ohimè, piangete anime innamorate,
You-weep, alas, you-weep, souls in-love,

e soccorso e pietate
and aid and pity,

sospirando, piangendo altrui chiedete.
sighing, weeping of-others you-ask.

Piangete, ohimè piangete
You-weep, alas you-weep

quando s'adira
when [herself]-grows-angry

beltà serena.
(a) beauty serene.

Chi non sospira indarno spera.
He-who not sighs in-vain hopes.
(He who does not sigh hopes in vain.)

Chi non piange, d'amor non si dia vanto;
He-who not weeps, of-love not [himself] let-him-give boast;
(Let him not boast of love who does not weep;)

è foco amor e lo sostiene il pianto.
is fire love, and it feeds [the] weeping.
(love is fire, and weeping feeds it.)

Soccorretemi, ch'io moro, occhi belli, o Dio, pietà!
Rescue-me, for-I die, eyes beautiful, O God, pity!

Negherete voi ristoro
Do-you-deny [you] comfort

a chi per voi piangendo a morir va?
to him-who for you weeping to die goes?

Il timor, la gelosia mi conducono alla morte;
[The] fear, [the] jealousy me conduct to-[the] death;

già del seno apron le porte
already of-[the] (my) bosom open the doors
(already my bosom opens)

per che fugga l'alma mia.
through which may-escape [the]-soul my.
(so that my soul may escape.)

Occhi belli, e che saria, se in tanto duolo
Eyes beautiful, and what would-it-be, if in [such] (my) pain

un guardo solo mi volgeste per mercè?
one glance alone to-me you-would-turn in pity?

Ah, non tardate, ohimè,
Ah, (do) not delay, alas,

che m'uccide il gran martoro!
for me-kills the great suffering!

La speranza sbigottita per fuggir ha pronte l'ale,
[The] hope terrified to flee has ready the-wings,

perchè vede, che mortale è del fianco
because it-sees, that mortal is [of-the] (in-my) side

la ferita.
the wound.

Occhi belli, e chi m'aita?
Eyes beautiful, [and] who me-helps?

Crudi sarete, se negherete
Cruel you-will-be, if you-will-deny

un sol guardo per mercè!
one only glance in pity!

Per la più vaga e bella terrena stella,
For the most lovely and beautiful earthly star,

che oggi oscuri di Febo i raggi d'oro,
which today darkens of Phoebus the rays of-gold
(darkens the rays of the sun,)

mio core ardeva; Amor rideva,
my heart burned; Love laughed,

vago di rimirare il mio martoro.
eager to see-again [the] my suffering.

Ma d'avermi schernito, tosto pentito
But of-having-me scorned, soon repented,

con la pietà di lei mi sana il petto.
with the pity of her for-me (love) heals the bosom.
(Love heals me with pity.)

Ond'io fò fede a chi nol crede,
Whence-I [make faith] (affirm) to him-who not-it believes,

che Amore è solo il dio d'ogni diletto.
that Love is alone the god of-every delight.

del Cavaliere IL TEMPO FUGGE
(Monologo del tempo)

Il tempo fugge, la vita si distrugge
[The] time flies, [the] life itself consumes

e già mi par sentire
and already [to-me it-seems to-hear] (I seem to hear)

l'ultima tromba e dire:
the-last trumpet [and say] (saying):

uscite da la fossa, ceneri sparse, ed ossa;
come-out from the grave, ashes dispersed, and bones;

sorgete anime ancora
arise souls again,

prendete i corpi or ora;
take-up [the] (your) bodies [now] (at once);

venite a dir'il vero se fu miglior pensiero
come to say-the truth if it-was (a) better thought

servire al mondo vano,
to-serve [to]-the world vain,

o al Re del Ciel soprano?
or [to]-the King of-[the] Heaven supreme?

Si che ciascun intenda, apra gli occhi e comprenda,
So that each-one may-hear, may-open the eyes and understand,

che questa vita è vento, che vola in un momento:
that this life is (a) wind, which flies-away in a moment:

oggi vien fore, doman si more:
today it-comes forth, tomorrow [itself] dies:

oggi n'appare, doman dispare.
today [from-there]-it appears, tomorrow it-disappears.

Faccia dunque ognun prova,
Let-make then each-one proof,

mentr'il tempo gli giova,
while-the time to-him permits,

lasciar quant'è nel mondo
to-leave what-ever-there-is in-the world,

quantunqu'in se giocondo;
whatever-in itself (is) gay;

ed opri con la man,
and let-him-work with [the] (his) hand,

opri col core,
let-him-work with-[the] (his) heart,

perchè del ben oprar frutto è l'onore.
because of-[the] well working (the) fruit is [the]-honor.
(because honor is the fruit of good works.)

Affè, mi fate ridere,
In faith, me you-make laugh,

amorosi, lascivetti,
amorous, lascivious,

d'ogni dama, che mirate
[of] (with-every) woman whom you-see

v'infiammate.
you-yourself-inflame.
(you fall in love.)

Come, come, in cento affetti
How, how, in (a) hundred affections

un sol cor si può dividere?
a single heart itself can divide?
(How can a heart divide itself in a hundred affections?)

V'imprigiona v'incatena
You-imprisons, you-enchains
(You are imprisoned and enchained by)

ogni crin, ch'un poco adorno vada intorno.
every head-of-hair, that-[a little elegant] goes about.

Da beltà veduta appena
By beauty seen scarcely

vi lasciate il cor dividere.
[yourself] you-let the heart divide.
(you let your heart be shared.)

Delizie contente, che l'alma beate,
Delights happy, that the-soul bless,

fermate, fermate.
cease, cease.

Su questo mio core, deh più non stillate
Upon [this] my heart, then more (do) not drop

le gioie d'amore.
the joys of-love.

Delizie mie care, fermatevi qui;
Delights mine dear, remain-[yourselves] here;

non so più bramare, mi basta così.
not I-know more to-desire, to-me it-suffices thus.

In grembo agli amori fra dolci catene
In (the) lap of-[the] love[s] in sweet chains

morir mi conviene.
to-die for-me it-is-necessary.

Dolcezza omicida, a morte mi guida
Sweetness murderous, to death me guide

in braccio al mio bene.
in (the) arm(s) of-[the] my beloved.

Donzelle, fuggite procace beltà!
Young-girls, flee (from a) bold handsome-young-man!

Se lucido sguardo vi penetra il core,
If (a) bright glance [to-you] penetrates [the] (your) heart,

lasciate quel dardo del perfido amore,
leave that dart of-[the] perfidious love,

che insidie scaltrite tramando vi sta!
which snares crafty weaving for-you [stands] (is)!
(which is setting traps for you!)

Un dì la bella Clori scherzando con Amor
One day [the] beautiful Chloris, playing with Love,

l'arco gli prese.
the-bow from-him took.

Saetta or tutti i cori,
She-shoots-with-arrows now all [the] hearts,

ferisce, ma il suo cor
she-wounds, but [the] her (own) heart

salvo lo rese.
safe [it] she-rendered.

Fuggite, amanti, si dolci incanti,
Flee, lovers, such sweet enchantments;

fuggite Amore, che il traditore
shun love, for the traitor

vi tradirà.
you will-betray.
(will betray you.)

E giovanetto, ma ben sagace,
He-is (a) young-boy, but very wise,

mostra il diletto, promette pace,
he-offers [the] pleasure, he-promises peace,

ma non la dà.
but not it gives.
(but he doesn't give it.)

Cesti   ADORISI SEMPRE
                         (I casti amori d'Orontea)

Recit. :
S'io non vedo Alidoro
If-I (do) not see Alidoro

par, che manchin gli spirti,
it-seems, that fail [the] (my) spirits,
             (my spirits fail)

e lungi dal suo bel quasi mi muoro.
and far from-[the] his beauty almost [myself] I-die.
                         (I almost die.)

S'io lo miro, respiro;
If-I him see, I-breathe (again);

il fulgor de'suoi sguardi il cor ricrea,
the splendor of-[the]-his glances the heart revives,
                         (revives my heart,)

e sento dirmi in tacita favella:
and I-hear say-to-me in silent speech:
(and I hear a silent voice say to me:)

adoralo, Orontea!
adore-him, Orontea!

Aria:
Adorisi sempre,
Let-one-adore always,

ne mai muti tempre.
nor ever change [quality] (intensity),

chi serve al suo bene
she-who serves [to-the] (her) beloved
(she who serves her beloved must always adore)

fra ceppi e catene!
among fetters and chains!

Le doglie e l'asprezze sian nuove dolcezze!
[The] pains and [the]-bitterness let-them-be new pleasures!

49

E chi d'amar desia, non si lamenti,
And she-who to-love desires, (let) not herself lament,
(let her who desires to love not complain,)

che le gioie d'amor sono i tormenti.
for the joys of-love are the torments.

Ah! quanto è vero
Ah! how-[much] it-is true

che il nudo arciero
that the naked archer (Cupid)

forza non ha!
strength not has!

Il nostro core ogni vigore solo gli dà!
[The] our heart all vigor alone to-him gives!

L'accesa face per cui si sface misero sen
The-lighted torch for which itself-destroys poor breast
(The lighted torch for which a poor heart destroys itself)

è sol del senso l'ardore intenso,
is only of-the sense(s) the-ardor intense,
(is only the intense ardor of the senses,)

che non hà fren!
which (does) not have restraint!

E dove t'aggiri
And where [yourself]-do-you-go

tra l'alme dolenti
among the-souls sorrowful,

se pianti e sospiri
if weeping and sighs

non altro qui senti?
not other here you-hear?
(are all that you hear?)

Se pene e tormenti
If pains and torments

ingombrano il tutto
fill [the] everything .

d'orror, di strida,
with-horror, with cries,

di querele e lutto!
with laments and mourning!

Intorno all'idol mio
Around [to-the] idol my

spirate pur, spirate, aure soavi e grate;
blow then, blow, breezes sweet and welcome;

e nelle guance elette
and on-the cheeks chosen
(and on his dear cheeks)

baciatelo per me, cortesi aurette.
kiss-him for me, kind breezes.

Al mio ben, che riposa
To-[the] my darling, who rests

su l'ali della quiete,
on the-wings of-[the] silence,

grati sogni assistete e il mio racchiuso ardore
welcome dreams be present and [the] my suppressed ardor

svelategli per me, larve d'amore.
reveal-to-him for me, spirits of-love.

Tu mancavi a tormentarmi,
You failed to torment-me,

crudelissima speranza
very-cruel hope,

e con dolce rimembranza
and with sweet remembrance

vuoi di nuovo avvelenarmi.
you-wish anew to-poison-me.

Ancor dura la sventura
Still lasts the misfortune

d'una fiamma incenerita.
of-a flame burned-to-ashes.

La ferita, ancora aperta,
The wound, still open,

par m'avverta nuove pene.
seems me-to-warn (of) new pains.

Dal rumor delle catene
From-the sound of-the chains

mai non vedo allontanarmi.
never (not) I-see remove-myself.
(I never can get away.)

Cesti

VIENI, ALIDORO, VIENI
(I casti amori d'Orontea)

Recit.:
Addio Corindo, addio!
Farewell Corindo, farewell!

Rivolto ad altra sfera,
Returned to (an)other realm,

della fiamma primiera,
of-the flame earlier,
(its first love)

non si rammenta più l'egro cor mio,
(let) not [itself] remember more [the]-sick heart my,

addio Corindo, addio!
farewell Corindo, farewell!

Aria:
Vieni, Alidoro, vieni,
Come, Alidoro, come,

consola chi si more!
console the-one-who [herself] dies!

E temprando il mio ardore
And tempering [the] my ardor

godi in grembo a Silandra i dì sereni!
enjoy in (the) bosom [to] (of) Silandra the days serene!

Vieni, mia vita, vieni!
Come, my life, come!

Vieni omai, deh, vieni o morte
Come now, ah, come, O death,

questo core a consolar.
this heart to console.

La mia vita, la mia sorte
[The] my life, [the] my fate

tu sarai se farai
you will-be if you-will-[make] (bring)

ch'abbia fine una volta il mio penar.
that-may-have (an) end [one time] [the] my suffering.
(an end to my suffering.)

Quel d'amore è un certo male
[That of]-love is a certain illness

che lo intende sol chi'l prova
for it understands only the-one-who-it experiences
(for only the one who experiences it can understand it)

e rimedio egli non ha;
and remedy it not has;

posta l'alma in stretti nodi,
having-placed the-soul in tight knots,

la combatte in mille modi
it it-fights in (a) thousand ways
(it fights the soul in a thousand ways)

e morire ognor la fa.
and to-die always it it-makes.
(and always makes it die.)

Ahi! che forse ai miei dì l'ultima aurora splende!
Alas! that perhaps on [the] my days the-last dawn shines!

ahi che il prence e l'amante
alas, that the prince and the-lover

e lo sposo che adoro,
and the husband whom I-adore,

mio scudo, mia difesa, lungi è da me.
my shield, my defense, far is from me.

Se d'un segreto imene io tradisco il mistero,
If of-a secret marriage I betray the secret,
(If I betray the secret of our marriage,)

del crudo genitor al tremendo furor
of [the] (a) cruel father to-the tremendous fury
(to the fury of a cruel father)

abbandonar degg'io lo sposo mio,
abandon must-I the husband mine,
(I must abandon my husband,)

e me pure legge crudel
and me also (a) law cruel
(and a cruel law)

per questo imen fatal me condanna a morir.
for this marriage fatal [me] condemns to die.
(for this marriage condemns me, also, to die.)

Madre! un periglio minaccia il caro figlio!
Mother, a danger threatens (the) dear son!

Sola quand'io vivea
Alone when-I lived

non mai per me tremai così.
[not] never for myself did-I-tremble so.

Vita al mio cor troppo cara,
Life to [the] my heart too dear,

spezzare i tuoi lacci dovrò:
break [the] your bonds I-must:

58

ma lasciar quel che s'adora si può mai senza dolor?
but leave that which one-adores one can ever without pain?
(can one ever leave that which one adores without pain?)

Se mi portate affetto,
If for-me you-bear affection,

se mi volete bene,
if me you-wish well,
(if you love me,)

nè beffe, nè dispetti
neither scorn[s], nor spite[s]

non mi dovete far;
[not] to-me you-must make;

dal pianto e dai sospiri
from-[the] weeping and from-[the] sighs

il cor mi balza in petto,
the heart [to-me] throbs in (my) bosom,

mi manca già il respiro,
[to-me] lacks already the breath,
(already I lack breath,)

non posso più parlar.
not can-I more speak.

Cimarosa   BEL NUME, CHE ADORO

Bel nume, che adoro,
Beautiful idol whom I-adore,

tu versi di speme un dolce ristoro
you pour of hope a sweet comfort

in questo mio sen.
in [this] my bosom.

Quel raggio amoroso pietoso mi dice:
That ray amorous compassionate(ly) to-me says:

contento, felice vivrai col tuo ben.
contented, happy you-will-live with [the] your beloved.

Nel lasciarti, o prence amato,
In-[the] leaving-you, O prince beloved,

mi si spezza in seno il cor.
to-me [itself] breaks in (the) bosom the heart.
(my heart breaks)

Di morirti almeno allato
To die-(with)-you at-least at-the-side
(To die at your side)

perchè a me si niega ancor?
why to me itself denies still?
(why is it denied to me?)

Ah, signor, si acerbo affanno,
Ah, my-Lord, such bitter anguish,

dolce amico o mio tesor,
sweet friend, O my treasure,

ah destin empio, tiranno!
ah, fate wicked, tyrant!

Deh m'uccida il tuo rigor.
Then me-let-kill [the] your severity.
(Ah, let your severity kill me.)

Voi che un dolce amor provate
You who a sweet love experience
(You who feel a sweet love)

deh spiegate il mio dolor.
then explain [the] my sorrow.

Cimarosa   QUEL SOAVE E BEL DILETTO

Quel soave e bel diletto
That sweet and beautiful pleasure

che fin'or provaste al core,
which until-now you-have-felt in-the heart,

già vi leggo nell'aspetto
already [to-you] I-read in-[the]-(your)-face
(already I read in your face)

che un velen diventa già.
that a poison becomes already.
(is becoming a poison)

Imparate che l'amore
Learn that [the]-love

è una brutta infermità.
is an ugly sickness.

Io ben stimo stravagante
I [well] consider extravagant

quello sciocco e folle amore
that stupid and foolish love

che ha piacer di farsi amante
which [has] (takes) pleasure in making (one a) lover

di chi amor per lui non ha.
of her-who love for him not has.
(of her who does not love him.)

Resta in pace, idolo mio,
Rest in peace, idol mine,

non scordar a chi sei sposa;
(do) not forget to whom you-are (the) wife;

qualche lagrima pietosa
some tear(s) sympathetic

non negare al tuo fedel.
(do) not deny to-[the] your faithful-one.

Cimarosa SE PIETA NEL COR SERBATE

Se pietà nel cor serbate,
If pity in-[the] (your) heart you-keep,

deh! calmate il vostro ardor,
then calm [the] your ardor,

che ve'l chiede, già mirate
for of-you-it asks, now behold
(for pity asks you to behold)

la mia pena il mio dolor.
[the] my pain, [the] my sorrow.

Tornerete armati in campo,
You-will-return armed into (the) field (of battle),

offrirete ai colpi il petto.
you-will-offer to-the blows [the] (your) bosom.

Ah, ritorni il dolce affetto
Ah, may-return [the] gentle affection
(Ah, may gentle affection return)

a regnar nel vostro cor.
to reign in-[the] your heart.
(to reign in your heart.)

Non posso disperar,
Not I-can despair,
(I cannot depair,)

sei troppo cara al cor.
you-are too dear to-[the]-(my) heart.

Il solo sperare d'aver da gioire
The only hope of-having to be-happy
(The only hope of being happy)

m'è un dolce languire,
to-me-is a sweet languishing,

m'è un caro dolor.
to-me-is a dear pain.

Dimmi, Amor, dimmi che fa
Tell-me, love, tell-me what [does] (is doing)

la mia cara libertà?
[the] my dear liberty?

Da che andò, come sai tu,
[From that] (since) it-went-away, as know you,
(Since it went away, as you know)

a legarsi ad un bel crine,
to tie-itself to a beautiful head-of-hair,

questo cor, pien di ruine
this heart, full of ruin[s]

non l'ha poi rivista più!
not it-has then seen more!
(has seen its liberty no more)

Un pensier il cor mandò
A thought [the] (my) heart sent

a trovarla in sue catene;
to find-it in its chains;

ma per crescer le mie pene
but to increase [the] my pains

il pensier mai non tornò!
the thought never [not] returned!

Donaudy   O DEL MIO AMATO BEN

O del mio amato ben perduto incanto,
O of-[the] my beloved treasure lost enchantment,
(O lost enchantment of my dearly beloved,)

lungi è dagli occhi miei
far is from-[the] eyes my

chi m'era gloria e vanto!
she-who to-me-was glory and pride!

Or per le mute stanze
Now through the empty rooms

sempre la cerco e chiamo con pieno il cor di speranze.
always her I-seek and I-call with full the heart of hopes.
                                    (a heart full of hope.)

Ma cerco invan, chiamo invan,
But I-seek in-vain, I-call in-vain,

e il pianger m'è si caro,
and [the] weeping to-me-is so dear,

che di pianto sol nutro il cor.
that with weeping alone I-nourish [the] (my) heart.

Mi sembra, senza lei triste ogni loco.
To-me it-seems, without her, sad every place.

Notte mi sembra il giorno mi sembra gelo il foco.
Night to-me seems the day, to-me seems cold the fire.

Se pur talvolta spero di darmi ad altra cura,
If however sometimes I-hope to give-myself to another care,

sol mi tormenta un pensiero:
alone me torments one thought:

ma, senza lei, che farò?
but, without her, what shall-I-do?

Mi par così la vita vana cosa
To-me seems thus [the] life (a) vain thing

senza il mio ben.
without [the] my beloved.

Perduta ho la speranza in voi mirare,
Lost have-I the hope on you to-look,

e di speranza sola nutrivo il core!
and with hope alone I-nourished [the] (my) heart!

Ahimè, ah, come farò,
Alas, ah, [how] (what) shall-I-do,

se per amare la fede ho già smarrita,
if through loving [the] faith I-have already lost,

la fede nell'amore?
[the] faith in-[the] love?

Donaudy   QUANDO TI RIVEDRO

Quando ti rivedrò,
When you shall-I-see,

infida amante che mi fosti si cara?
unfaithful lover, (you) who to-me were so dear?

Tante lagrime ho piante
So-many tears I-have wept

or che altri ci separa,
now that another us separates,

che temo sia fuggita ogni gioia
that I-fear to-be fled every joy
(that I fear that every joy has fled)

per sempre di mia vita.
for ever from my life.

Eppur più mi dispero,
But (the) more [myself] I-despair,

più ritorno a sperare.
(the) more I-return to hope.

Più t'odio nel pensiero
(The) more you-I-hate in-[the] (my) thought(s)

e più ancora l'anima mia ti torna ad amar.
[and] (the) more still [the]-soul my you returns to love.
(the more my soul returns to love you.)

Quando ti rivedrò,
When you shall-I-see,

infida amante che mi fosti cara così?
unfaithful lover, (you) who to-me were dear so?

Spirate pur, spirate
Blow then, blow

attorno a lo mio bene,
about [to the] my beloved,

aurette, e v'accertate
breezes, and [yourselves]-find-out

s'ella nel cor mi tiene.
if-she in-[the] (her) heart me holds.

Spirate, aurette.
Blow, breezes.

Se nel cor mi tiene
If in-[the] (her) heart me she-holds,

v'accertate, aure beate,
find-out, breezes blessed,

aure lievi e beate.
breezes light and blessed.

Donaudy VAGHISSIMA SEMBIANZA

Vaghissima sembianza d'antica donna amata,
Very-lovely image of-(an)-ancient woman loved,
(Charming portrait of a beautiful woman loved long ago,)

Chi, dunque, v'ha ritratta con tanta simiglianza
who, then, you-has painted with so-much similitude
(who has depicted you with so much life)

ch'io guardo, e parlo e credo
that-I look, and I-speak, and I-believe

d'avervi a me davanti, come ai bei dì d'amor?
to-have-you to me before, as in-the beautiful days of-love?
(that I have you before me)

La cara rimembranza
The dear memory

che in cor mi s'è destata
that in (my) heart [to-me] itself-is awakened
(which has been awakened in my heart)

si ardente v'ha già fatta rinascer la speranza,
so ardent here-has now made to-be-reborn [the] (my) hope,

che un bacio, un voto, un grido d'amore
so-that a kiss, a pledge, a cry of-love

più non chiedo che a lei che muta è ognor.
more not I-ask but of her who silent is forever.
(I ask only of her, who is silent, forever.)

Donizetti   AH! UN FOCO INSOLITO
         (Don Pasquale)

Ah! Un foco insolito mi sento addosso,
Ah, a fire unaccustomed [myself] I-feel upon-me,

omai resistere io più non posso.
now to-resist I longer not can.
(I can't resist it any longer.)

Dell'età vecchia scordo i malanni,
Of-[the]-age old I-forget the illnesses,

mi sento giovine come a vent'anni.
[myself] I-feel young like at twenty-years.

Deh! cara, affrettati. Vieni, sposina!
Ah, dear-one, hurry-[yourself]! Come, little-bride!

Ecco, di bamboli mezza dozzina
Behold, [of] babies (a) half dozen

già veggo nascere, già veggo crescere,
already I-see to-be-born, already I-see to-grow-up,

A me d'intorno veggo scherzar.
To me around I-see to-play.
(I see them playing around me.)

Vieni, vieni. che un foco insolito mi sento addosso,
Come, come, for a fire unaccustomed ⌊myself⌋ I-feel upon-me.

o casco morto quà.
or I-fall dead here.

Deh! vieni, affrettati, bella sposina!
Ah, come, hurry-[yourself] beautiful little-bride!

Già, già, di bamboli mezza dozzina
Already, already [of] babies (a) half dozen

a me d'intorno veggo scherzar.
to me around I-see to-play.
(I see them playing around me.)

Donizetti   BELLA SICCOME UN ANGELO
                             (Don Pasquale)

Bella siccome un angelo in terra pellegrino,
Beautiful as an angel ⌈in⌉ (on) earth (a) pilgrim,
(Beautiful as an angel wandering on earth,)

fresca siccome il giglio, che s'apre sul mattino,
fresh as the lily, that [itself]-opens on-the morning,
                        (that opens in the morning,)

occhio che parla e ride,
(an) eye that speaks and laughs,

sguardo che i cor conquide,
(a) look that the hearts conquers,
(a look that conquers all hearts,)

chioma che vince l'ebano, sorriso incantator.
hair that surpasses [the]-ebony, (a) smile enchanting.

Alma innocente, ingenua, che sè medesma ignora
(A) soul innocent, ingenuous, that herself [the-same] ignores,
                        (completely self-effacing,)

modestia impareggiabile, bontà che v'innamora, ah!
modesty incomparable, goodness that you-inspires-with love, ah!
                        (goodness that inspires you with love)

Ai miseri pietosa, gentil, dolce, amorosa, ah!
To-the poor sympathetic, kind, sweet, loving, ah!

Il ciel l'ha fatta nascere per far beato un cor.
The heaven her-has made to-be-born to make happy a heart.
(Heaven caused her to be born to make a heart happy.)

Donizetti   CERCHERO LONTANA TERRA
                             (Don Pasquale)

Recit.:
Povero Ernesto! Dallo zio cacciato,
Poor Ernesto! By-[the] (my) uncle expelled,

da tutti abbandonato,
by all abandoned,

mi restava un amico e un coperto nemico
to-me remained one friend, and a hidden enemy

discopro in lui, che a' danni miei congiura.
I-discover in him, who to harm[s] my conspires.

Perder Norina, oh Dio!
To-lose Norina, oh, God!

Ben feci a lei d'esprimere in un foglio i sensi miei.
Well did-I to her to-express in a leaf [the] sentiments my.
(I was right to express my sentiments to her in a letter.)

Ora in altra contrada
Now in another country

i giorni grami a trascinar si vada.
the days wretched to drag-out one let-go.
(let me now go and drag out my wretched days.)

Aria:
Cercherò lontana terra dove gemer sconosciuto,
I-will-seek (a) far-off land where to-sigh unknown,
                         (where I can sigh, unknown,)

là vivrò col cuore in guerra
there I-will-live with-the heart in war
                    (with my heart at war,)

deplorando il ben perduto. Ma nè sorte a me nemica,
lamenting the beloved lost. But neither fate, to me enemy,
(lamenting my lost love.   But neither unkind fate,)

nè frapposti monti e mar,
nor interposed mountains and seas,
(nor mountains and seas between us,)

76

ti potranno, dolce amica, dal mio core cancellar,
you can, sweet friend, from-[the] my heart erase,
(can erase your image from my heart,)

e se fia che ad altro oggetto
and if it-shall-be that to another object

tu rivolga un giorno il core,
you may-turn one day [the] (your) heart,

se mai fia che un altro affetto
if ever it-shall-be that an other affection

spenga in te l'antico ardore,
may-extinguish in you the-old ardor,

non temer che un infelice
not to-fear that an unhappy-one
(do not fear your unhappy-one)

te spergiura accusi al ciel;
you sworn-falsely accuses to-[the] heaven;
(may accuse you before heaven of swearing falsely;)

se tu sei, ben mio felice,
if you are, beloved my, happy,

sarà pago il tuo fedel.
will-be compensated [the] your faithful-one.
(your faithful one will be satisfied.)

Donizetti

COM'E GENTIL
(Don Pasquale)

Com'è gentil... la notte a mezzo april!
How-is pleasing... the night in mid-April!

E azzurro il ciel!.. la luna è senza vel.
Is blue the sky!.. the moon is without veil.
                (the moon is clear.)

Tutt'è languor... pace, mistero, amor!
Everything-is languor... peace, mystery, love!

Ben mio, perchè ancor non vieni a me?
Beloved my, why yet not come-you to me?

Formano l'aure d'amore accenti!
Shape the-breezes of-love words!
(The breezes are shaping words of love!)

Del rio nel mormore sospiri senti.
Of-the brook in-the murmur sighs you-hear.
(You hear sighs in the murmur of the brook.)

Poi quando sarò morto piangerai,
Afterwards when I-will-be dead, you-will-weep,

ma richiamarmi in vita non potrai.
but to-call-me-back to life not you-will-be-able.

Il tuo fedele si strugge di desir,
[The] your faithful-one [himself] pines-away with desire,

Nina crudele, mi vuoi veder morir?
little-Norina cruel, me do-you-wish to-see die?

Donizetti   SO ANCH'IO LA VIRTU MAGICA
                                     (Don Pasquale)

Cavatina:
Quel guardo il cavaliere in mezzo al cor traffisse,
That look the knight in middle to-the heart transfixed,
(That look transfixed the knight,)

piegò il ginocchio e disse: son vostro cavalier.
he-bent the knee and said: I-am your knight.

E tanto era in quel guardo sapor di paradiso
And so-much was in that look taste of paradise
(And there was such a taste of paradise in that look)

che il cavalier Riccardo, tutto d'amor conquiso,
that the knight, Richard, completely by-love conquered,

giurò che ad altra mai non volgeria il pensier. Ah!
swore that to another never ⌊not⌋ would-he-turn the thought. Ah!
(swore that he would never think of another.)

Aria:
So anch'io la virtù magica d'un guardo a tempo e loco,
Know also-I the virtue magic of-a look at time and place,
(I, too, know the magic power of a look at the right time
and place,)

So anch'io come si bruciano i cori a lento foco;
Know I-also how [themselves] burn the hearts at slow fire;
(I, too, know how hearts burn with a slow fire;)

d'un breve sorrisetto conosco anch'io l'effetto,
of-a brief little-smile know also-I the-effect,

di menzognera lagrima, d'un subito languor.
of (a) deceitful tear, of-a sudden faintness.

Conosco i mille modi dell' amorose frodi,
I-know the thousand ways of-[the] loving deceptions,

i vezzi e l'arti facili per adescare un cor.
the caresses and the-skills easy to entice a heart.

So anch'io la virtù magica per inspirare amor,
Know also-I the virtue magic to inspire love,
(I also know the magic power to inspire love,)

conosco l'effetto ah! si, per inspirare amor.
I-know the-effect, ah, yes, to inspire love.

Ho testa bizzarra, son pronta, vivace,
I-have head whimsical, I-am alert, vivacious
(I have a whimsical mind; I am alert, vivacious;)

brillare mi piace, mi piace scherzar.
to-scintillate me it-pleases, me it-pleases to-banter.

Se monto in furore di rado sto al segno,
If I-mount in fury of rare I-remain to-the sign,
(If I become angry, I rarely remain that way,)

ma in riso lo sdegno fo presto a cangiar.
but in laughter the wrath I-make quickly to change.
(but I turn wrath quickly into laughter.)

Ho testa bizzarra, ma core eccellente, ah!
I-have head whimsical, but heart excellent, ah!
(I have a whimsical mind, but a very fine heart.)

Donizetti   UNA FURTIVA LAGRIMA
                             (L'elisir d'amore)

Una furtiva lagrima negl' occhi suoi spuntò:
A furtive tear in-[the] eyes her burst-forth:

quelle festose giovani invidiar sembrò:
those merry young-girls to-envy she-seemed:

Che più cercando io vo?
What more searching I go?
(Do I need to look further?)

M'ama, sì, m'ama, lo vedo, lo vedo.
Me-she-loves, yes, me-she-loves, it I-see, it I-see.

Un solo istante i palpiti
One sole moment the beating

del suo bel cor sentir!
of-[the] her beautiful heart to-feel!

I miei sospir confondere per poco a suoi sospir!
[The] my sighs to-mingle for little to her sighs!
(My sighs to mingle with hers for a little while!)

I palpiti, i palpiti sentir!
The beating, the beating to-feel!

Confondere i miei co' suoi sospir!
To-mingle [the] mine with-[the] her sighs!

Cielo, si può morir, di più non chiedo.
Heaven, one can die, [of] more not I-ask.
(Heavens, one could die happy; I would not ask for more.)

81

Donizetti   O MIO FERNANDO
                           (La Favorita)

Recit.:
Fia dunque vero? O ciel! Desso, Fernando,
Will-it-be then true? O heavens! He, Fernando,

lo sposo di Leonora! Ah! Tutto mel dice,
the husband of Leonora! Ah! Everything me-it tells,
                             (Everything says it is true,)

e dubbia è l'alma ancora all'inattesa gioia?
and doubtful is the-soul still to-the-unexpected joy?
(and is my soul still doubtful of this unexpected joy?)

O Dio! sposarlo! oh mia vergogna estrema...
Oh, God, to-marry-him...oh, my shame extreme...

In dote al prode recar il dishonor! No!...mai!
In dowry to-the valiant-one to-bring [the] disonor! No, never!
(To bring dishonor as a dowry to the valiant one!)

Dovesse esecrarmi...fuggir! saprà in brev'ora
Should-he curse-me....to-flee! He-will-know in brief-hour
                                 (very soon)

chi sia la donna che cotanto adora.
who is the woman whom so-much he-adores.
(what kind of woman it is that he adores so much.)

Aria:
O mio Fernando, della terra il trono
O my Fernando, of-the earth the throne
                     (an earthly throne)

a possederti avria donato il cor;
to possess-you would-have given the heart;
(my heart would have given to possess-you;)

ma puro l'amor mio, come il perdono,
but pure [the]-love my, like the pardon,
(but my pure love, as well as pardon,)

dannato ahi lassa! è a disperato orror!
damned, alas, unhappy one, is to desperate horror!
(is damned, alas, to desperate horror!)

Il ver fia noto, e in tuo dispregio estremo
The truth will-be known, and in your contempt extreme,

La pena avrommi che maggior si de'!...ah!
The punishment I-will-have that greater itself gave! ah!
(I will have the greatest punishment that was ever given.)

Se il giusto tuo disdegno allor fia scemo,
If [the] just your disdain then will-be diminished,
(If your disdain will be lessened,)

piombi, gran Dio, la folgor tua su me!
hurl, great God, [the] thunderbolt your on me!
(send your lightning down on me, O God!)

Su, crudeli... e chi v'arresta?
On, cruel-ones..and who you-stops?
(Come on, cruel ones, who is stopping you?)

Scritto è in cielo il mio dolor.
Written is in heaven [the] my sorrow.
(My sorrow is written in heaven.)

Su, venite ell'è una festa,
On, come, it-is a holiday,
                (an occasion for celebration,)

sparsa l'ara sia di fior,
scattered the-altar will-be with flowers,

già la tomba a me s'appresta,
already the tomb to me itself-prepares,
(already the tomb is being prepared for me,)

e coperta in negro vel sia la trista fidanzata,
and covered in black veil let-be the sad betrothed.

che rejetta, disperata, non avrà perdono in ciel,
who, rejected, desperate, not will-have pardon in heaven,

maledetta, disperata, non avrà perdono in ciel.
cursed, desperate, not will-have pardon in heaven.

Donizetti

O LUCE DI QUEST'ANIMA
(Linda di Chamounix)

Recit.:
Ah! tardai troppo,
Ah, I-delayed too-much,

e al nostro favorito convegno
and [to] (at)-[the] our favorite meeting (place)

io non trovai il mio diletto Carlo;
I not found [the] my beloved Carlo;

e chi sa mai quanto egli avrà sofferto!
and who knows [ever] how-much he will-have suffered!

Ma non al par di me! Pegno d'amore
But not [to]-the same as I! (As a) token of-love

questi fior mi lasciò! Tenero core!
these flowers for-me he-left! Tender heart!

E per quel core io l'amo, unico di lui bene.
And for that heart I him-love, only of him wealth.
                                (his only wealth.)

Poveri entrambi siamo, viviam d'amor, di speme:
Poor both we-are, we-live [of] (on)-love, [of] (on) hope:

pittore ignoto ancora egli s'innalzerà
painter unknown yet, he himself-will-raise

coi suoi talenti!
with-[the] his talents!

Sarà mio sposo allora.   Oh, noi contenti!
He-will-be my husband then. Oh, we (will be) happy!

Aria:
O luce di quest'anima, delizia, amore e vita,
O light of this-soul, delight, love and life,

la nostra sorte unita in terra, in ciel sarà.
[the] our fate united [in] (on) earth, in heaven will-be.

Deh vieni a me, riposati su questo cor
Ah, come to me, rest-yourself on this heart

che t'ama, che te sospira e brama,
that you-loves, that you longs-for and desires,
(that loves you, longs for you and desires you,)

che per te sol vivrà.
that for you only will-live.

Donizetti   IL DOLCE SUONO MI COLPI (MAD SCENE)
(Lucia di Lammermoor)

Il dolce suono mi colpì di sua voce!
The sweet sound me struck of his voice!
(The sweet sound of his voice struck me!)

Ah, quella voce m'è qui nel cor discesa!
Ah, that voice to-me-is here in-the heart descended!
(That voice is embedded in my heart!)

Edgardo! Io ti son resa; Edgardo! Ah! Edgardo mio!
Edgardo! I to-you am restored; Edgardo! Ah! Edgardo mine!

Si, ti son resa! Fuggita io son da' tuoi nemici.
Yes, to-you I-am restored! Escaped I am from your enemies.

Un gelo mi serpeggia nel seno! Trema ogni fibra!
A chill to-me creeps into-the bosom! Trembles each fiber!
(A chill creeps into my bosom! Each fiber trembles!)

Vacilla il piè!
Hesitates [the] (my) foot!

Presso la fonte meco t'assidi alquanto...
Near the fountain with-me [yourself]-sit a-little-while...

Ohimè! Sorge il tremendo fantasma, e ne separa! Ohimè!
Alas! Rises the terrible phantom, and us separates! Alas!

Ohimè! Edgardo!... Edgardo!
Alas! Edgardo!... Edgardo!

Ah! Il fantasma, il fantasma ne separa!
Ah, the phantom, the phantom us separates!

Qui ricovriamo, Edgardo, a piè dell'ara.
Here we-will-take-(refuge) Edgardo, at (the) foot of-the-altar.

Sparsa è di rose!
Scattered it-is with roses!

Un'armonia celeste, dì, non ascolti? Ah!
A-harmony celestial, say, not do-you-hear? Ah!

L'inno suona di nozze!
The-hymn sounds of marriage!

Il rito per noi s'appresta! Oh me felice!
The ceremony for us itself-prepares! Oh, me happy!
(It is time for the ceremony; oh, how happy I am!)

Ardon gli incensi...
Burn the incense[s]...
(The incense burns...)

splendon le sacre faci, splendon intorno!
shine the sacred torches, they-shine all-around!

Ecco il Ministro! Porgimi la destra...
Here-is the Minister! Give-me [the] (your) right-hand...

Oh lieto giorno!
Oh, happy day!

Alfin son tua, alfin sei mio,
At-last I-am yours, at-last you-are mine,

a me ti dona un Dio...
to me you gives [a] God...
(God gives you to me...)

Ogni piacer più grato, mi fia con te diviso,
Each pleasure more pleasing, to-me will-be with you shared,
(Each pleasure will be more pleasing shared with you,)

del Ciel clemente un riso la vita a noi sarà!
of [the] Heaven merciful a smile [the] life to us will-be!
(for us life will be a merciful smile from heaven!)

Spargi d'amaro pianto il mio terrestre velo,
Shed of-bitter tears [the] my terrestrial veil,
(Shed bitter tears over my mortal remains,)

mentre lassù nel Cielo io pregherò per te.
while up-there in-[the] Heaven I will-pray for you.

Al giunger tuo soltanto fia bello il Ciel
At-[the] arrival your only will-be beautiful the Heaven
(Only when you arrive there will heaven be beautiful)

per me! Ah sì!
for me! Ah, yes.

Donizetti   FRA POCO A ME RICOVERO
                              (Lucia di Lammermoor)

Recit.:
Tombe degli avi miei,
Tombs of-[the] family my,

l'ultimo avanzo d'una stirpe infelice
the-last remnant of-a family unhappy

Deh! raccogliete voi. Cessò dell'ira il breve foco...
Ah, receive [you]. Ended of-the-wrath the brief fire...
                  (The fire of my wrath ended quickly.)

Sul nemico acciaro abbandonar mi vo'.
On-the enemy sword to-abandon myself I-wish

Per me la vita è orrendo peso!
For me [the] life is (a) horrible burden!

L'universo intero è un deserto per me senza Lucia!
The-universe entire is a desert for me without Lucia!

Di faci tuttavia splende il Castello! Ah!
With torches still shines the castle! Ah!

Scarsa fu la notte al tripudio! Ingrata donna!
Short was the night to-the merry-making! Ungrateful woman!
(The night was so short for merry-making!)

Mentr'io mi struggo in disperato pianto,
While-I myself destroy in desperate weeping,

tu ridi, esulti accanto al felice consorte!
you laugh, you-exult near [to-the] (your) happy consort!

Tu delle gioie in seno, io della morte!
You of-[the] joys in (the) bosom, I of-[the] death!

Aria:
Fra poco a me ricovero darà negletto avello,
Shortly to me shelter will-give (a) neglected grave,
(Soon a neglected grave will give me shelter,)

una pietosa lagrima non scenderà su quello!
a compassionate tear not will-fall on [that] it!

Ah! fin degli estinti, ahi misero!
Ah, even of-the deceased, alas, miserable-one.
(Ah, not even in death, miserable one,)

manca il conforto a me.
is-lacking the comfort to me.
(is there comfort for me.)

Tu pur, tu pur dimentica quel marmo dispregiato:
You, too, you, too, forget that marble despised:

mai non passarvi, o barbara,
never [not] pass-there, O cruel-one,

del tuo consorte a lato.
with-[the] your consort at (your) side.

Ah! rispetta almen le ceneri di chi morìa per te!
Ah, respect at-least the ashes of him-who died for you!

Mai non passarvi, tu lo dimentica,
Never [not] pass-there, you it forget,
(Do not pass by my grave; forget it exists;)

rispetta almeno chi muore per te.
respect at-least him-who dies for you.

O barbara, io moro per te!
O cruel-one, I die for you!

89

Donizetti　　　　　　　REGNAVA NEL SILENZIO
　　　　　　　　　　　　(Lucia di Lammermoor)

Regnava nel silenzio alta la notte e bruna,
Reigned in-the silence deep the night and dark,
(Silence reigned in the dark and deep night,)

colpia la fonte un pallido raggio di tetra luna...
struck the fountain a pallid ray of dull moon...
(a pallid ray of dull moonlight struck the fountain.)

quando un sommesso gemito
when a low groan

fra l'aure udir si fe';
through the-breezes to-hear itself made;
(broke the quiet air;)

ed ecco, su quel margin, ah,
and here, on this edge, ah,

l'ombra mostrarsi a me! Ah!
the-spectre showed-itself to me! Ah!

Qual di chi parla, muoversi il labbro suo vedea,
As of one-who speaks, move-itself [the] lip(s) its I-saw,
(As if to speak, I saw it move its lips,)

e con la mano esanime chiamarmi a se parea.
and with the hand lifeless to-call-me to itself it-seemed.
(and with its lifeless hand it seemed to beckon me.)

Stette un momento immobile, poi ratta dileguò...
It-stood a moment immobile, then swiftly it-disappeared...

E l'onda pria sì limpida di sangue rosseggiò, sì,
And the-water, before so limpid, with blood reddened, yes.
　　　　　　　　　　　　　　　(turned the color of blood.)

Quando rapito in estasi del più cocente ardore,
When carried-away in ecstasy of-the most burning ardor,

col favellar del core,
with-[the] speaking of-the heart,

mi giura eterna fè,
to-me he-swears eternal faith,

gli affanni miei dimentico, gioia diviene il pianto.
[the] anxieties my I-forget, joy replaces [the] weeping.
(I forget my anxieties, my weeping becomes joy.)

Parmi che a lui d'accanto
It-seems-to-me that to him near
(It seems to me what when I am near him)

si schiuda il ciel per me.
itself opens [the] heaven for me.
(heaven opens itself for me.)

Durante   DANZA, DANZA

Danza, danza, fanciulla gentile al mio cantar.
Dance, dance, girl gentle to [the] my singing.

Gira, leggera, sottile,
Turn, light, slender,

al suono dell'onde del mar,
to-the sound of-the-waves of-the sea.

Senti il vago rumore dell'aura scherzosa
Hear the lovely sound of-the-breeze playful

che parla al core con languido suon
which speaks to-the heart with (a) languid sound

e che invita a danzar senza posa.
and which invites to dance without rest.

Vergin tutto amor
Virgin, all love,

o madre di bontade, o madre pia,
O mother of mercy, O mother holy,

ascolta, dolce Maria,
hear, sweet Mary,

la voce del peccator.
the voice of-the sinner.

Il pianto suo ti muova,
The weeping his-her you let-move,
(Let his or her weeping move you,)

giungano a te i suoi lamenti,
let-arrive to you [the] his-her laments,
(let his or her laments reach you,)

suo duol, suoi tristi accenti
his-her sorrow, his-her sad accents

senti* pietoso quel tuo cor.
let-hear merciful that your heart.
(let your merciful heart hear.)

*Some texts have "oda" instead of "senti." The
meaning is the same.

Bella porta di rubini
Beautiful [door of rubies] (lips)

ch'apri il varco ai dolci accenti,
which-opens the path to-[the] sweet accents,

che nei risi peregrini scopri perle rilucenti,
which in-[the] smiles exquisite uncovers pearls gleaming,

tu d'amor dolce aura spiri
you of-love (the) sweet air breathe

refrigerio ai miei martiri.
comfort to-[the] my suffering[s].

Vezzosetta e fresca rosa umidetto e dolce labbro,
Charming and fresh rose, moist and sweet lip(s),

ch'hai la manna rugiadosa
who-have the manna dewy

sul bellissimo cinabro.
on-the very-beautiful vermilion.

Non parlar, ma ridi e taci;
(Do) not speak, but smile and be-silent;

sien gli accenti i nostri baci.
let-be the words (the) our kisses.
(Let our kisses be the words.)

O bellissimi capelli, miei dolcissimi diletti
O very-beautiful tresses, my sweetest delights,

amorosi serpentelli, che ritorti in anelletti,
amorous little-snakes, that twisted in little-rings,

discendete infra le rose de le guancie rugiadose.
descend among the roses of the cheeks dewy.

Treccie ombrose, ove s'asconde,
Tresses shadowy, where himself-hides,

per ferir, l'alato arciero,
to wound, the-winged archer, (Cupid),

cedan più le chiome bionde,
(let) yield more the tresses blond,
(blond tresses must yield,)

belle treccie, al vostro nero,
beautiful tresses, to-[the] your(s) black,

che scherzando al viso intorno
for playing to-the face about,
(playing about your face,)

notte siete e gli occhi giorno.
night you-are and the eyes day.
(you are night, and the eyes are day.)

Occhietti amati, che m'incendete
Dear-eyes beloved, that me-inflame,

perchè spietati omai più siete?
why cruel now more are-you?

Splendan sereni di gioia pieni
Let-shine serene with joy filled

vostri splendori, fiammi de'cori.
your splendors, flames of-the-hearts.

Bocca vermiglia ch'hai per confini,
Mouth vermilion which-has for borders,

o meraviglia, perle e rubini,
O marvel, pearls and rubies,

quando ridente, quando clemente
when smiling, when merciful,

dirai: ben mio, io ardo anch'io?
will-you-say: treasure mine, I burn also-[I]?

Vezzosette e care pupillette ardenti,
Charming and dear eyes ardent,

chi v'ha fatto avare
who you-has made miserly
(who has made you miserly)

dei bei rai lucenti?
of-[the] beautiful [rays] (glances) glowing?

S'io rimiro i vostri sguardi
If-I consider [the] your glances,

scorgo sol fulmini e dardi:
I-perceive only lightning[s] and arrows:

nè veder so più quel riso
nor to-see know-I-how more that smile
(nor do I see any longer that smile)

che rendea sì vago il viso.
which rendered so lovely the face.
(which made your face so lovely.)

Cangia, cangia tue voglie,
Change, change your desires,

o mio cor, che fedele fosti a donna crudele.
O my heart, for faithful you-were to (a) woman cruel.

Non t'accorgi, meschin, che sei ferito?
(Do) not you-perceive, poor-fellow, that you-are wounded?

Lascia d'amar chi t'ha tradito.
Leave (off) to love (her) who you-has betrayed.
(Stop loving the one who has betrayed you.)

Lascia d'amare chi ti finge col riso,
Cease from-loving (her) who pretends with-[the] (a) smile,

col mostrarti il bel viso.
with-[the] showing-to-you [the] (her) beautiful face.

Vedi pur come il canto
See also how [the] song

è cagion di tue doglie.
is (the) reason [of] (for) your sorrows.

Lungi, lungi è amor da me
Far, far is love from me

da che fui tradito già
since [that] I-was betrayed already

da te, donna senza fè.
by you, woman without faith.

Vanne pur, superba, va
Go-from-here then, haughty-one, go

dov'è amor con l'arco altero,
where-is love with the-bow proud,
(where love dwells, with the proud bow,)

ch'ogni cor fa prigioniero.
which-every heart makes prisoner.
(which enslaves every heart.)

Più non amo, non bramo ahimè
More not I-love, not I-desire alas
(I no longer love, I do not desire)

d'amar donna, ch'è senza fè.
to-love (a) woman who-is without faith.

La cagion tu sai perchè
The reason you know why

da te lungi il piè rivolsi,
from you far the foot I-turned,
(I went away from you,)

donna rea, senza mercè,
woman guilty, without pity,

e dai lacci il cor disciolsi
and from-[the] bonds [the] (my) heart I-loosened

e sprezzai d'amor il regno
and I-despised of-love the rule

per seguir l'ira e lo sdegno,
to follow [the] wrath and [the] indignation.

99

Frescobaldi   SE L'AURA SPIRA

Se l'aura spira tutta vezzosa,
If the-breeze blows all caressing,

la fresca rosa ridente sta;
the fresh rose smiling stands;

la siepe ombrosa di bei smeraldi
the hedge shady of beautiful emeralds

d'estive caldi timor non ha.
of-summer heat fear not has.
(does not fear the summer heat.)

Ai balli, ai balli liete venite,
To-the dances, to-the dances happy come,

ninfe gradite, fior di beltà,
nymphs welcome, flower of beauty,

or che si chiaro il vago fonte
now that so clear the charming spring

dall'alto monte al mar sen va.
from-the-high mountain to-the sea [itself-from-there] goes.

Suoi dolci versi spiega l'augello,
His sweet verses displays the-bird,

e l'arboscello fiorito sta;
and the-shrub in-blossom stands;

un volto bello all'ombra accanto
one face beautiful to-the-shade near

sol si dia vanto d'aver pietà.
alone [itself] can boast of-having compassion.

Al canto, ninfe ridenti,
To-[the] (your) singing, nymphs smiling,

scacciate i venti di crudeltà.
chase the winds of cruelty.

Gabrielli BELLEZZA TIRANNA, LANGUISCO PER TE
(Il Clearco in Negroponte)

Bellezza tiranna, languisco per te!
Beauty tyrannical, I-languish for you!

Mi sprezzi io t'adoro,
Me you-despise, I you-adore,

mi fuggi, ed io muoro,
me you-shun, and I die,

crudele, perchè?
cruel-one, why?

Gabrielli   VUOI TU, CH'IO SPERI, AMORE
                             (Flavio Cuniberto)

Vuoi tu, ch'io speri, Amore?
Wish you, that-I may-hope, Love?

Rispondi: no o sì!
Reply: no or yes!

Quel labbro sdegnoso di strali è ripieno
That lip disdainful of arrows is full
(Those disdainful lips are full of arrows)

ma il ciglio amoroso pur anche è sereno.
but the eye amorous nevertheless [also] is serene.

Sì o no, no o sì?
Yes or no, no or yes?

S'ancor gli stai nel core
If-still to-him you-are in-the heart
(If you are still in his heart, Love)

sarò felice un dì.
I-shall-be happy one day.

Recit. :
Lungi dal ben, ch'adoro,
Far from-[the]-(my) beloved, whom-I-adore,

miserabile amante,
(a) miserable lover,

per chi più non m'ascolta, invan sospiro,
for her-who more not me-hears, in-vain I-sigh,
(I sigh for her, who no longer hears me,)

e d'un vago sembiante, per cui languisco,
and of-a lovely face, for which I-languish,

in mille lacci astretto,
in (a) thousand snares constrained,

lungi è il bel foco,
far is the beautiful fire,

e pur le fiamme ho in petto.
and yet the flames I-have in (my) bosom.

Aria:
D'un bel crin tra i biondi stami
Of-a beautiful head-of-hair among the blond strands
(By the blond strands of her beautiful hair)

il mio cor avvinto sta.
[the] my heart tied-up is.

Mi dan pena quei legami
To-me give pain those bonds

ma se son legami d'oro,
but [if] (since) they-are bonds of-gold,

piango i nodi e i lacci adoro,
I-bewail the knots and the snares I-adore,

nè più bramo libertà.
nor longer do-I-desire liberty.

Luci vezzose, dunque sarete
Eyes charming, then will-you-be

sempre sdegnose così ver me?
always disdainful thus toward me?

Sempre spietate, mi negherete qualche mercè?
Always pitiless, to-me will-you-deny some compassion?

Sempre spietate, luci adorate,
Always pitiless, eyes adored,

luci vezzose, sempre sdegnose
eyes charming, always disdainful

dunque sarete così per me?
then will-you-be thus toward me?

Si può rimirar vaghi rai,
One can see-again lovely [rays] (eyes),

che mi dite, si può?
what to-me do-you-say, [one can]?

S'io chiedo al mio ben
If-I ask of-[the] my beloved

mi sento nel sen
[to-myself] I-feel in-[the] (my) heart

risponder di no, no, no.
reply [of] no, no, no.

Si può vegheggiar vago ciglio,
One can admire lovely [eye-lash] (eyes),

vago ciglio, si può, che mi di?
lovely eyes, [one can] what to-me do-you-say?

S'io chiedo ad Amor mi sento nel cor
If-I ask [to] (of) love [to-myself] I-feel in-the heart

risponder di sì, sì, sì.
reply [of] yes, yes, yes.

(Shall I see again those lovely eyes?
If I ask my beloved, I feel my heart say, no,
but if I ask love, the heart replies, yes.)

E pena troppo barbara sentirsi,
It-is pain too fierce to-feel-oneself,

O Dei, morir e non poter mai dir:
O God, to-die and not to-be-able ever to-say:

morir mi sento.
to-die myself I-feel.
(I feel myself dying.)

V'è nel lagnarsi e piangere
There-is in-[the] grieving and weeping

qualch'ombra di piacer
some-shadow of pleasure

ma struggersi e tacer
but to-pine-away and remain-silent

troppo è tormento.
too-great is torment.
(is too great a torment.)

Augellin vago e canoro,
Little-bird lovely and melodious,

tu sospiri il colle, il prato,
you sigh-for the hill, the meadow,

e pur sei tra lacci d'oro
and nevertheless you-are [among traps] (in a cage) of-gold

dolcemente imprigionato.
sweetly imprisoned.

Pur senza mai posare e l'ali e'l piede
But without ever resting [both the]-wings and-[the] foot

sempre in perpetui giri,
always in perpetual circles,

vago augel, ti raggiri, e i tuoi concenti
lovely bird, [yourself] you-turn, and [the] your harmonies

sembran note di gioia e son lamenti.
seem notes of joy and are laments.

Io t'intendo, canoro augelletto,
I you-understand, melodious little-bird,

vai piangendo la tua servitù:
you-go lamenting [the] your slavery:

e vorresti d'ameno boschetto
and you-would-like of (the)-pleasant grove

le bell'ombre godere anche tu.
the beautiful-shadows to-enjoy also [you].

Caro laccio, dolce nodo
Dear snare, sweet knot

che legasti il mio pensier,
which tied [the] my thought,

so ch'io peno e pur ne godo;
I-know that-I suffer and nevertheless [of-it] I-am-happy;

son contento e prigionier.
I-am content and (a) prisoner.

Gasparini   LASCIAR D'AMARTI

Lasciar d'amarti per non penar,
To-cease from-loving-you in-order not to-suffer,

caro mio bene, non si può far.
dear my treasure, not [one] (I) can do.

A forza di pene,
[By-force] (In spite) of pains,

di strali e catene
of arrows and chains

non voglio lasciarti;
not I-want to-leave-you;

ti voglio adorar.
you I-want to-adore.

Voi, amanti, che vedete quanto amor mi sia d'affanno,
You, lovers who see how-much love to-me is [of]-anguish,

imparate dal tiranno a fuggir la crudeltà.
learn from-the tyrant to flee [the] (his) cruelty.

Pria piacer promette e pace,
First pleasure he-promises and peace,

poi ne cinge di catene
then [of]-them he-binds with chains

e sperar non ci conviene di tornare in libertà.
and to-hope not to-us is-permitted to return to liberty.

Giordani   CARO MIO BEN

Caro mio ben credimi almen,
Dear my beloved, believe-me at-least

senza di te languisce il cor.
without [of] you languishes [the] (my) heart.

Il tuo fedel sospira ognor;
[The] your faithful-one sighs always;

cessa crudel, tanto rigor.
cease cruel-one, so-much severity.

O del mio dolce ardor bramato oggetto
O of-[the] my sweet ardor desired object,
(O desired object of my sweet ardor,)

l'aura che tu respiri, alfin respiro.
the-air which you breathe, at-last I-breathe.

Ovunque il guardo io giro
Wherever [the] (my) glance I turn

le tue vaghe sembianze amore in me dipinge:
[the] your lovely features love [in] (for) me paints:

il mio pensier si finge
[the] my thought [to-itself pretends] (imagines)

le più liete speranze;
the most happy hopes;

e nel desio che così m'empie il petto
and in-the longing which thus [to-me]-fills [the] (my) bosom

cerco te chiamo te spero e sospiro.
I-seek you, I-call you, I-hope and I-sigh.

Gluck CHE FARO SENZA EURIDICE (RECITATIVE VERSION I)
(Orfeo ed Euridice)

Recit.:
Ahimè! dove trascorsi,
Alas! Where have-I-come,

ove mi spinse un delirio d'amor?
where me has-driven a madness of-love?
(where has the madness of love driven me?)

Sposa...Euridice...Euridice...Consorte...
Wife...Euridice...Euridice...Consort...

Ah! più non vive... la chiamo invan!
Ah! longer not she-lives...her I-call in-vain!

Misero me! la perdo e di nuovo e per sempre!
Wretched me! her I-lose [and] anew and forever!

Oh legge! oh morte! oh ricordo crudel!
Oh law (of the underworld)! O death! O memory cruel!

Non ho soccorso...non m'avanza consiglio...
Not have-I aid... not to-me-remains counsel
                    (there remains no solution for me)

Io veggo solo (Oh fiera vista!) il luttuoso aspetto
I see only (O fierce prospect!) the mournful aspect

dell'orrido mio stato!
of-[the] horrid my condition!

Saziati, sorte rea... son disperato!
Satisfy-yourself, fate cruel...I-am desperate!

Aria:
Che farò senza Euridice?
What will-I-do without Euridice?

Dove andrò senza il mio ben?
Where will-I-go without [the] my beloved?

Che farò? Dove andrò?
What will-I-do? Where will-I-go?

Che farò senza il mio ben?
What will-I-do without [the] my beloved?

Dove andrò senza il mio ben?   Euridice!   Euridice!
Where will-I-go without [the] my beloved? Euridice! Euridice!

Oh Dio! rispondi...rispondi...
O God!   answer... answer...

Io son pure il tuo fedele!
I am still [the] your faithful-one!

Ah!   Non m'avanza più soccorso, più speranza,
Ah! Not to-me-remains any help, any hope,

nè dal mondo, nè dal ciel!
neither from-[the] earth, nor from-[the] heaven!

Gluck   CHE FARO SENZA EURIDICE (RECITATIVE VERSION II)
(Orfeo ed Euridice)

Recit. :
Che ho fatto io?
What have done I?
(What have I done?)

Dove mai quest'amore, dove spinsemi il pianto suo?
Where [ever] this-love, where drove-me [the] weeping her?
(Where have my love and her weeping driven me?)

Cara sposa! Euridice, Euridice! Ah, diletta!
Dear wife! Euridice, Euridice! Ah, beloved!

Ah, non più m'ode morta è di dolor.
Ah, not longer me-hears-she; dead she-is of sorrow.

Son'io, son'io, le diedi io la morte;
It-is I, it-is-I, to-her gave I the death;
                    (I caused her death;)

quanto, quanto sgraziato sono!
how-[much,] how-[much,] wretched am-I!

Il duol mio dir non posso!
[The] sadness my to-say not can-I!
(My sadness is beyond telling!)

In tal terribil ora mi resta solo
In such (a) terrible hour to-me remains only

del morir la via; e tutto cessa.
of-[the] death the way; and everything ceases.

(The text of the aria is identical with Version I)

115

Vieni, che poi sereno
Come, for then serene

alla tua bella in seno
to-[the] your beautiful-one in (the) bosom
(in the bosom of your beloved)

ti troverà l'aurora quando riporta il dì.
you will-find the-dawn when it-brings-back the day.
(dawn will find you.)

Farai d'invidia allora impallidir gli amanti,
You-will-make with-envy then grow-pale the lovers,

e senza affanni e pianti
and without anxieties and weeping[s]

tu goderai così.
you will-be-happy thus.

(Text as in Metastasio libretto.)

Ah mio cor, schernito sei.
Ah, my heart, scorned you-are.

Stelle, Dei, nume d'amore!
Stars, Gods, deity of-love!

Traditore, t'amo tanto;
Traitor, you-I-love so-much;

puoi lasciarmi sola in pianto?
can-you leave-me alone in weeping?

Handel   AL FUROR

Al furor che ti consiglia,
To-the fury which you counsels,

ad Augusto alle sue squadre
to Augustus, to-[the] his troops

offri pur quest'alma ancor.
offer moreover this-soul also.

E delitto esser ti figlia;
It-is (a) crime to-be to-you (a) daughter;

è castigo aver per padre
it-is punishment to-have for (a) father

un sì crudo genitor.
[a] so cruel (a) parent.

Handel   BENCHE MI SIA
                                (Ottone)

Recit.:
Sî me traete, alme malvagie,
Yes, me you-drag, souls savage,

a morte, che a vergine reale
to death, for to (a) virgin royal

convien, morendo, prevenire oltraggio.
it-is-necessary, dying, to-prevent outrage.

Serbarò questa spoglia ad Ottone, intatta e pura;
I-will-preserve this body for Ottone, intact and pure;

che forse in questo punto istesso
who perhaps in this ⌊moment same⌋ (very moment)

ad altra donna in grembo,
to another woman in-(the)-bosom,
(in the arms of another woman,)

la mia salvezza e'l proprio onor trascura.
[the] my safety and-[the] (his) own honor neglects.
(forgets my safety and his honor.)

Aria:
Benchè mi sia crudele,
Although to-me he-may-be cruel,

benchè infedel mi sia,
although unfaithful to-me he-may-be,

infida l'alma mia, no non sarà cosî.
unfaithful [the]-soul my, no, not will-be thus.
(my heart will not be so unfaithful.)

Senta le mie querelle il Nume Dio d'amore
Let-hear [the] my complaints the [divinity] God of-love
(Let the God of love hear my complaints)

poi renda a questo core
then may-he-return to this heart

il ben che lo tradî.
the treasure which it betrayed.
(the lover who betrayed it.)

Handel   CARE SELVE

Care selve, ombre beate,
Dear woods, shadows blessed,

vengo in traccia del mio cor.
I-come in trace of-[the] my heart.
(I come seeking my heart.)

Chi sprezzando il sommo bene
He-who despising the highest good

colpe a colpe accumulò,
sins to sins accumulated,
(sin upon sin has accumulated,)

pensi a crude e giuste pene
let-him-think of (the) cruel and just punishments

se il mal frutto maturò.
if the evil fruit matured.
(if the evil fruit has matured.)

Handel   AURE, DEH PER PIETA
                                (Giulio Cesare)

Recit.:
Dall'ondoso periglio salvo mi porta al lido
From-the-watery danger safe me carries to-the shore

il mio propizio fato.
[the] my favorable destiny.

Qui la celeste parca non tronca ancor
Here the heavenly fate (does) not cut-off yet

lo stame alla mis vita.
the thread [to-the] (of) my life.

Ma dove andrò, e chi mi porge aita?
But where shall-I-go, and who to-me offers help?

Ove son le mie schiere?
Where are [the] my troops?

Ove son le legioni che a tante mie vittorie
Where are the legions which to so-many (of) my victories

il varco apriro?
the pathway opened?

Solo in queste erme arene,
Alone [in] (on) these deserted beaches,

al monarca del mondo errar conviene?
to-the monarch of-the world to-wander is-it-necessary?

Aure!
Breezes!

Aria:
Aure, deh der pietà, spirate al petto mio
Breezes, then in pity, breathe into-[the] bosom my

per dar conforto, o Dio, al mio dolor.
to give comfort, O God, to-[the] my sorrow.

Dite, dov'è, che fa,
Speak, where-is-she, what is-she doing,

l'idolo del mio sen?
the-idol of-[the] my heart?

L'amato e dolce ben di questo cor?
The-beloved and sweet treasure of this heart?

Ma d'ogni intorno io veggio
But from-all around I see

sparse d'armi e d'estinti l'infortunate arene!
scattered with-arms and with-dead the-unfortunate beaches!

Segno d'infausto annunzio alfin sarà!
Sign of-unhappy news at-last it-will-be!

Handel   DA TEMPESTE
                              (Giulio Cesare)

Da tempeste il legno infranto
By tempests the ship wrecked,

se poi salvo giunge in porto
if then safe it-arrives in port,

non sa più che desiar.
not knows more what to-desire.

Così il cor tra pene e pianto,
So the heart, amid pains and weeping,

or che trova il suo conforto,
now that it-finds [the] its comfort,

torna l'anima a bear.
returns the-soul to bless.
(makes the soul happy again.)

Handel

NON E SI VAGO E BELLO
(Giulio Cesare)

Non è si vago e bello il fior nel prato
Not is so lovely and beautiful the flower in-the field

quanto è vago e gentile il tuo bel volto.
as is lovely and pleasing [the] your beautiful face.

D'un fiore il pregio a quello solo vien dato,
Of-a flower the praise to that-one alone comes given,
(The praise of only one flower is given to that one,)

ma tutto un vago Aprile è in te raccolto.
but all [a] lovely April is in you gathered.

Handel   PIANGERO LA SORTE MIA
                                (Giulio Cesare)

Recit. :
E pur così in un giorno perdo fasti e grandezze?
And moreover thus in one day (do) I-lose pomp and grandeur?

Ahi, fato rio!
Alas, fate cruel!

Cesare, il mio bel nume, è forse estinto!
Caesar, [the] my handsome God, is perhaps dead!

Cornelia e Sesto inermi son
Cornelia and Sextus unarmed are,

nè sanno darmi soccorso.
nor do-they-know-how to-give-me aid.

O Dio! Non resta alcuna speme al viver mio.
O God! Not remains any hope of living my.

Aria:
Piangerò la sorte mia
I-shall-weep (for) [the] fate my

si crudele e tanto ria
so cruel and so wicked

finchè vita in petto avrò.
as-long-as life in (my) bosom I-shall-have.

Ma poi morta, d'ogni intorno
But then dead, from-all around,

il tiranno e notte e giorno,
the tyrant, both night and day,

fatta spettro, agiterò.
having-become (a) ghost, I-shall-molest.

Handel   PRESTI OMAI
                          (Giulio Cesare)

Presti omai l'Egizia terra
Let-give now the-Egyptian land
(Let the Egyptian land now give)

le sue palme al vincitor.
[the] its palms to-the conqueror.

Handel   QUEL TORRENTE
                          (Giulio Cesare)

Quel torrente che cade dal monte
That torrent which falls from-the mountain

tutto atterra ch'incontro lo sta.
all overthrows which-against it stands.
(overthrows everything which resists it.)

Tale anch'io a chi oppone la fronte
So also-I to him-who opposes the forehead
(So also he who raises his head against me)

dal mio brando atterrato sarà.
by-[the] my sword overthrown shall-be.
(shall be overthrown by my sword.)

Handel   SE PIETA DI ME NON SENTI
                          (Giulio Cesare)

Se pietà di me non senti,
If pity [of] (for) me not you-feel,

giusto ciel, io morirò.
just heaven, I shall-die.

Tu dà pace a miei tormenti,
You give peace to my torments,

o quest'alma spirerò.
or this-soul will-expire.

Handel   V'ADORO, PUPILLE
                          (Giulio Cesare)

V'adoro, pupille, saette d'Amore,
You-I-adore, eyes, lightnings of-Love,

le vostre faville son grate nel sen.
[the] your sparks are welcome in-[the] (my) heart.

Pietose vi brama il mesto mio core
Compassionate you desires [the] sad my heart
(My sad heart desires you to be compassionate,)

ch'ogn'ora vi chiama, l'amato suo ben.
for-always you it-calls, the-beloved its treasure.
(for it always calls you, its beloved treasure.)

Il mio crudel martoro crescer non può di più:
[The] my cruel suffering increase not can [of] more:

Morte, dove sei tu, che ancor non moro?
Death, where are you, for yet not do-I-die?

Vieni, de'mali miei, no, che il peggior non sei,
Come, of-[the]-pains mine, no, for the worst not you-are,
(Come, for you are not the worst of my pains)

ma sei ristoro.
but you-are (the) relief.

Recit. :
Aspide sono a'detti tuoi d'amore,
(A) serpent*I-am at-[the]-words your of-love,
(I am a serpent against your words of love)

nè vuò macchiar d'infedeltà il mio core.
nor do-I-wish to-soil with-infidelity [the] my heart.

Aria:
Ne men con l'ombra d'infedeltà
Not even with the-shadow of-infidelity

voglio tradire l'anima mia,
do-I-wish to-betray [the]-soul my,

e se'l mio bene suo mal si fa
and if-[the] my beloved [his] evil [himself] does

incolpi amore, non gelosia.
blame love, not jealousy.

*I am a shield (archaic meaning)

O grati orrori!   O solitarie piante!
O welcome horrors!   O solitary trees!

date sollievo, O Dio al core amante!
give relief, O God to-[the] (a) heart loving!

Al conforto dell'alma
To-the comfort of-[the]-(my)-soul

il piè qui porto.
the foot here I-carry.
(I come here.)

Fonti, antri, ascoltate i miei lamenti,
Fountains, caves, hear [the] my laments,

e se potesse omai pace le date.
And if it-is-possible now peace to-her give.

Lungi dal patrio tetto abbandonata sola
Far from-the paternal roof, abandoned, alone,

io qui mi volgo;
I here [myself] turn;

non ho chi mi consoli o mi conforti.
not I-have who me may-console or me comfort.
(I have no one to console me and comfort me.)

Misera, i miei sospiri a voi rivolgo;
Miserable-one, [the] my sighs to you I-turn;

O Dio, date sollievo!
O God, give relief!

S'io dir potessi al mio crudele,
If-I say could to-[the] my cruel-one,

la tua fedele penando va,
[the] your faithful-one suffering goes,

con un sospir del mio martir
with a sigh [of-the] (for) my martyrdom

discoprirebbe qualche pietà.
he-would-reveal some pity.

Handel   OMBRA MAI FU
                          (Serse)

Frondi tenere e belle
Branches tender and beautiful

del mio platano amato,
of-[the] my [plane-tree] (sycamore) beloved,

per voi rispende il fato;
for you shines [the] destiny;

tuoni, lampi e procelle
thunders, lightnings and tempests

non v'oltraggino mai la cara pace,
(do) not let-them-outrage ever [the] (your) dear peace,

ne giunga a profanarvi, austro rapace!
nor let-arrive to profane-you, west-wind rapacious!
(nor may the west-wind ever damage you!)

Ombra mai fu di vegetabile,
Shade never there-was of-(a) plant,

cara ed amabile, soave più.
dear and agreeable, sweet more.
(more dear and pleasant than yours.)

Handel   QUELL'AMOR

Recit.:
L'infelice Medea!
[The]-unhappy Medea!

Innocente saria, se amor non conoscesse.
Innocent she-would-be, if love not she-did-know.

Il germano ed i figli,
The brother and the children,

vittime al mio furore,
victims [to-the] (of) my fury,

furon cosa d'amore:
were (a) thing of-love:

e se freme l'inferno al suon dei detti miei
and if trembles the-inferno at-the sound of-[the] words mine

questi non sanno render al mio conforto
these (do) not know-how to-render to-[the] my comfort

altro che danno.
other than harm.

Aria:
Quell'amor, ch'è nato a forza
That-love which-is born by violence

non contenta un cor amante.
(does) not satisfy a heart loving.

Qual s'accende tal s'ammorza
As itself-it-kindles so itself-it-extinguishes
(As it is kindled so it is extinguished)

e si perde in un istante.
and itself loses in a moment.
(and is lost in a moment.)

135

Se il timore il ver mi dice,
If [the] fear the truth to-me says,
(If fear tells me the truth,)

infelice, abbandonata, sorte ingrata, io morirò.
unhappy, abandoned, fate cruel, I shall-die.

Ma diletta a mia costanza
But dear to my constancy

la speranza a dir mi viene,
[the] hope to say to-me comes,

che il mio bene io placherò.
that [the] my beloved I shall-appease.

Handel   SOMMI DEI!
                                (Radamisto)

Sommi Dei!
Highest Gods!

Che scorgete i mali miei,
(You) who behold [the] wrongs mine,

proteggete un mesto cor!
protect a sad heart!

Sorge nel petto certo diletto
(There) arises in-the bosom (a) certain delight

che bella calma promette al cor.
which beautiful calm promises to-the heart.

Sarà il contento, dopo gran stento
It-will-be [the] (a) satisfaction, after great difficulty

coglier la palma del nostro ardor.
to-gather the palm of-[the] our ardor.
(to reap the reward of our ardor.)

Haydn   NON V'E CHI MI AJUTA
                               (La canterina)

Non v'è chi mi ajuta,
Not there-is one-who me helps,
(There is no one to help me,)

non v'è chi mi sente,
not there-is one-who me hears,
(there is no one to hear me,)

afflitta e dolente,
afflicted and sorrowful,

più voce non ho.
more voice not I-have.
(I can scarcely speak.)

Haydn   COME PIGLIA SI BENE LA MIRA
                         (L'infedeltà delusa)

Come piglia si bene la mira
How takes-he so well [the] aim
(How can Cupid aim so well)

s'ha la benda sugli occhi l'amor;
if-he-has [the] (a) blind-fold on-[the]-(his) eyes [the] love;
(if he is blindfolded;)

come ha l'ali e d'intorno s'aggira
how has-he [the]-wings and around roams-about
(how can he have wings and roam about)

se mi sta sempre fitto nel cor?
if [to-me] he-is always fixed in-[the] (my) heart?

Come fanciullo ch'ama il trastullo
How (a) boy who-loves [the] amusement
(How can he be a boy who loves amusement)

se per diletto c'impiaga il petto
if for pleasure to-us-he-wounds the bosom
(if for pleasure he wounds our bosom)

e poi si ride del nostro dolor?
and then [himself] laughs [of-the] (at) our pain?
(and then derides our pain?)

Mi dicean ch'è una pecchia l'amore
To-me they-said that-is a bee [the]-love
                         (that love is a bee)

che dà il mele, ma pizzica il cor;
which gives [the] honey, but bites the heart;

ei m'ha punto, ne sento il bruciore,
he me-has stung, of-it I-feel the burning,

ma del mele non porgemi ancor.
but of-the honey not he-gives-me yet.

140

Haydn   E LA POMPA UN GRAND IMBROGLIO
                            (L'infedeltà delusa)

E la pompa un grand imbroglio
Is [the] ostentation a great perplexity
(Ostentation is a great confusion)

per un'alma che disprezza
for a-soul that despises

fasto, onor e la richezza.
pomp, honor and [the] wealth.

Io non cerco ed io non voglio
I (do) not seek and I (do) not want
(I seek only and I want only)

che la pace del mio cor.
but [the] peace [of-the] (in) my heart.
(peace in my heart.)

141

Haydn TRINCHE VAINE ALLEGRAMENTE
(L'infedeltà delusa)

Trinche vaine allegramente
Drink wine happily

che Patrone oggi sposar tu ballare, tu cantar.
for padrone today gets-married; you dance, you sing.
    (the master)

Je, foller imbriacar, lustig paesan.
Hey, wild get-drunk, jolly country-man.

Spaisen vuol non pagar niente
To-eat he-wants [not] pay nothing
(The master charges nothing!)

paesan allegramente che Patrone far scialar.
countryman happily for padrone make spend.
                    (let the master spend his money.)

Je, tu cantar, lustig paesan.
Hey, you sing, jolly country-man.

(The German inn-keeper is drunk
and tries to sing in Italian.)

Haydn   O LUNA LUCENTE
                         (Il Mondo della luna)

O luna lucente, di Febo sorella,
O moon shining, of Pheobus (the) sister,

che candida e bella resplendi lassù,
which white and beautiful shine(s) up-there,

deh, fa che i nostri occhi
ah, make that [the] our eyes

s'accostano a tuoi
themselves-approach to yours

e scopriti a noi che cosa sei tu.
and reveal-[yourself] to us what [thing] are you.

Haydn QUESTA MANO E QUESTO CUORE
(Le pescatrici)

Questa mano e questo cuore
This hand and this heart

caro bene, a voi prometto;
dear treasure, to you I-promise;

a voi giuro eterno amore e costante fedeltà;
to you I-swear eternal love and constant fidelity;

ma sia pari il vostro affetto,
but let-be equal [the] your affection,

pari in voi sia l'onestà.
equal in you let-be the-honesty.

Il tradirmi, o mio diletto,
[The] to-betray-me, O my beloved,

saria troppa crudeltà.
would-be too-much cruelty.

Haydn   VOGLIO AMAR E VUO SCHERZARE
                                         (Le pescatrici)

Voglio amar e vuò scherzare
I-want to-love and I-want to-play

con ogn'un di fè e d'amor,
with everyone of faith and of-love,

ma ad un solo vuò serbare
but for one only I-want to-preserve

tenerino questo cor.
tender this heart.
(this tender little heart.)

Chi vuol comprar le bella calandrina
Who wants-to-buy the beautiful little-lark

che canta da mattina fino a sera?
that sings from morning until [to] evening?

Chi vuol comprarla venga a contratto,
He-who wants to-buy-her let-him-come to agreement,

sempre a buon patto la venderò.
always at (a) good price her I-will-sell.

E si gentile, ha così dolce il canto
She-is so tame, she-has so sweet the song

e venderla degg'io che l'amo tanto;
and sell-her must-I who her-love so-much;
(and I who love her so much must sell her;)

ma questo è il mio mestiere
but this is [the] my trade

e nol fo per piacere.
and not-it I-do for pleasure.
(and I don't do it for pleasure.)

Che fiero costume d'aligero nume
What (a) fierce custom of-(a)-winged god*(Cupid)

che a forza di pene si faccia adorar!
who by force of punishment[s] himself should-make adored!

E pur nell'ardore il dio traditore
And nevertheless in-[the] (my) ardor the god traitorous

un vago sembiante mi fe' idolatrar.
a lovely face me made to-worship.
(made me worship a lovely face.)

Che crudo destino che un cieco bambino
What (a) cruel fate that a blind child

con bocca di latte si faccia stimar!
with (a) mouth of milk himself should-make esteemed!
(scarcely weaned, should make himself esteemed!)

Ma questo tiranno con barbaro inganno
But this tyrant with barbarous deception

entrando per gli occhi mi fe' sospirar.
entering though [the] (my) eyes me made to-sigh.

*Cupid, represented as a child, has wings, is blind, and
carries a bow and arrows.

Non mi dir di palesar, O mio cor adolorato,
(Do) not to-me say to reveal, O my heart tormented,

al bell'idolo spietato
to-the handsome-idol cruel

la cagion del tuo penar!
the reason [of-the] (for) your suffering!

Non è degno di salir il tuo foco ad alta sfera.
Not is worthy to rise [the] your fire to (such a) high realm.

E fallace consigliera
Is (a) false counsellor

la speme a risanar empio martir.
[the] hope to heal inhuman martyrdom.
(Hope is a false counsellor to heal cruel suffering.)

Pena, sospira e taci! E sol t'avanza,
Suffer, sigh and be-silent! And only to-you-remains,

vincer l'aspro dolor con la costanza.
to-conquer the-bitter pain with [the] constancy.

Sotto il manto del tacer
Under the mantle of-[the] silence

dell'ardor copri la forza
of-[the]-longing cover the strength

che sepolta, più rinforza ogni fiamma il suo poter!
for buried, more increases every flame [the] its power!
(for every flame increases in power when it is buried!)

Che, se poi t'afflige il duol,
So, if then you-torments the pain,
          (pain torments you)

tu con pioggia di gran pianto,
[you] with (a) rain of great weeping,

che dagli occhi scorra intanto,
which from-[the] (your) eyes would-run meanwhile,

148

porta l'anima tua stillata al suol.
carry [the]-soul your in-drops to-the ground.

Muto pianger talor pietade impetra;
Silent weeping sometimes pity obtains;

rende molle la pioggia anco la pietra.
renders soft the rain even [the] stone.
(the rain softens even the stone.)

Leo   SE CERCA, SE DICE

Recit. :
Io vado.
I go.

Deh pensa ad Aristea!
Ah, [think of] (care for) Aristea!

(Che dirà mai quando in se tornerà!
(What will-she-say [ever] when in herself she-will-return!
                              (when she recovers!)

Tutte ho presenti tutte le smanie sue.)
All I-have present [all] [the] agitations her.)
(I can imagine her agitation.)

Licida, ah senti:
Licida, ah, listen:

Aria:
Se cerca, se dice:
If she-seeks, if she-says:

l'amico dov'è?
[the-friend] (my beloved) where-is-he?

L'amico infelice, rispondi, morî!
[The]-(my)-lover unfortunate, reply, he-died!

Ah, no! Si gran duolo non darle per me!
Ah, no! Such great sorrow (do) not give-her for me!

Rispondi, ma solo: piangendo partî!
Reply, but only: weeping he-left!

Che abisso di pene
What (an) abyss of suffering[s]

lasciare il suo bene,
to-leave [the] one's treasure,

lasciarlo per sempre, lasciarlo così!
to-leave-it for ever, to-leave-it thus!

Leoncavallo   O COLOMBINA (HARLEQUIN'S SERENADE)
                 (Pagliacci)

O Colombina, il tenero fido Arlecchin è a te vicin!
O Colombina, the tender, faithful Harlequin is to you near!

Di te chiamando e sospirando
[Of] (for) you calling and sighing

aspetta il poverin! La tua faccetta mostrami,
waits the poor-little-one! [The] your little-face show-me,

ch'io vo' baciar senza tardar la tua boccuccia.
that-I wish to-kiss without delay [the] your little-mouth.
(because)

Amor mi cruccia e mi sta a tormentar!
Love me afflicts and me stands to torment!
                         (is tormenting me!)

O Colombina, schiudimi il finestrin,
O Colombina, open-to-me the little-window,

che a te vicin di te chiamando e sospirando
that to you near [of] (for) you calling and sighing,
(because near you, calling and sighing)

è il povero Arlecchin! A te vicin è Arlecchin!
is [the] poor Harlequin! To you near is Harlequin!

151

Leoncavallo   SI PUO? (PROLOGO)
                          (Pagliacci)

Si può? Signore! Signori! Scusatemi
One may? Ladies! Gentlemen! Excuse-me
(May I?)

se da sol mi presento. Io sono il Prologo.
if [by] alone myself I-present. I am the Prologue.

Poichè in iscena ancor
Since on (the) stage again

le antiche maschere mette l'autore,
the old masks puts the-author,
(the author wishes to put the old characters,)

in parte ei vuol riprendere le vecchie usanze,
in part, he wishes to-take-again the old customs,

e a voi di nuovo inviami.
and to you again he-sends-me.

Ma non per dirvi come pria:
But not to tell-you as before:

"Le lagrime che noi versiam son false!
"The tears that we shed are false!

Degli spasimi e dei nostri martir
By-the sufferings and by-[the] our torments

non allarmatevi." No.
(do) not alarm-yourselves." No.

L'autore ha cercato invece
The-author has searched instead

pingervi uno squarcio di vita.
to-paint-for-you a slice of life.

Egli ha per massima sol che l'artista è un uom,
He has for (his) maxim only that the-artist is a man,

e che per gli uomini scrivere ei deve,
and that for [the] men write he must,

ed al vero ispiravasi.
and at-the truth inspired-himself.
(and truth was his inspiration.)

Un nido di memorie in fondo a l'anima
A nest of memories in (the) depth [to] (of) [the]-(his)-soul

cantava un giorno, ed ei con vere lacrime scrisse,
sang one day, and he with real tears wrote,

e i singhiozzi il tempo gli battevano!
and the sobs the time for-him beat!

Dunque, vedrete amar
Now-then, you-will-see (men) love

sì come s'amano gli esseri umani
just as themselves-love the beings human,
(just as human beings love each other,)

vedrete de l'odio i tristi frutti,
you-will-see of [the]-hatred the wretched fruits,

del dolor gli spasimi,
of-[the] sadness the spasms,

urli di rabbia, udrete, e risa ciniche!
howls of rage, you-will-hear, and laughter cynical!

E voi, piuttosto che le nostre povere gabbane d'istrioni,
and you, rather than [the] our poor garb of-actors,

le nostr'anime considerate,
the our-souls consider,

poichè siam uomini di carne e d'ossa,
since we-are men of flesh and of-bone,

e che di quest'orfano mondo
and that of this-orphan world

al pari di voi spiriamo l'aere!
[to]-the same [of] (as) you we-breathe the-air!
(we breathe the same air of this orphan world as you!)

Il concetto vi dissi.
The concept to-you I-have-told.

Or ascoltate com'egli è svolto. Andiam! Incominciate!
Now listen how-it is unfolded.   Let's go!   Begin!

Leoncavallo STRIDONO LASSU (BALLATELLA)
(Pagliacci)

Recit. :
Qual fiamma avea nel guardo! Gli occhi abbassai
What fire he-had in-the look! The eyes I-lowered
(What fire in his gaze! I lowered my eyes)

per tema ch'ei leggesse il mio pensier segreto!
for fear that-he might-read [the] my thought secret!
(my secret thought!)

Oh! s'ei mi sorprendesse brutale come egli è!
Oh, if-he me were-to-surprise, brutal as he is!

Ma basti, orvia. Son queste sogni paurosi e fole!
But enough, come,-now. Are these dreams fearful and foolish!

O che bel sole di mezz'agosto!
Oh, what (a) beautiful sun of mid-August!

Io son piena di vita, e tutta illanguidita
I am full of life, and completely languid

per arcano desio, non so che bramo!
with secret desire; not know-I what I-desire!

Oh! che volo d'augelli, e quante strida!
Oh, what (a) flight of-birds, and how-many cries!

Che chiedon? Dove van? Chissà!
What do-they-seek? Where are-they-going? Who knows?

La mamma mia, che la buona ventura annunziava
[The] mother my, who [the] good fortune predicted,

comprendeva il lor canto e a me bambina
understood [the] their song, and to me (as a) child

così cantava: Hui! Hui!
thus sang: Hui! Hui!

Aria:
Stridono lassù, liberamente lanciati a vol,
They-cry up-there, freely launched in flight,

a vol come frecce, gli augel. Disfidano le nubi,
in flight like arrows, the birds. They-defy the clouds,

155

e'l sol cocente, e vanno per le vie del ciel.
and-the sun burning, and they-go through the paths of-the sky.

Lasciateli vagar per l'atmosfera,
Let-them wander through the-atmosphere,

questi assetati d'azzurro e di splendor:
these thirsting for-blue (sky) and for splendor:

seguono anch'essi un sogno, una chimera, e vanno
follow too,-they, a dream, an illusion, and they-go

per le nubi d'or!
through the clouds of-gold!

Che incalzi il vento e latri la tempesta,
That mounts the wind and howls the storm,
(Though the wind mounts and the storm howls,)

con l'ali aperte san tutto sfidar;
with [the]-wings spread they-know-how everything to-defy;

la pioggia, i lampi nulla mai li arresta,
the rain, the lightning, nothing ever them stops,

e vanno sugli abissi e i mar. Vanno laggiù
and they-go over-the abysses and the seas.   They-go, far-off,

verso un paese strano che sognan forse
toward a country strange that they-dream-of, perhaps,

e che cercano invan. Ma i boëmi del ciel
and that they-seek in-vain. But the gypsies of-the sky

seguon l'arcano poter che li sospinge e van!
follow the-secret power that them drives, and they-go-on!

Leoncavallo   VESTI LA GIUBBA
                           (Pagliacci)

Recit. :
Recitar! Mentre preso dal delirio
To-perform! While taken with-[the] delirium,

non so più quel che dico e quel che faccio!
not know-I any-more that which I-say and that which I-do!

Eppur...è d'uopo... sforzati!
Yet... it-is necessary...force yourself!

Bah, se' tu forse un uom? tu se' Pagliaccio!
Bah, are you [perhaps] a man? You are (a) clown!

Aria:
Vesti la giubba e la faccia infarina.
Put-on the smock and the face cover-with-powder.

La gente paga e rider vuole quà.
The people pay, and to-laugh they-wish here.

E se Arlecchin t'invola Colombina,
And if Harlequin from-you-steals Colombine,

ridi, Pagliaccio, e ognun applaudirà!
laugh, Clown, and everyone will-applaud!

Tramuta in lazzi lo spasmo ed il pianto;
Change into buffoonery the suffering and the tears;

in una smorfia il singhiozza e il dolor...
into a grimace the sob(s) and the sadness...

Ridi Pagliaccio, sul tuo amore infranto!
Laugh, Clown, at-[the] your love shattered!

Ridi del duol che t'avvelena il cor!
Laugh at-the sorrow that to-you-poisons the heart!
                           (poisons your heart!)

157

Tu partisti; idolo amato,
You (have) departed; idol beloved,

me lasciasti fra le pene!
me you-left among [the] griefs!

Duri lacci e rie catene
Hard snares and cruel chains

soffre un petto innamorato.
suffers a heart in-love.

Pur dicesti o bocca bella,
Yet you-said, O mouth beautiful,

quel soave e caro sî
that sweet and dear "yes"

che fa tutto il mio piacer.
which makes all [the] my pleasure.

Per onor di sua facella
For (the) honor of his [banner] (reputation)

con un bacio amor t'aprî,
with a kiss love you-opened,
(love opened you with a kiss,)

dolce fonte del goder.
sweet fountain of-[the] pleasure.

Marcello   IL MIO BEL FOCO

Il mio bel foco, o lontano o vicino
[The] my beautiful fire, either distant or near

ch'esser poss'io, senza cangiar mai tempre,
that-be can-I, without changing ever [quality],
(that I may be,)

per voi care pupille, arderà sempre.
for you, dear eyes, will-burn always.

Quella fiamma che m'accende
That flame which me-kindles

piace tanto all'alma mia
pleases so-much to-[the]-soul mine

che giammai s'estinguerà.
that never itself-will-it-extinguish.

E se il fato a voi me rende,
And if [the] fate to you me returns,

vaghi rai del mio bel sole,
lovely rays of-[the] my beautiful sun,

altra luce ella non vuole
other light it (does) not want
(my soul does not desire any other light)

nè voler giammai potrà.
nor wish ever will-it-be-able-to.
(nor will it ever want any other.)

Mascagni   O LOLA, BIANCA
                              (Cavalleria Rusticana)

O Lola, bianca come fior di spino,
O Lola, white as (the) flower of (the) thorn,

quando t'affacci te s'affaccia il sole;
when yourself-present you, itself presents the sun;
(when you appear, the sun appears;)

chi t'ha baciato il labbro porporino
he-who (of) you-has kissed the lip(s) bright-red

grazia più bella a Dio chieder non vole,
grace more beautiful [to] (from) God to-ask not desires,
(does not expect anything more beautiful from God,)

c'è scritto sangue sopra la tua porta,
there-is written blood over [the] your door,

ma di restarci a me non me n'importa;
but to remain-there to me not (for) me [not]-is-important;

se per te mojo e vado in paradiso
if for you I-die and go into paradise,

non c'entro se non vedo il tuo bel viso. Ah!
not there-I-enter if not I-see [the] your beautiful face. Ah!

Mascagni   VOI LO SAPETE
                                 (Cavalleria Rusticana)

Voi lo sapete, o mamma, prima d'andar soldato
You it know, O mamma, before to-go soldier
                    (before going away as a soldier)

Turiddu aveva a Lola eterna fè giurato.
Turiddu had to Lola eternal faith sworn.

Tornò, la seppe sposa,
He-returned, her he-knew married,
            (he learned she had married,)

e con un nuovo amore volle spegner
and with a new love he-wished to-extinguish

la fiamma che gli bruciava il core.
the flame which to-him burned the heart.
(the flame that burned his heart.)

M'amò. L'amai. Ah, l'amai.
Me-he-loved. Him-I-loved. Ah, him-I-loved.

Quell' invida d'ogni delizia mia,
That-one, envious of-each joy my,
(Lola, envious of my every joy,)

del suo sposo dimentica,
of-[the] her husband forgetful,

arse di gelosia, me l' ha rapito.
burned with jealousy, from-me him has stolen.

Priva dell' onor mio, dell' onor mio rimango:
Deprived of-[the] honor my, of-[the] honor my I-am-left:

Lola e Turiddu s'amano, io piango!
Lola and Turiddu love-each-other; I weep!

Presto, presto io m'innamoro,
Quickly, quickly I [myself]-fall-in-love,

ma più presto il cor n'è sciolto!
but more quickly [the] (my) heart from-it-is untied!
(but even more quickly I fall out of love!)

Riverisco oggi un bel volto,
I-salute today a pretty face,

ma diman più non l'adoro!
but tomorrow more not it-do-I-adore!

E un effimero e cadente
Is [an] ephemeral and failing
(Ephemeral and failing is)

quell'amor che m'ha piagato;
that-love which me-has wounded;
(that love which has wounded me;)

oggi sono egro e languente
today I-am sick and languishing

ma diman son risanato!
but tomorrow I-am well-again!

Più non sia, che m'innamori
More not let-it-be, that me-should-captivate
(No longer shall I be captivated)

vaga rosa in nobil viso!
(a) lovely rose in (a) noble face!
(by a face, lovely as a rose!)

Spesso giace angue tra fiori,
Often lies (a) serpent among (the) flowers,

che altri poi ne rest'anciso.
so-that another then [by-it remains]-(is)-killed.

Ostro ed or di fresca etade
Purple and gold of fresh age (youth)

non lushinghi un cor fedele!
(do) not let-flatter a heart faithful!

Veste pur spoglie dorate
Wears also clothing gilded

per le piagge angue crudele.
on the beaches (the) serpent cruel.

Non vi mova o riso o canto
Not you let-move either laughter or song

di bellezza allettatrice!
of beauty enticing!

Pur cantando invita al pianto
Also by-singing invites to-[the] weeping

la sirena ingannatrice.
the siren deceptive.

Ahi, troppo è dura, crudel sentenza,
Alas, too-much is severe, cruel sentence,
(Alas, too severe is the cruel sentence,)

e viepiù cruda pena: tornare a lagrimar
and much-more cruel punishment: to-return to weep
(and much more cruel is the punishment to return to weep)

nell'antro oscuro!
in-the-cave dark!

Aer sereno e puro, addio per sempre!
Air serene and pure, goodbye for ever!

O cieli, o sole, addio, lucide stelle!
O heaven, O sun, goodbye, bright stars!

Apprendete pietà, donne e donzelle!
Learn (to-show) pity, women and maidens!

Ardo e scoprir ahi lasso, non ardisco
I-burn, and to-reveal, alas, unhappy -one, not do-I-dare

quel che porto in sen rinchiuso ardore.
that which I-carry in (my) bosom suppressed longing.
(that suppressed longing which I carry in my bosom.)

E tanto più dolente ognor languisco,
And the more painfully always I-languish,

quanto più sta celato il mio dolore.
the more remains hidden [the] my pain.

Fra me talor mille disegni ordisco
Within myself sometimes (a) thousand plans I-contrive

colla lingua discior anche il timore.
with-[the] (my) tongue to-dissolve also [the] (my) fear.

Ed allor, fatto ardito
And then, becoming daring

io non pavento gridar soccorso!
I (do) not fear to-cry (for) help!

Soccorso a micidial tormento!
Help against (this) murderous torment!

Ma s'avvien ch'io m'appresso a lei davanti
But if-it-happens that-I [myself] approach to her [before]

per provar, al mio mal, pace e diletto,
to experience, for-[the] my pain, peace and pleasure,

divengo tosto pallido in sembiante,
I-become immediately pale in countenance,

e chinar gli occhi a terra son costretto.
and to-lower [the]-(my)-eyes to (the) ground I-am obliged.

Dir, vorrei dir, ma non oso.
Speak, I-would speak, but not do-I-dare.

Indi tremante. Ah, e mi ritengo.
Therefore, trembling. Ah, and myself I-restrain.
                    (I tremble, and I remain silent.)

Al fin l'affetto s'aprir
At last the-emotion itself to-open

nunzia del cor la lingua vuole!
messenger of-the heart the tongue wants!
(At last the heart makes the tongue speak!)

Si troncan sulle labbra le parole!
Themselves break on-[the] (my) lips the words!

Monteverdi   CHIOMA D'ORO

Chioma d'oro, bel tesoro,
Hair of-gold, beautiful treasure,

tu mi leghi in mille nodi,
you me tie in (a) thousand knots,

se t'annodi se ti snodi.
if you-yourself-tie-up, if you yourself untie.
(whether you wear your hair up or down.)

Candidette perle elette
White-little pearls chosen

se le rose che coprite
if the rose which you-cover
(if your rosy lips, which cover your pearly teeth)

discoprite, mi ferite.
you-uncover, me you-wound.
(smile to uncover your teeth, you wound me.)

Vive stelle che si belle e si vaghe risplendete,
Living stars, which ao beautiful and so lovely shine

se ridete m'ancidete.
If you-laugh, me-you-kill.

Preziose, amorose coralline labbra amate,
Precious, amorous little-coral lips beloved,

se parlate mi beate.
if you-speak, me you-bless.

O bel nodo per cui godo,
O beautiful knot for which I-rejoice,

O soave uscir di vita,
O sweet departure from life,

O gradita mia ferita.
O welcome my wound.
(Oh, my welcome wound.)

168

Monteverdi   CON CHE SOAVITA

Con che soavità, labbra odorate,
With what sweetness, lips fragrant,

e vi bacio e v'ascolto;
both you I-kiss and you-I-listen-to;
(I both kiss you and listen to you;)

ma se godo un piacer, l'altro m'è tolto,
but if I-enjoy one pleasure, the-other from-me-is taken,

come i vostri diletti s'ancidono
as [the] your pleasures [themselves]-fight

fra lor.
between them(selves).

Se dolcemente vive per ambedue l'anima mia,
If sweetly lives for both [the]-soul my,
            (my soul lives for both,)

che soave armonia fareste, o cari baci,
what sweet harmony you-would-make, o dear kisses,

che soave armonia fareste, o dolci detti,
what sweet harmony you-would-make, o sweet words,

se foste unitamente d'ambedue le dolcezze
if you-were jointly of-both the sweetnesses

ambo capaci,
[both] capable,

baciando i detti e ragionando i baci.
kissing the words and discussing the kisses.

Monteverdi   IL LAMENTO D'ARIANNA (LASCIATEMI MORIRE)
(Complete version)

Lasciatemi morire, e chi volete voi che mi conforte
Let-me die, and who wish you that me should-comfort
(whom do you wish to comfort me)

in cosî dura sorte, in cosî gran martire?
in such cruel fate, in such great martyrdom?

O Teseo mio, si che mio ti vo'dir,
O Theseus mine, indeed that mine to-you I-want-to-say,
(I want to call you mine,)

che mio pur sei,
since mine moreover you-are,

benchè t'involi, ahi crudo,
although yourself-you-take-away, alas, cruel-one,

a gli occhi miei,
[to] (from) [the] eyes mine,

volgiti, Teseo mio,
turn-yourself, Theseus mine,

o Dio, volgiti indietr'a rimirar colei,
oh, God, turn-yourself back-to behold-again her,

che lasciato ha per te la patria e'l regno,
who left has for you the homeland and-the kingdom,

e'n queste arene ancora,
and-(who)-in these sands yet,

cibo di fere dispietate e crude,
food of wild-beasts pitiless and cruel,

lascerà l'ossa ignude.
will-leave [the] (her) bones naked.

O Teseo mio, se tu sapessi, o Dio, se tu sapessi ohimè
O Theseus mine, if you knew, oh, God, if you knew, alas,

come s'affanna la povera Arianna,
how [herself]-[she]-grieves the poor Ariadne,
(how Ariadne grieves,)

170

forse pentito
perhaps having-repented,

rivolgeresti ancor la prora al lito.
you-would-turn again the prow (of-your-ship) to-the shore.

Ma con l'aure serene tu te ne vai felice,
But with-the breezes serene you [yourself] from-here go happy,

ed io qui piango;
and I here weep;

a te prepara Atene liete pompe superbe,
for you prepares Athens happy celebrations proud,

ed io rimango,
and I remain,

cibo di fere in solitarie arene;
food of wild-beasts in solitary deserts;

te l'uno e l'altro tuo vecchio parente
you the-one and the-other your old parents

stringeran lieti,
will-embrace happy,

ed io più non vedrovvi, o madre, o padre mio.
and I more not will-see-you, O mother, O father mine,

Dove è la fede che tanto mi giuravi?
Where is the faith that so-much to-me you-swore?

Così nell'alto sede tu mi ripon degli Avi?
Thus in-the-high place you me place of-the ancestors?
(Thus do you place me on a level with your ancestors?)

Son queste le corone,
Are these the crowns,

onde m'adorni il crine?
with-which to-me-you-adorn [the] (my) hair?

Questi gli scettri sono, queste le gemme e gli ori?
These the scepters are, these the gems and the gold?

Lasciarmi in abbandono:
To-leave-me in abandon:

Monteverdi IL LAMENTO D'ARIANNA (LASCIATEMI MORIRE)
(continued)

Ah, fera che mi strazi e mi divori.
Ah, wild-beast which me tears-up and me devours.

Ah, Teseo mio, lascerai tu morire, invan piangendo,
Ah, Theseus mine, will-let you die, in-vain weeping,

invan gridando aita la misera Arianna
in-vain crying (for) help the wretched Ariadne
(Ah my Theseus, will you let wretched Ariadne die, weeping
    and calling for help in vain,)

che a te fidossi, e ti diè gloria e vita?
who to you trusted-herself, and to-you gave glory and life?

Ahi, che non pur risponde;
Alas, that not even he-replies;
(Alas, he does not even reply;)

Ahi, che più d'aspe è sordo a miei lamenti.
Alas, that more than-(a)-serpent, he-is deaf to my laments.

O nembi, O turbi, O venti,
O storms, O whirlwinds, O winds,

sommergete lo voi dentro a quell'onde;
submerge him [you] within [to] those-waves;

correte, orche e balene,
run, monsters and whales,

e delle membra immonde
and of-[the] (his) limbs filthy

empite le voragini profonde.
fill the abysses profound.

Che parlo, ahi, che vaneggio? Misera, Ohimè,
What do-I-say, alas, [that] do-I-rave? Wretched-one, alas,

che veggio? O Teseo mio non son,
what do-I-see? O Theseus mine, not I-am,

non son quell'io
not I-am that-one-[I]

che i feri detti sciolse;
who the wild words released;

parlò l'affanno mio, parlò il dolore,
spoke [the]-anguish mine, spoke the pain,
(it was my anguish that spoke, it was my pain,)

172

parlò la lingua, sî, ma non già il core.
spoke the tongue, yes, but not really [the] (my) heart.
(it was my tongue, yes.)

Misera ancor do loco a la tradita speme
Wretched still I-[give place] (yield) to the betrayed hope;

e non si spegne fra tanto scherno
and not itself extinguishes amid so-much scorn
(not yet is extinguished, even amid so much scorn)

ancor d'amor il foco.
yet of-love the fire.
(the fire of love.)

Spegni tu, morte, omai le fiamme indegne.
Extinguish [you], death, now the flames unworthy.

O madre, O padre,
O mother, O father,

O dell'antico regno superbi alberghi,
O of-the-ancient kingdom proud dwellings,
(O ancient royal palaces,)

ov'ebbi d'or la cuna;
where-I-had of-gold the cradle;
(where I had a golden cradle;)

o servi, o fidi amici (ahi, fato indegno) mirate
O servants, O faithful friends (alas, fate unworthy) behold

ove m'ha scorto empia fortuna,
where me-has discovered cruel fortune,

mirate di che duol m'ha fatto erede l'amor mio,
behold of what sorrow me-has made heir [the]-love mine,
(behold to what sorrow love has made me the heir,)

la mia fede e l'altrui inganno.
[the] my faith and the-[of-others] deceit (of others).

Così va chi tropp'ama e troppo crede.
Thus goes one-who too-much-loves and too-much believes.
(Thus it goes with one who loves too much.)

Monteverdi   LASCIATEMI MORIRE!

Lasciatemi morire!
Let-me die!

E che volete che mi conforte
And what do-you-wish that me should-comfort
(And what consolation is there for me)

in così dura sorte,
in such hard fate,

in così gran martire?
in such great [suffering] (martyrdom)?

Lasciatemi morire!
Let-me die!

Monteverdi   IN UN FIORITO PRATO
                   (Orfeo)

In un fiorito prato con l'altre sue compagne
In a flowery meadow with [the]-other her companions

giva cogliendo fiori
she-went gathering flowers

par farne una ghirlanda alle sue chiome;
to make-of-them a garland for-[the] her tresses;

quando angue insidioso,
when (a) serpent treacherous,

ch'era tra l'erbe ascoso
which-was among the-grass[es] hidden

le punse un piè con velenoso dente.
to-her bit a foot with poison tooth.
(stung her foot with its poison tooth.)

Ed ecco immantinente scolorirsi il bel viso
And behold immediately grew-pale-[itself] the beautiful face

e ne'suoi lumi sparir quei lampi,
and in-[the]-her eyes disappeared those lightnings,

onde fa scorno al sole.
with-which she-makes scorn to-the sun.
(with which she puts the sun to scorn.)

Allor noi tutte sbigottite e meste le fummo intorno,
Then we, all dismayed and sad, to-her were near,

richiamar tentando gli spirti in lei smarrite
to-recall trying the spirits in her lost

con l'onda fresca e coi possenti carmi.
with [the]-water cool and with powerful charms.

Ma nulla valse, ahi lassa,
But nothing availed, alas, un-happy-one,

ch'ella i languidi lumi alquanto aprendo
for-she the languid eyes somewhat opening

e te chiamando, Orfeo, Orfeo.
and you calling, Orfeo, Orfeo.
(and called you, "Orfeo, Orfeo.")

Dopo un grave sospiro
After a deep sigh

spirò fra queste braccia ed io rimasi
she-died within these arms and I remained,

piena il cor di pietade e di spavento.
full the heart of pity and of terror.
(my heart full of pity and terror.)

Mozart   AH, NON LASCIARMI, NO
                          K. 486a

Recit. :
Basta, vincesti, eccoti il foglio.
Enough, you-have-won, here-is-for-you the letter.

Vedi quanto t'adoro ancora ingrato.
See how-much you-I-adore still ungrateful-one.
(See how much I still adore you.)

Con un tuo sguardo solo
With a your glance one
(With one glance of yours)

mi togli ogni difesa
from-me you-take-away every defense

e mi disarmi;
and me you-disarm;

ed hai cor di tradirmi?
and do-you-have (the) heart to betray-me?

e poi lasciarmi?
and then to-leave-me?

Aria:
Ah, non lasciarmi, no, bell'idol mio,
Ah, (do) not leave-me, no, beautiful-idol mine,

di chi mi fiderò, se tu m'inganni?
in whom [myself] shall-I-trust, if you me-deceive?

Di vita mancherei, nel dirti: addio,
Of life I-would-lack, in-[the] telling-you goodbye,

che viver non potrei, fra tanti affanni!
since live not I-could, among so-many anxieties!

177

Mozart   AH! NON SAI QUAL PENA
                              K. 416

Recit.:
Mia speranza adorata!
My hope adored!
(My beloved hope!)

Ah! troppo è a noi l'ira del ciel funesta;
Ah, too-much is to us the-wrath of-[the] heaven calamitous;
(Ah, the wrath of heaven is too calamitous for us;)

l'ultima volta è questa, ch'io ti stringo al mio seno.
the-last time is this, that-I you clasp to-[the] my breast.

Anima mia, io più non ti vedrò, deh, tu l'assisti,
Soul my, I more not you will-see; ah, [you] her-assist,

tu per me la consola.
[you] for me her console.

Addio, Zemira, ricordati di me!
Goodbye, Zemira, remember-[yourself of] me!

senti... che vedo? tu piangi, o mio tesoro,
listen...what do-I-see? you weep, O my treasure,

oh, quanto accresce quel pianto il mio martir.
oh, how-much increases that weeping [the] my suffering.

Chi prova mai stato peggior del mio?
Who experiences ever condition worse than-[the] mine?
(Who can experience a condition worse than mine?)

Addio per sempre, amata sposa, addio!
Goodbye for ever, beloved spouse, goodbye!

Aria:
Ah! non sai qual pena sia il doverti, oh Dio! lasciar,
Ah, not know-you what pain is [the] having-you, oh, God,
    to-leave,
(Oh, God, you do not know the pain of having to leave you,)

Ma quel pianto, anima mia, fa più grave il mio penar,
But that weeping, soul my, makes more grave [the] my
    suffering,

                        178

Deh, mi lascia, oh fier momento! Cara sposa,
Ah, me leave, O fierce moment! Dear wife,

ah, ch'io mi sento per l'affanno il cor mancar!
ah, how-I [myself] feel through [the]-anguish the heart to-fail!
(ah, how I feel as if anguish will make my heart fail!)

A quai barbare vicende mi servaste, avversi Dei,
To what savage vicissitudes me you-kept, adverse gods,

Dite voi, se i casi miei non son degni di pietà.
Say you, if [the] cases my not are worthy of pity.
(Tell me if my situation is not worthy of pity.)

Mozart   AH! NON SON IO CHE PARLO
                          K. 369

Recit. :
Misera, dove son!
Unhappy-one, where am-I!

L'aure del Tebro son queste ch'io respiro?
The-air[s] of-the Tiber are these that-I breathe?

Per le strade m'aggiro di Tebe e d'Argo?
Through the streets [myself]-do-I-go of Thebes and of-Argos?

O dalle greche sponde, di tragedie feconde,
Or from-the Grecian shores, with tragedies fruitful,

le domestiche furie vennero a questi lidi,
the domestic furies have-come to these shores,

della prole di Cadmo, e degli Atridi?
of-the offspring of Cadmus, and of-the sons-of-Atreus?

Là, d'un monarca ingiusto,
There, of-a monarch unjust,

l'ingrata crudeltà m'empie d'orrore,
the-ungrateful cruelty me-fills with-horror,

d'un padre traditore quà la colpa m'agghiaccia:
of-a father traitorous here the guilt me-chills:

e lo sposo innocente ho sempre in faccia.
and the husband innocent I-have always in face.
                                    (before my eyes.)

O immagini funeste! O memorie! O martiro!
O images fatal! O memories! O torture!

Ed io parlo, infelice, ed io respiro? Ah no!
And I speak, unhappy-one, and I breathe? Ah no!

Aria:
Ah! non son io che parlo, è il barbaro dolore
Ah! not am I who speak, it-is the cruel pain
(It is not I who speak,)

                          180

che mi divide il core,
which [to-me] divides [the] (my) heart,

che delirar mi fa.
which [to-rave] (delirious) me makes.

Non cura il ciel tiranno l'affanno
Not heeds [the] heaven tyrannical the-anguish
(Heaven does not heed the anguish)

in cui mi vedo:
in which myself I-see:
(in which I see myself:)

un fulmine gli chiedo, e un fulmine non ha.
a thunderbolt of-it I-ask, and a thunderbolt not it-has.
(I ask heaven for death, but heaven does not strike me with
lightning.)

Mozart   AH SE IN CIEL, BENIGNE STELLE
                                      K. 538

Ah se in ciel, benigne stelle, la pietà non è smarrita,
Ah, if in heaven, kind stars, [the] pity not is lost,

o toglietemi la vita,
either take-away-(from)-me [the] (my) life,

o lasciatemi il mio ben.
or leave-to-me [the] my beloved.

Voi, che ardete ognor si belle
You, that burn always so beautifully,

del mio ben nel dolce aspetto,
of-[the] my beloved in-the sweet face,
(in the sweet face of my beloved)

proteggete il puro affetto
protect the pure affection

che inspirate a questo sen.
that you-inspire [to] (in) this breast.

Mozart   AH, T'INVOLA
                           K. 272

Recit.:
Ah, lo previdi!
Ah, it I-foresaw!

Povero prence, con quel ferro istesso che mi salvò
Poor prince, with that weapon same which me saved

ti lacerasti il petto.
to-yourself you-tore the bosom.
(you tore your bosom.)

Ma tu si fiero scempio perchè non impedir?
But [you] such fierce slaughter why (did you) not prevent?

Come, o crudele,
How, O cruel-one,

d'un misero a pietà non ti movesti?
of-a miserable-one to pity not yourself did-you-move?
(how could you not have pity on a miserable one?)

Qual tigre ti nodrî? Dove, dove, nascesti?
What tiger you nourished? Where, where, were-you-born?
(What tiger nourished you?)

Ah, t'invola, agli occhi miei!
Ah, yourself-take-away from-[the] eyes mine!
(Take yourself away from my eyes!)

Aria:
Ah, t'invola agli occhi miei!
Ah, take-yourself-away from-[the] eyes mine!
(Ah, take yourself away from my eyes!)

Alma vile, ingrato cor!
Soul vile, ungrateful heart!

La cagione, o Dio, tu sei del mio barbaro dolor.
The reason, O God, you are of-the my bitter pain.

Va crudele! Va, spietato!
Go cruel-one! Go, pitiless-one!

Va, tra le fiere ad abitar.
Go, among the savage-beasts to live.

Recit. :
Misera! invan m'adiro,
Wretched-one! in-vain [myself]-I-grow-angry,

e nel suo sangue intanto
and in-[the] his blood meanwhile

nuota già l'idol mio.
swims already [the]-idol my.

Con quell'acciaro, O Perseo, che facesti?
With that-sword, O Perseus, what have-you-done?

Mi salvasti poc'anzi, or m'uccidesti!
Me you-saved a-little-before, now me-you-have-killed!

Col sangue, ahi, la bell'alma
With-the blood, oh, the beautiful-soul

ecco, già uscì dallo squarciato seno.
see, already has-gone from-the wounded bosom.

Me infelice! Si oscura il giorno agli occhi miei,
Me unhappy! [Itself] darkens the day to-[the] eyes my,

e nel barbaro affanno il cor vien meno.
and in-[the] cruel anguish the heart [comes less] (faints).

Ah, non partir, ombra diletta,
Ah, (do) not depart, spirit beloved,

io voglio unirmi a te.
I want to-unite-myself to you.

Sul grado estremo, intanto che m'uccide il dolor,
On-the step last, while [that] me-kills the pain,

intanto fermati, fermati alquanto!
meanwhile stop-[yourself], stop [some] (a little while)!

Deh, non varcar quell'onda, anima del cor mio,
Ah, (do) not cross that-stream, soul of-[the] heart my,

di Lete all'altra sponda, ombra, compagna anch'io
of Lethe to-the-other shore, spirit, companion, also-I

voglio venir con te!
I-want to-come with you!

Mozart   AL DESIO DI CHI T'ADORA
                      K. 577

Al desio di chi t'adora
To-the desire of her-who you-adores,

vieni, vola, o mia speranza!
come, fly, O my hope!

Morirò, se indarno ancora tu mi lasci sospirar!
I-will-die, if in-vain still you me leave to-sigh!

Le promesse, i giuramenti, deh rammenta, o mio tesoro!
The promises, the vows, alas, remember, O my treasure!

E i momenti di ristoro, che mi fece Amor sperar!
And the moments of refreshment, that me made love to-hope!
                              (for which love made me hope!)

Ah! ch'omai più non resisto
Ah, that-now longer not I-resist
(Ah, I can resist no lònger)

all'ardor, che in sen m'accende!
[to]-the-ardor that in breast me-kindles!
(the ardor that burns in my breast!)

Chi d'amor gli affetti intende,
He-who of-love the emotions understands,

compatisca il mio penar!
let-(him)-pity [the] my suffering!

186

Mozart   ALMA GRANDE E NOBIL CORE
                          K. 578

Alma grande e nobil core le tue pari ognor disprezza,
Soul great and noble heart [the] your likes always scorns,
(A great soul and noble heart scorns the likes of you,)

Sono dama al fasto avvezza
I-am (a) lady, to-[the] magnificence accustomed,

e so farmi rispettar.
and I-know to-make-myself to-respect.
(and I know how to make myself respected.)

Va, favella a quell'ingrato,
Go, speak to that-ingrate,

gli dirai che fido io sono.
to-him you-will-say that faithful I am.
(tell him that I am still faithful.)

Ma non merita perdono, sì mi voglio vendicar.
But not he-merits pardon; truly myself I-wish to-avenge.

Mozart   CHI SA, CHI SA, QUAL SIA
                          K. 582

Chi sa qual sia l'affanno del mio bene.
Who knows what may-be the-anguish of-[the] my beloved.

se sdegno, gelosia, timor, sospetto, amor.
if (it be) wrath, jealousy, fear, suspicion, love.

Voi che sapete, o Dei, i puri affetti miei,
You that know, O Gods, [the] pure affections my,
(O Gods, you that know my pure affection,)

voi questo dubbio amaro toglietemi dal cor.
you this doubt bitter take-away-to-me from-the heart.
(take away this bitter doubt from my heart.)

Mozart   IO NON CHIEDO
                          K. 316

Recit. :
Popoli di Tessaglia!
People[s] of Thessaly!

Ah, mai più giusto fu il vostro pianto.
Ah, never more justified was [the] your weeping.

A voi non men che a questi innocenti fanciulli
To you not less than to these innocent children,

Admeto è padre.
Admetus is (the) father.

Io perdo l'amato sposo,
I lose [the]-(my)-beloved husband,

e voi l'amato rè;
and you [the]-(your)-beloved king;

la nostra sola speranza,
[the] our only hope,
(our only hope,)

il nostro amor c'invola
[the] our love from-us-takes-away
(our love is taken away from us)

questo fato crudel.
this destiny cruel.
(by this cruel destiny.)

Nè so che prima in si grave sciagura
Nor do-I-know that first in so heavy (a) disaster

a compianger m'appigli del regno,
to pity [for-me]-I-should-choose [of]-the kingdom,
(I should choose to pity the kingdom,)

di me stessa, o de'miei figli.
[of me] myself, or [of-the]-my children.
(myself, or my children.)

La pietà degli Dei sola ci resta
The pity of-the Gods alone to-us remains

189

a implorare, a ottener.
to implore, to obtain.

Verrò compagna alle vostre preghiere,
I-shall-come companion to-[the] your prayers,
(I shall come to pray with you,)

ai vostri sacrifizi;
to-[the] your sacrifices;

avanti all'ara una misera madre,
before [to]-the altar a poor mother,

due bambini infelici,
two children unhappy,

tutto un popolo in pianto presenterò così.
all a people in tears I-shall-offer thus.
(an entire people)

Forse con questo spettacolo funesto,
Perhaps with this spectacle sad,
(Perhaps by this sad spectacle,)

in cui dolente gli affetti,
in which sorrowing the emotions,
(in which, sorrowing,)

i voti suoi dichiara un regno,
the vows its declares a kingdom,
(a kingdom declares its vows,)

placato al fin sara del ciel lo sdegno.
appeased at last will-be of-[the] heaven the wrath.
(the wrath of heaven will at last be appeased.)

Aria:
Io non chiedo, eterni Dei,
I (do) not ask, eternal Gods,

tutto il ciel per me sereno,
all [the] heaven for me serene,

ma il mio duol consoli almeno
but [the] my sorrow let-console at-least
(but let my sorrow be consoled, at least,)

qualche raggio di pietà.
some ray of pity.
(by some ray of pity.)

Non comprende i mali miei
Not understands [the] pains mine
(One cannot understand my pains)

nè il terror, che m'empie il petto
nor the terror, which to-me-fills the bosom
(nor the terror that fills my bosom)

chi di moglie il vivo affetto,
one-who of (a) wife the strong affection,
(unless he feels the strong affection that a wife feels,)

chi di madre il cor non ha.
one-who of (a) mother the heart not has.
(or has the heart of a mother.)

Mozart   NO, NO, NO, CHE NON SEI CAPACE
                                K. 419

No, no, no, che non sei capace di cortesia, d'onore,
No, no, no, why, not you-are capable of courtesy, of-honor,

e vanti a torto un core, ch'arde d'amor per me;
and you-boast wrongfully a heart, that-burns with-love for me;

vanne! t'abborro, ingrato,
go-from-this-place! You-I-abhor, ingrate,

e più me stesso abborro,
and more [me] myself I-abhor,

che t'ho un istante amato,
that you-I-have (for) an instant loved,

che sospirai per te.
that I-sighed for you.

Mozart   NON SO D'ONDE VIENE
                          K. 294

Recit.:
Alcandro, lo confesso, stupisco di me stesso.
Alcandro, it I-confess, I-am-astonished at [me] myself.

Il volto, il ciglio, la voce di costui
The face, the eye(s), the voice of him
(The face, the eyes, his voice)

nel cor mi desta un palpito
in-[the] heart to-me awakens a palpitation sudden
(in my heart awaken a sudden palpitation)

che lo risente in ogni fibra il sangue.
so-that it feels in every fiber the blood.
(which the blood feels in every fiber.)

Fra tutti i miei pensieri la cagion ne ricerco,
Among all [the] my thoughts the reason of-it I-seek,

e non la trovo.
and not it do-I-find.

Che sarà, giusti Dei, questo ch'io provo?
What can-be, just Gods, this that-I experience?

Aria:
Non so d'onde viene quel tenero affetto,
Not do-I-know from-whence comes that tender emotion,

quel moto, che ignoto mi nasce nel petto,
that impulse, which unknown to-me is-born in-[the] (my)
     bosom,

quel gel, che le vene scorrendo mi va.
that chill, that the veins running-through to-me goes.
(that chill which goes running through my veins.)

Nel seno a destarmi si fieri contrasti,
In-the bosom to awaken-for-me such bitter contrasts,
(To awaken such bitter conflicts in my bosom,)

non parmi che basti la sola pietà.
not does-it-seem-to-me that is-enough [the] alone pity.
(it does not seem to me that pity alone is enough.)

Mozart   NON TEMER, AMATO BENE
                          K. 490

Recit. :
Venga la morte! intrepida l'attendo,
Let-come [the] death! fearless it-I-await,

ma, ch'io possa struggermi ad altra face,
but, that-I could destroy-myself for another torch,
                    (long for another man,)

ad altr'oggetto donar gl'affetti miei,
to another-object to-give [the]-affections my,

come tentarlo? Ah! di dolor morrei!
how to-attempt-it? Ah, of sorrow I-would-die!

Aria:
Non temer, amato bene, per te sempre il cor sarà.
(Do) not fear, beloved well, for you always the heart will-be.
(Fear not, well beloved, my heart will always be yours.)

Più non reggo a tanto pene,
More not I-bear to so-much pain,
(I cannot bear so much pain any longer,)

l'alma mia mancando va.
[the]-spirit my, lacking, goes.
(my spirit faints.)

Tu sospiri? o duol funesto!
You sigh? O grief fatal!

Pensa almen, che istante è questo!
Think at-least, what (a) moment is this!

Non mi posso, oh Dio! spiegar.
Not myself I-can, O God, explain!
(O God, I cannot explain!)

Stelle barbare, stelle spietate,
Stars barbarous, stars merciless,

perchè mai tanto rigor?
why ever so-much severity?

194

Alme belle, che vedete le mie pene in tal momento,
Souls beautiful, who see [the] my pains in such-a moment,

dite voi s'egual tormento può soffrir un fido cor.
say [you], if-equal torment can suffer a faithful heart.

Mozart   NON TEMER, AMATO BENE
                          K. 505

Recit. :
Ch'io mi scordi di te?
That-I [myself] forget [of] you?

Che a lei mi doni puoi consigliarmi?
That to her myself I-give, you-can counsel-me?

E puoi voler ch'io viva?
And can-you wish that-I live?

Ah no, sarebbe il viver mio di morte assai peggior!
Ah, no would-be [the] life my [of] (than) death much worse!
     (my life would be much worse than death!)

(Remainder of recitative, and aria, have identical text with
"Non temer, amato bene," K. 490.)

Mozart   OR CHE IL CIELO
                          K. 374

Recit. :
A questo seno, deh vieni, idolo mio.
To this bosom, ah, come, idol mine.

Quanti timori, quanti lacrime, o Dio,
How-many fears, how-many tears, o God,

costi alla sposa tua.
you-cost [to-the] wife your.

Dunque tu vivi, O contento! O certezza!
Then you live, O happiness! O certainty!

O premio! O speme! O amor!
O reward! O hope! O love!

Numi clementi, nell'offrirmi,
Gods merciful, in-[the]-offering-to-me,

pietose un sî bel dono,   \
compassionate(ly) [a] so beautiful (a) gift,

tutto il vostro rigore io vi perdono.
all [the] your severity I [to-you] forgive.

Aria:
Or che il cielo a me ti rende,
Now that [the] heaven to me you renders,
(Now that heaven gives you back to me,)

cara parte del mio cor,
dear part of-[the] my heart,

la mia gioia, ah, non comprende
[the] my joy, ah, (does) not understand
(He cannot understand my joy)

chi non sa che cosa è amor.
he-who not knows what thing is love.
   (who does not know what love is.)

Sono all'alma un grato oggetto
Are to-the-soul a welcome object

                    197

le sue barbare vicende,
[the] its cruel vicissitudes,

ed in sen dolce descende
and into (the) heart sweet(ly) descende

la memoria del dolor.
the memory of-[the] sorrow.

Mozart   RESTA, OH CARA
                          K. 528

Recit. :
Bella mia fiamma, addio!
Beautiful my flame, goodbye!

Non piacque al cielo di renderci felici,
Not it-pleased [to-the] heaven to render-us happy,

Ecco reciso, prima d'esser compito, quel purissimo nodo,
Here-is cut, before [of]-being completed, that purest knot,

che strinsero fra lor gl'animi nostri
that bound between them [the]-souls our

con il solo voler.
with a single wish.

Vivi! cedi al destin! cedi al dovere!
Live! Yield to-[the] destiny! Yield to-[the] duty!

Della giurata fede la mia morte t'assolve;
From-the sworn faith [the] my death you-absolves;
(My death absolves you from your oath;)

a più degno consorte...o pene!
[to] (with a) more worthy consort... Oh, grief[s],

unita vivi più lieta e più felice vita.
united live (a) more joyous and more happy life.

Ricordati di me, ma non mai turbi
Remember-[yourself of] me, but [not] never let-disturb

d'un infelice sposo la rara rimembranza il tuo riposo!
of-an unhappy husband the rare remembrance [the] your
   repose!
(may the memory of an unhappy husband never disturb your
   rest.)

Ah, tutto finisca il mio furor col morir mio.
Ah, completely let-end [the] my rage with-[the] death my.

Cerere, Alfeo, diletta sposa, addio!
Ceres, Alfeo, beloved wife, goodbye!

Aria:
Resta, oh cara!　Acerba morte me separa, oh Dio, da te.
Stay, O beloved!　Harsh death me separates, oh, God, from
　you.

Prendi cura di sua sorte, consolarla almen procura.
Take care of her fate, to-console-her at-least procure.
(Look after her, console her.)

Vado...ahi lasso! addio per sempre!
I-go...alas, unhappy-one!　Goodbye for ever!

Quest'affanno, questo passo è terribile per me.
This-anguish, this step is terrible for me.

Ah, dov'è il tempio?　dov'è l'ara?
Ah, where-is the temple?　where-is the-altar?

Vieni affretta la vendetta!
Come, hasten the vengeance!

Questa vita così amara più soffribile non è, no.
This life, so bitter, longer sufferable not is, no.
　　　　　　　　　　　(is no longer bearable.)

Mozart   SPERAI VICINO IL LIDO
                                 K. 368

Recit. :
Ma che vi fece, o stelle, la povera Dircea,
But what to-you has-done, O stars, [the] poor Dircea,
(What has poor Dircea done to you, O stars,)

che tante unite sventure contro lei!
that so-many you-unite misfortunes against her!
(that you unite so many misfortunes against her!)

Voi, che inspiraste i casti affetti alle nostr'alme;
You, who inspired the pure affections to-[the] our-souls;

voi, che al pudico Imeneo foste presenti,
you, who at-the chaste wedding were present,

difendetelo, o Numi; io mi confondo.
defend-it, O Gods; I [myself] am-perplexed.

M'oppresse il colpo a segno
Me-overwhelmed the blow exactly
(The blow struck me exactly)

che il cor mancommi, e si smarrì l'ingegno.
so-that the heart lacked-me, and itself lost the-skill
(so that my heart failed me, and my skill was lost.)

Aria:
Sperai vicino il lido
I-hoped near the shore,
(I hoped the shore was near,)

credei calmato il vento,
I-believed calmed the wind,
(I believed the wind had abated,)

ma trasportar mi sento fra le tempeste ancor.
but transported myself I-feel among the tempests again.

E da uno scoglio infido mentre salvar mi voglio
And from one rock treacherous while to-save myself I-want
(And while I try to save myself from one treacherous rock)

urto in un altro scoglio del primo assai peggior.
I-strike upon another rock than-the first much worse.
(I strike upon another, much worse than the first.)

Mozart   VADO, MA DOVE?
                          K. 583

Vado, ma dove? o Dei! se de' tormenti suoi,
I-go, but where? O Gods! if [of-the] (for) torments his
                            (if for his torments,)

se de' sospiri miei non sente il ciel pietà!
if [of-the] (for) sighs my not feels [the] heaven pity!
(if for my sighs heaven does not feel pity!)

Tu che mi parli al core,
You that to-me speak to-the heart,
(You, who speak to my heart,)

guida i miei passi, amore;
guide [the] my steps, love;

tu quel ritegno or togli che dubitar me fa.
[you] that restraint now remove that to-doubt me makes.
(remove that restraint that makes me doubt.)

Voi avete un cor fedele,
You have a heart faithful,

come amante appassionato
like (a) lover passionate,

ma mio sposo dichiarato
but (as) my husband declared,

che farete? cangerete?
what will-you-do? will-you-change?

Dite, allora che sarà?
Say, then what will-be?

Manterrete fedeltà?
Will-you-keep faith?
(Will you be faithful?)

Ah! non credo, già prevedo,
Ah! not I-believe; already I-foresee,
    (I believe not;)

mi potreste corbellar.
me you-could deceive.

Non ancora, non per ora
Not yet, not [for] now

non mi vuò di voi fidar.
not [myself] do-I-wish [of] (in) you to-trust.

Mozart   VORREI SPIEGARVI, OH DIO!
                          K. 418

Vorrei spiegarvi, oh Dio!
I-would-like to-explain-to-you, oh, God,
(Oh, God, how I would like to explain to you)

qual è l'affanno mio
what is the-anguish my;
(what my anguish is;)

ma mi condanna il fato, a piangere e tacer.
but me condemns the fate, to weep and to-be-silent.
(but fate condemns me to weeping and silence.)

Arder non può il mio core per chi vorrebbe amore
To-burn not can [the] my heart for whom it-would-wish love,
(My heart can not burn for whom it would wish to love,)

e fa che cruda io sembri, un barbaro dover.
and makes that cruel I seem, a barbarous duty.
(And a barbarous duty makes me seem cruel.)

Ah conte, partite, correte, fuggite lontano da me;
Ah, Count, depart, run,   flee far from me;

la vostra diletta Emilia v'aspetta,
[the] your beloved Emilia you-awaits,

languir non la fate, è degna d'amor.
to-languish not her make, she-is worthy of-(your)-love.
(do not make her languish)

Ah stelle spietate! nemiche mi siete.
Ah, stars merciless! enemies to-me you-are.

Mi perdo s'ei resta, oh Dio! mi perdo.
Myself I-lose if-he remains, oh God! myself I-lose.
(I am lost if he remains. Oh, God, I am lost.)

204

Mozart   DAL TUO GENTIL SEMBIANTE
                          (Ascanio in Alba)

Dal tuo gentil sembiante
From-[the] your gentle appearance
(Through your gentle appearance)

risplende un'alma grande.
shines a-soul great.

E quel chiaror che spande
And that light which shines-forth

quasi adorar ti fà.
almost adore you makes (one).
(almost makes one adore you.)

Se mai divieni amante
If ever you-become (a) lover,

felice la donzella
happy the maiden

che a fiamma così bella
who [to] (by a) flame so beautiful

allor s'accenderà.
then herself-will-kindle.
(will be kindled to love.)

Mozart   L'OMBRA DE' RAMI TUOI
                                (Ascanio in Alba)

L'ombra de' rami tuoi l'amico suolo aspetta.
The-shade of-[the] branches your the-friendly soil awaits.
(The friendly soil awaits the shade of your branches.)

Vivi mia pianta eletta: degna sarai di me.
Live, my plant choice: worthy you-will-be of me.
      (my choice plant)

Già questo cor comprende
Already this heart comprehends

quel che sarai di poi;
that which you-will-be in-the-future;

già di sue cure intende
certainly of its care[s] understands
(certainly because of its solicitude)

l'opra lodarsi in te.
the-work to-praise-itself in you.
(its work will be praised in you.)

Mozart   SI, MA D'UN ALTRO AMORE
                           (Ascanio in Alba)

Recit.:
Del suo gran padre in lui il magnanimo cor
Of-[the] his great father in him the magnanimous heart
(With the magnanimous heart of his great father,)

chi dice impresso:
one says, he-is-stamped;
(it is said, he is endowed;)

chi de la dea celeste
one (says) from the goddess celestial
(it is said that the celestial goddess')

l'immensa carità trasfusa in esso.
the-immense charity is-transfused in him.
(immense charity is transfused in him.)

Aria:
Sì, ma d'un altro amore
Yes, but of-another love

sento la fiamma in petto:
I-feel the flame in (my) breast:

e l'innocente affetto solo a regnar non è.
and the-innocent affection only to reign not is.
(and it is not just innocent affection.)

Mozart AH, SE FOSSE INTORNO AL TRONO
(La Clemenza di Tito)

Recit. :
Se grata appieno essermi vuoi, Servilia,
If pleasing completely to-be-to-me you-wish, Servilia,

agli altri inspira il tuo candor.
[to-the] others inspire (with) [the] your candor.

De publicar procura, che grato a me si rende,
To publish attain, that pleasing to me itself becomes,
(Let it be known that it is pleasing to me,)

più del falso che piace, il ver che offende.
more (than) [of]-the lie that pleases, the truth that offends.
(to hear more the truth that offends than the lie that pleases.)

Aria:
Ah, se fosse intorno al trono ogni cor così sincero!
Ah, if were near to-the throne every heart so sincere!
(Ah, if everyone near my throne were so sincere!)

Non tormento un vasto impero, ma saria felicità.
Not torment a vast empire, but it-would-be happiness.
(This empire would bring me happiness instead of torment.)

Non dovrebbero i regnanti tollerar sì grave affanno,
Not should the rulers endure such heavy grief,

per distinguer dall-inganno l'insidiata verità.
to distinguish from-the-deceit the-insidious truth.
(in distinguishing between deceit and flattery.)

Mozart   DEH, PER QUESTO ISTANTE
                          (La Clemenza di Tito)

Deh, per questo istante solo ti ricorda il primo amore,
Ah, for this moment only yourself remember the first love,
(Ah, for only a moment, remember our former friendship,)

che morir mi fa di duolo, il tuo sdegno,
For to-die me makes of sorrow your disdain,

il tuo rigor.
[the] your severity.

Di pietade indegno, è vero,
Of pity I-am-unworthy, it-is true,

sol spirar io deggio orror,
only to-inspire I must horror,
(I must inspire only horror,)

pur saresti men severo, se vedesti questo cor.
yet you-would-be less severe, if you-were-to-see this heart.

Disperato vado a morte, ma il morir non mi spaventa,
Despairingly I-go to death, but [the] to-die not me terrifies,

il pensiero mi tormenta che fui teco un traditor.
the thought me torments that I-was with-you a traitor.

Tanto affanno soffre un core,
So-much grief suffers a heart,

nè si more di dolor.
nor itself dies of sorrow.
(that it dies of sorrow.)

Mozart   DEH SE PIACER MI VUOI
                          (La Clemenza di Tito)

Deh se piacer mi vuoi, lascia i sospetti tuoi;
Ah, if to-please me you-wish, leave [the] suspicions your;

non mi stancar con questo molesto dubitar.
(do) not me tire with this troublesome doubt.

Chi ciecamente crede, impegna a serbar fede;
Whoever blindly believes, pledges to keep faith;

chi sempre inganni aspetta, alletta ad ingannar.
whoever always deceits awaits, invites [to] being-deceived.

Mozart   DEL PIU SUBLIME SOGLIO
                                (La Clemenza di Tito)

Del più sublime soglio l'unico frutto è questo:
Of-the most high throne, the-only reward is this:

tutto è tormento il resto, e tutto è servitù.
all is torment the rest, and all is servitude.
(all the rest is torment and servitude.)

Che avrei, se ancor perdessi
What would-I-have, if now I-were-to-lose

le sole ore felici,
the only hours happy,

ch'ho nel giovar gli oppressi,
that-I-have in-[the] being-useful to-the oppressed,

nel sollevar gli amici,
in-[the] raising-up [the] friends,

nel dispensar tesori al merto,
in-[the] distributing treasures [to-the] (for) merit,

e alla virtù?
and [to-the] (for) virtue?

211

Mozart   NON PIU DI FIORI
                              (La Clemenza di Tito)

Recit.:
Ecco il punto, o Vitellia,
Here-is the moment, O Vitellia,

d'esaminar la tua costanza.
to-examine [the] your steadfastness.

Avrai valor, che basti, a rimirar
Will-you-have courage, that might-suffice, to behold-again
(Will you have sufficient courage to behold once more,)

esangue il tuo Sesto fedel?
bloodless [the] your Sextus faithful?
(lifeless, your faithful Sextus?)

Sesto che t'ama più della vita sua?
Sextus, who you-loves more than-[the] life his?
        (who loves you more than his own life?)

Che per tua colpa divenne reo?
Who through your guilt became (a) criminal?

Che t'ubbidì, crudele? Che ingiusta t'adora?
Who you-obeyed, cruel-one? Who, unjust-one, you-adores?
(Who obeyed you, cruel one? Who adores you, unjust one?)

Che in faccia a morte sì gran fede
Who in (the) face of death such great loyalty

ti serba? E tu frattanto,
to-you maintains? And you, meanwhile,

non ignota a te stessa,
not unaware to you yourself,
(well aware of your guilt,)

andrai tranquilla al talamo d'Augusto?
will-go tranquilly to-the nuptial-bed of-Augustus?

Ah mi vedrei sempre Sesto d'intorno.
Ah, to-me I-would-see always Sextus around.
(Ah, I would always see Sextus around me.)

E l'aure e i sassi temerei
And the-breezes and the rocks, I-would-fear,

212

che loquaci mi scoprissero a Tito.
that talkative me might-reveal to Titus.
(might speak and reveal my true self to Titus.)

A piedi suoi vadasi il tutto a palesar.
At feet his let-one-go [the] everything to reveal.
(I shall go to reveal everything at his feet.)

Si scemi il delitto di Sesto,
Itself let-diminish the crime of Sextus,
(Let the crime of Sextus be lessened.)

se scusar non si può, col fallo mio.
if to-excuse not one can, with [the] fault my.
(if it cannot be excused, by my guilt.)

D'imperi e d'imenei speranze, addio.
Of-empires and of-marriage[s] hopes goodbye.
(Goodbye to hopes of empire and marriage.)

Aria:
Non più di fiori vaghe catene discenda Imene
No more of flowers pretty chains let-descend Hymen
(No more let Hymen descend, pretty chains of flowers)

ad intrecciar.
to weave.

Stretta fra barbare aspre ritorte
Squeezed between cruel, sharp fetters,

veggo la morte ver me avanzar. Infelice!
I-see [the] death toward me advance. Unhappy-one!

Qual orrore!   Ah, di me che si dirà?
What horror!   Ah, of me what one will-say?
                (Ah, what will they say of me?)

Chi vedesse il mio dolore,
Whoever might-see [the] my sorrow,

pur avria di me pietà.
surely would-have on me pity.

Mozart   PARTO, PARTO
                           (La Clemenza di Tito)

Parto, parto, ma tu ben mio meco ritorna in pace;
I-go, I-go, but you, love my, with-me return in peace;
           (but you, my love, make peace with me;)

sarò qual più ti piace,
I-will-be what more you pleases,
(I will be whatever pleases you more,)

quel che vorrai farò.
that which you-will-like I will-do.
(I will do what you like.)

Guardami e tutto obblio,
Look-at-me, and everything I-forget,

e a vendicarti io volo.
and to avenge-you I fly.

A questo sguardo solo da me si penserà.
To this glance only by myself one will-think.
(I will think of this glance alone.)

Ah qual poter, O Dei! donaste alla beltà!
Ah, what power, O Gods, have-you-given to-[the] beauty!

Mozart   S'ALTRO CHE LAGRIME
                          (La Clemenza di Tito)

S'altro che lagrime per lui non tenti,
If-other than tears for him not you-attempt,

tutto il tuo piangere non gioverà.
all [the] your weeping not is-useful.

A quest'inutile pietà che senti,
To this-useless pity that you-feel,

o quanto è simile la crudeltà.
oh, how-[much] is similar [the] cruelty.
(cruelty is so similar.)

Mozart   SE ALL'IMPERO, AMICI DEI!
                          (La Clemenza di Tito)

Se all'impero, amici Dei! necessario è un cor severo,
If to-the-empire, friendly gods, necessary is a heart severe,

o togliete a me l'impero,
either, take-away ⌊to⌋ (from) me the-empire,

o a me date un altro cor.
or to me give another heart.

Se la fè de regni miei coll'amor non assicuro,
If the faith of realms my with-the-love not I-secure,
(If with my love I do not secure the confidence of my realm,)

d'una fede non mi curo
of-a faith not for-me I-value
(I do not desire loyalty)

che sia frutto del timor.
which might-be (the) fruit of-[the] fear.

216

Mozart   TARDI S'AVVEDE
        (La Clemenza di Tito)

Tardi s'avvede d'un tradimento
(Too)-late himself-perceives of-a treason
(He perceives treason too late)

chi mai di fede mancar non sà;
who never of faith to-lack not knows;
(who himself is never lacking in fidelity;)

un cor verace, pieno d'onore, non è portento
a heart true, full-of-honor, not is marvel
(it is not to be wondered at if a true heart, full of honor,)

se ogn'altro core crede incapace d'infedeltà.
if every-other heart it-believes incapable of-infideltiy.
(believes every other heart incapable of dishonor.)

Mozart TU FOSTI TRADITO
(La Clemenza di Tito)

Tu fosti tradito, ei degno è di morte,
You were betrayed; he deserving is of death,

ma il core di Tito pur lascia sperar.
but the heart of Titus yet lets (us) hope.

Deh! prendi consiglio, Signor, dal tuo core;
Ah, take counsel, (my) Lord, from-[the] your heart;

il nostro dolore ti degna mirar.
[the] our sorrow [you] deign to-behold.

Mozart   AH! LO VEGGIO QUELL'ANIMA BELLA
(Così Fan Tutte)

Ah! lo veggio quell'anima bella
Ah, it I-see that-soul beautiful
(Ah, I see it: that beautiful soul)

al mio pianto resister non sa:
to-[the] my weeping to-resist not knows-how:

non è fatta per esser rubella
not she-is made to be rebellious

agli affetti di amica pietà.
to-the affections of loving pity.

In quel guardo, in quei cari sospiri
In that look, in those dear sighs

dolce raggio lampeggia al mio cor:
(a) sweet ray flashes to-[the] my heart:

già rispondi a miei caldi desiri,
already you-respond to my hot desires,

già tu cedi al più tenero amor.
already you surrender to-the most tender love.

Ma tu fuggi, spietata tu taci,
But you flee, merciless-one, you are-silent,

ed invano mi senti languir?
and in-vain me you-perceive languish?
(do you see me languish in vain?)

Ah, cessate speranze fallaci
Ah, cease, hopes deceitful,

la crudel mi condanna a morir!
the cruel-one me condemns to die!

Mozart   UN'AURA AMOROSA
                           (Così Fan Tutte)

Un'aura amorosa del nostro tesoro
A-breath amorous of-[the] our treasure

un dolce ristoro al cor porgerà.
a sweet refreshment to-the heart will-bring.

Al cor che nudrito da speme d'amore,
To-the heart which, nourished with hope of-love,

d'un esca migliore bisogna non ha.
[of]-a food better need not has.
(does not need a better food.)

Mozart
COME SCOGLIO IMMOTO RESTA
(Così Fan Tutte)

Recit. :
Temerari, sortite fuori questo loco!
Audacious-ones, leave [outside-of] this place!

e non profani l'alito infausto
and not let-profane the-breath unpropitious
(and let not the unpropitious breath)

dagli infami detti nostro cor, nostro orecchio,
of-the infamous words our heart, our ear,
(of your infamous words profane our hearts, our ears,)

e nostri affetti! Invan per voi,
and our affections! (It is) useless for you,

per gli altri invan si cerca
for the others useless, (that) one seeks

le nostre alme sedur:
[the] our souls to-seduce:

l'intatta fede che per noi già
the-intact faithfulness which by us already

si diede ai cari amanti saprem
[itself] (was) pledged to-the dear lovers we-shall-know-how

loro serbar infino a morte,
[to-them] to-preserve until [to] death,

a dispetto del mondo e della sorte.
in spite of-the world and of-[the] fate.

Aria:
Come scoglio immoto resta
As (a) rock steadfast remains

contra i venti e la tempesta,
against the winds and the tempest,

così ognor quest'alma è forte nella fede e nell'amor.
thus always this-soul is strong in-the faith and in-the-love.

Con noi nacque quella face che ci piace, e ci consola;
With us was-born that torch that us pleases, and us consoles;

221

e potrà la morte sola
and will-be-able the death only
(and only death will be able)

far che cangi affetto il cor.
to-make that change affection the heart.
(to make the heart change its affection.)

Rispettate, anime ingrate, questo esempio di costanza,
Respect, souls ungrateful, this example of constancy,

e una barbara speranza non vi renda audaci ancor!
and a barbarous hope (let) not you render bold again!
(and let not a barbarous hope make you bold again!)

Mozart　　　　　　　　　UNA DONNA A QUINDICI ANNI
　　　　　　　　　　　　(Così Fan Tutte)

Una donna a quindici anni
A lady, at fifteen years (of age),

dee saper ogni gran moda,
must know each great fashion,

dove il diavolo ha la coda,
where the devil has [the] (his) tail,

cosa è bene, e mal cos'è,
what is good, and bad what-is,

dee saper le maliziette,
must know the malicious (ways),

che innamorano gli amanti,
that make-fall-in-love [the] lovers,

finger riso, finger pianti,
feign laughter, feign tears,

inventar i bei perchè.
invent [the] fine reasons.

Dee in un momento dar retta a cento,
She-must in a moment give attention to (a) hundred (people),

colle pupille parlar con mille,
with-the eyes talk with (a) thousand,

dar speme a tutti, sien belli o brutti,
to-give hope to all, whether handsome or ugly,

saper nascondersi, senza confondersi,
to-know-how to-hide-herself; without embarrassment,

senza arrossire, saper mentire,
without blushing, to-know-how to-lie,

e qual regina dall'alto soglio
and like (a) queen from-the-high throne

col posso e voglio farsi ubbidir.
with-[the] "I can" and "I wish" make-herself obeyed.

Par ch'abbian gusto di tal dottrina,
It-seems that-they-have (a) taste for such (a) doctrine;

viva Despina, che sa servir.
long-live Despina, who knows-how to-serve.

Mozart   DONNE MIE, LA FATE A TANTI
                          (Così Fan Tutte)

Donne mie, la fate a tanti
Ladies mine, it you-do to so-many

che, se il ver vi deggio dir,
that, if the truth to-you must-I say,

se si lagnano gli amanti,
if [themselves] they-complain the lovers,
(if lovers complain,)

li comincio a compatir.
them I-begin to pity.

Io vo'bene al sesso vostro,
I like well [to-the] sex your,

lo sapete, ognun lo sa, ogni giorno ve lo mostro,
it you-know, everyone it knows, each day to-you it I-show,

vi do segno d'amistà.
to-you I-give sign of-friendship.

Ma quel farla a tanti e tanti
But that to-do-[it] to so-many and so-many
(But to act that way to so many)

m'avvilisce in verità.
me-offends in truth.

Mille volte il brando presi per salvar il vostro onor,
(A) thousand times the sword I-took to defend [the] your honor,

Mille volte vi difesi
(A) thousand times you I-defended

colla bocca e più col cor.
with-the mouth and more with-the heart.
(with my lips and my heart.)

Ma quel farla a tanti e tanti
But that to-do- [it] to so-many and so-many
(But to act that way to so many)

225

è un vizietto seccator.
is a little-bad-habit boring.

Siete vaghe, siete amabili,
You-are charming, you-are lovable,

più tesori il ciel vi diè,
many treasures [the] heaven to-you gave,

e le grazie vi circondano dalla testa sino a piè.
and the graces you surround from-the head until to foot.
(and the graces surround you from head to foot.)

Ma, la fate a tanti e tanti
But, it you-do to so-many and so-many

che credible non è,
that believable not it-is,

che se gridano gli amanti
that if cry-out [the] lovers

hanno certo un gran perchè.
they-have certainly a great reason.

Mozart   E AMORE UN LADRONCELLO
                          (Così Fan Tutte)

E amore un ladroncello, un serpentello è amor.
Is love a little-thief, a little-serpent is love.

Ei toglie e dà la pace,
He takes-away and gives [the] peace

come gli piace, ai cor.
as him it-pleases, to-the heart.

Per gli occhi al seno appena
Through the eyes to-the breast no-sooner

un varco aprir si fa,
a path to-open [himself] he-makes,

che l'anima incatena e toglie libertà.
than the-spirit he-enchains and takes-away liberty.

Porta dolcezza e gusto,
He-bears sweetness and pleasure,

se tu lo lasci far;
if you it allow (him) to-do;

ma t'empie di disgusto,
but you-he-fills with disgust,

se tenti di pugnar.
if you-attempt to fight.

Se nel tuo petto ei siede,
If in-[the] your [breast] (heart) he sits,

s'egli ti becca qui,
if-he you pecks here,

fa tutto quel ch'ei chiede
do everything that [which]-he asks

che anch'io farò così.
[that] (for) also-I will-do thus.

Mozart   IN UOMINI, IN SOLDATI
                          (Così Fan Tutte)

In uomini, in soldati sperare fedeltà?
In men, in soldiers, to-hope-for fidelity?

non vi fate sentire per carità!
not you make to-hear for charity!
(don't let anyone hear you, for heaven's sake!)

Di pasta simile son tutti quanti,
Of dough same are all of-them
(They are all made of the same stuff.)

le fronde mobili, l'aure incostanti
the leaves mobile, the-breezes inconstant

han più degli uomini stabilità.
have more than-the men stability.
(have more stability than men.)

Mentite lagrime, fallaci sguardi, voci ingannevoli,
Lying tears, deceitful looks, expressions false,

vezzi bugiardi, son le primarie lor qualità.
caresses lying, are [the] primary their traits.

In noi non amano che il cor diletto,
In us not they-love but the heart beloved,
(They love only our hearts,)

poi ci dispregiano, neganci affetto,
then us they-despise, they-deny-us affection,

nè val da' barbari chieder pietà.
nor is-it-worth from-[the] barbarians to-ask pity.

Paghiam, o femmine, d'ugual moneta
We-pay, o Women, with-(the)-same money

questa malefica razza indiscreta;
this pernicious breed indiscreet;

amiam per comodo, per vanità.
Let-us-love for convenience, for vanity.

Mozart   NON SIATE RITROSI, OCCHIETTI VEZZOSI
                    (Così Fan Tutte)

Non siate ritrosi, occhietti vezzosi,
(Do) not be stubborn, little-eyes pleasing,

due lampe amorosi vibrate un po' quà.
two lights loving, vibrate a little here.

Felici rendeteci, amate con noi, e noi felicissimi
Happy make-us, love with us, and we very-happy

faremo anche voi.
shall-make also you.

Guardate, toccate, il tutto osservate:
Look, touch, [the] everything observe:

siam forti e ben fatti, e come ognun vede,
we-are strong and well made, and as everyone sees,

sia merto, o caso, abbiamo bel piede,
be-it-through merit, or chance, we-have (a) fine foot,

bell'occhio, bel naso, guardate bel piede,
fine-eye, fine nose; look: fine foot,

osservate bell'occhio, toccate bel naso,
observe: fine eye; touch: fine nose,

il tutto osservate:
[the] everything observe:

e questi mustacchi chiamare si possono
and these mustaches to-call themselves can
                         (might be called)

trionfi degli uomini, pennacchi d'amor,
triumphs of-the men, plumes of-love,
(masculine triumphs)

trionfi, pennacchi, mustacchi!
triumphs, plumes, mustaches!

229

Mozart   PER PIETA, BEN MIO, PERDONA
                          (Così Fan Tutte)

Recit.:
Ei parte... senti... ah no! partir si lasci,
He leaves... listen... ah, no! to-leave him let,
                          (let him leave,)

si tolga ai guardi miei
himself let-remove [to-the] (from) glances my

l'infausto oggetto della mia debolezza.
the-unhappy object of-[the] my weakness.

A qual cimento il barbaro mi pose!
To what (a) test the barbarous-one me placed!
(What a test the barbarous one has placed before me!)

Un premio è questo ben dovuto a mie colpe!
A reward is this well owed [to] (for) my sins!
(This is a just reward for my sins!)

In tale istante dovea di nuovo amante,
In such-a moment should-I of (a) new lover,

i sospiri ascoltar?
the sighs listen-to?

L'altrui querele dovea volger in gioco?
The-others' quarrels should-I take into consideration?

Ah, questo core a ragione condanni, o giusto amore!
Ah, this heart rightly you-condemn, O true love.

Io ardo e l'ardo mio non e più effetto
I burn, and [the]-ardor my not is longer (the) pretense

d'un amor virtuoso: è smania, affanno, rimorso,
of-a love virtuous; it-is frenzy, affliction, remorse,

pentimento, leggerezza, perfidia, e tradimento!
penitence, fickleness, perfidy, and betrayal!

Aria:
Per pietà, ben mio, perdona
[For] (have) pity, love my, pardon

230

all'error d'un alma amante
[to]-the-error of-a soul loving;

fra quest'ombre, e queste piante
among these-shadows, and these trees

sempre ascoso, oh Dio, sarà.
always hidden, O God, it-will-be.

Svenerà quest'empia voglia l'ardir mio, la mia costanza,
Will-sever this impious desire the-ardor my [the] my constancy,
(My ardor will sever this impious desire; my constancy)

perderà la rimembranza che vergogna e orror mi fa.
will-lose the memory that shame and horror me gives.

A chi mai mancò di fede questo vano, ingrato cor,
To him-who never lacked [of] faith this vain, ungrateful
      heart,
(To him, in whom this vain, ungrateful heart never lacked
    faith)

si dovea miglior mercede, caro bene,
one owed better reward, dear beloved,
(was owed a better reward,)

al tuo candor!
[to-the] (for) your purity.

Mozart RIVOLGETE A LUI LO SGUARDO
(Così Fan Tutte)

Rivolgete a lui lo sguardo
Turn to him [the] (your) glance

e vedrete come sta: tutto dice,
and you-will-see how he-is: (listen to) everything he says:

io gelo... io ardo...idol mio, pietà.
I freeze...I burn...idol my, (have) pity.

E voi, cara, un sol momento
And you, dear, an only moment
    (for only a moment)

il bel ciglio a me volgete,
[the] (your) beautiful eye(s) to me turn,

e nel mio ritroverete
and in-[the] my (eyes) discover-again

quel che il labbro dir non sa.
that which the lip(s) to-say not know-how.

Un Orlando* innamorato non è niente in mio confronto,
An Orlando in-love [not] is nothing in my comparison,
    (compared to me,)
un Medoro* il sen piagato
A Medoro, [the] (his) breast wounded,

verso lui per nulla io conto:
toward him for nothing I count:
(counts for nothing compared to me;)

son di foco i miei sospiri,
are of fire [the] my sighs,

son di bronzo i suoi desiri,
are of bronze [the] his desires,

se si parla poi di merto
if one speaks then of merit,

certo io sono, ed egli è certo
certain I am, and he is certain

*Orlando and Medoro: characters in Ariosto's Orlando Furioso.
232

che gli uguali non si trovano
that to-us equals not themselves find
(that our equals are not to be found)

da Vienna al Canada.
from Vienna to-[the] Canada.

Siam due Cresi per richezza'
We-are two Croesuses for richness,
(We are both rich as Croesus,)

due Narcisi per bellezza,
two Narcissuses for beauty,
(we are both handsome as Narcissus,)

in amor i Marcantoni verso noi sarian buffoni,
in love the Mark Anthonys toward us would-be buffoons,
(as lovers we would make Mark Anthony look like a clown,)

siam più forti d'un ciclopo,
we-are more strong than-a Cyclops,
(we are stronger than Cyclops,)

letterati al par di Esopo,
men-of-letters to-the same of Aesop,
(we are writers equal to Aesop,)

se balliamo, un Pich* ne cede,
if we-dance, a Pich to-us yields,

si gentil e snello è il piede,
so genteel and nimble is the foot,
(so light-footed we are,)

se cantiam col trillo solo
if we-sing, with-the trill alone

facciam torto all'usignuolo,
we-do wrong to-the-nightingale,

e qualch'altro capitale abbiam
and some-other capital we-have
(and we have some other qualities)

*The celebrated Italian dancer, Carlo le Pick (or Picq).

poi che alcun non sa.
then that someone not knows.
(that nobody knows about.)

Bella, tengon sodo
(It is) beautiful, they-hold (their) ground,

se ne vanno, ed io ne godo!
themselves from-here they-go, and I of-it enjoy!
(they are going away, and I am gratified!)

Eroine di costanza, specchi son di fedeltà
Heroines of constancy, mirrors they-are of faithfulness.

Mozart
SMANIE IMPLACABILI
(Così Fan Tutte)

Recit.:
Ah scostati! paventi il tristo effetto
Ah, go away! fear the sad effect

d'un disperato affetto!
of-a desperate affection!

Chiudi quelle finestre...odio la luce,
Close those windows...I-hate the light,

odio l'aria che spiro...odio me stessa!
I-hate the-air that I-breathe...I-hate [me] myself!

Chi schernisce il mio duol? Chi mi consola?
Who scorns [the] my sadness? Who me consoles?

Deh fuggi, per pietà, lascimi sola.
Ah, flee, for pity('s sake), leave-me alone.

Aria:
Smanie implacabili, che m'agitate
Frenzies implacable, that me-agitate

entro quest'anima più non cessate,
within this-soul [more] (do) not cease,

finchè l'angoscia mi fa morir.
until [the]-anguish me makes to-die.

Esempio misero d'amor funesto,
Example miserable of-love fatal,
(Miserable example of fatal love,)

darò all' Eumenidi se viva resto
I-will-give to-the Furies, if living I-remain

col suono orribile de' miei sospir.
with-the sound horrible of-[the] my sighs.

Mozart   TRADITO, SCHERNITO DAL PERFIDO COR
(Così Fan Tutte)

Recit. :
In qual fiero contrasto, in qual disordine di pensieri,
In what fierce conflict, in what confusion of thoughts,

e di affetti io mi ritrovo.
and of affections I myself find-again.

Tanto insolito e novo è il caso mio,
So-[much] rare and new is [the] case my,

che non altri non io basto per consigliarmi.
that not others, not I suffice to counsel-myself.
(that neither others nor I myself can counsel me.)

Alfonso, quanto rider vorrai
Alfonso, how-much to-laugh you-will-wish

della mia stupidezza.   Ma mi vendicherò,
[of-the] (at) my stupidity.   But myself I-will-vindicate,

saprò dal seno
I-will-know-how from-[the] (my) breast

cancellar quell'iniqua.   Cancellarla?
to-erase that-wicked-one.   Erase-her?

Troppo, oh Dio! questo cor per lei mi parla.
Too-much, O God, this heart for her to-me speaks.
                     (this heart speaks to me of her.)

Aria:
Tradito, schernito dal perfido cor,
Betrayed, scorned by-[the] (her) perfidious heart,

Io sento che ancora quest'alma l'adora,
I feel that still this-soul her-adores,

Io sento per essa le voci d'amor.
I hear for her the voices of-love.

Mozart   AH CHI MI DICE MAI
                                      (<u>Don Giovanni</u>)

Ah chi mi dice mai quel barbaro dov'è?
Ah, who me tells ever that cruel-one where-is?
(Ah, who can tell me where that wretch is?)

Che per mio scorno amai, che mi mancò di fè.
Whom for my shame I-loved, who to-me lacked of faith.
                              (who broke faith with me.)

Ah se ritrovo l'empio,
Ah, if I-find-again the-inhuman-one

e a me non torna ancor,
and to me not he-returns again,

vo' farne orrendo scempio,
I-want to-make-of-him (a) horrible slaughter,

gli vo' cavar il cor!
to-him I-want to-cut-out the heart!
(I want to cut out his heart!)

Mozart   AH FUGGI IL TRADITOR
                                (Don Giovanni)

Ah fuggi il traditor,
Ah, flee (from) the traitor,

non lo lasciar più dir!
not him let more speak!
(do not let him say more!)

Il labbro è mentitor,
The lip is liar,
(His lips lie,)

fallace il ciglio.
deceitful the eye.
(his glances are deceitful.)

Da miei tormenti impara
From my torments learn (how much)

a creder a quel cor,
to believe in that heart,

e nasca il tuo timor
and (let) be-born [the] your fear

dal mio periglio!
from my peril!

238

Mozart   BATTI, BATTI, O BEL MASETTO
                                (Don Giovanni)

Batti, batti, o bel Masetto, la tua povera Zerlina;
Beat, beat, O handsome Masetto, [the] your poor Zerlina;

starò qui come agnellina,
I-will-remain here like (a) little-lamb,

le tue botte ad aspettar.
[the] your blows to await.

Lascierò straziarmi il crine;
I-will-let tear-out-me the hair;
(I'll let you tear my hair out;)

Lascierò cavarmi gli occhi;
I-will-let scratch-out-me the eyes;
(I will let you scratch out my eyes;)

e le care tue manine
and [the] dear your little-hands
(and your dear little hands)

lieta poi saprò baciar.
happy then I-will-know-how to-kiss.

Ah! lo vedo, non hai core!
Ah! it I-see, not you-have heart!
     (I see that you don't have the heart!)

Pace, pace, o vita mia!
Peace, peace, o life my!
            (O darling!)

In contenti, ed allegria,
In contentment, and (in) merriment,

notte e dì vogliam passar.
night and day we-wish to-pass.
(we'll spend our nights and days.)

Mozart   DALLA SUA PACE
                                 (Don Giovanni)

Dalla sua pace la mia depende...
From-[the] her peace [the] mine depends...
(My peace depends on hers...)

Quel ch'a lei piace vita mi rende;
That which-to her pleases life to-me gives;
(What pleases her gives life to me;)

quel che le incresce morte mi dà;
that which her saddens death to-me gives;
(what saddens her gives death to me;)

s'ella sospira, sospiro anch'io;
if-she sighs, sigh also-I;

è mia quell'ira quel pianto è mio...
is mine that-wrath, that weeping is mine...
(her wrath and tears are also mine...)

E non ho bene s'ella non l'ha.
And not have-I well-being if-she not it-has.
(And I do not have happiness if she does not have it.)

Mozart   DEH VIENI ALLA FINESTRA
                          (Don Giovanni)

Deh vieni alla finestra, o mio tesoro,
Ah, come to-the window, O my treasure,

deh vieni a consolar il pianto mio.
ah, come to console [the] weeping my.
(ah, come to console my sorrow.)

Se neghi a me di dar qualche ristoro,
If you-deny to me to give some comfort,

davanti agli occhi tuoi, morir vogl'io.
before to-[the] eyes your, to-die wish-I.
(I'll die before your eyes.)

Tu ch'hai la bocca dolce, più del miele,
You that-have the mouth sweet, more than honey,
(You that have a mouth sweeter than honey,)

tu che il zucchero porti in mezzo al core,
you that the sugar carry in middle of-the heart,
(you whose heart is made of sugar,)

non esser, gioja mia, con me crudele,
(do) not be, joy my, with me cruel,

lasciati almen veder, mio bell'amore!
let-yourself at-least be-seen, my beautiful-love.

Mozart   FINCH'HAN DAL VINO
                           (Don Giovanni)

Finch'han dal vino calda la testa,
Until-they-have of-the wine hot the head,
(So that their heads may be warmed by wine,)

una gran festa fa preparar;
a great feast make to-prepare;
(prepare a great feast;)

se trovi in piazza qualche ragazza,
if you-find in (the city) square some girl(s),

teco ancor quella cerca menar;
with-you yet that-one seek to-guide;
(bring them along with you;)

senz'alcun ordine, la danza sia,
without-any order, the dancing let-be,
(let the dancing be without any set plan,)

ch'il minuetto, chi la follia,
some-the minuet, some the follia,

chi l'alemanna farai ballar.
some the-allemande you-will-make to-dance.

Ed io frattanto, dall'altro canto
And I, meanwhile, in-the-other corner,

con questa e quella vo'amoreggiar.
with this-one and that-one want-to-make-love.

Ah la mia lista, doman mattina
Ah, [the] my list, (by) tomorrow morning

d'una decina devi aumentar.
with-a ten you-must increase.
(must grow by ten.)

Mozart   HO CAPITO
                                (Don Giovanni)

Ho capito, signor sì!
I-have understood, my-lord, yes!

Chino il capo, e me ne vo'
I-bend the head, and [myself] from-here go,

giacchè piace a voi così
because it-pleases [to] you thus,

altre repliche non fo'. Cavalier voi siete già.
other replies not do-I-make.   Nobleman you are, certainly.
(I must not argue.)

Dubitar non posso affè, me lo dice la bontà,
To-doubt not I-can in-faith, me it tells the goodness,
(I cannot doubt the goodness)

che volete aver per me.
that you-wish to-have for me.

Bricconaccia! malandrina! Fosti, ognor, la mia ruina!
Rascal! Wicked-one! You were, always, [the] my ruin!

Vengo, vengo. Resta! Resta!
I-am-coming, I-am-coming. Stay! Stay!

E una cosa molto onesta;
It-is a thing very honest;

faccia il nostro cavaliere,
let-make [the] our nobleman,
(our nobleman will make)

cavaliera ancora te.
noblewoman yet you.
(a noblewoman of you yet.)

Mozart   IL MIO TESORO
                         (Don Giovanni)

Il mio tesoro intanto andate a consolar,
[The] my treasure meanwhile go to console,

e del bel ciglio il pianto cercate di asciugar.
and of-the beautiful eye the weeping seek to dry.
(and try to dry her tears.)

Ditele che i suoi torti a vendicar io vado.
Tell-her that [the] her wrongs to avenge I go.

Che sol di stragi e morti
That only of destruction and death

nunzio vogl'io tornar.
(a) messenger wish-I to-return.

Mozart MADAMINA! IL CATALOGO E QUESTO (Catalog Aria)
(Don Giovanni)

Madamina! Il catalogo è questo,
Little lady! The catalog is this,

delle belle, che amò il padron mio!
of-the beautiful-ones, that loved [the] master my!
(of the beautiful ones that my master loved!)

Un catalogo egli è ch'ho fatto io:
A catalog it is that-have made I;
(It is a catalog that I have made;)

osservate, leggete con me!
observe, read with me!

In Italia sei cento e quaranta,
In Italy six hundred and forty,

in Alemagna due cento trent'una;
in Germany two hundred thirty-one;

cento in Francia, in Turchia novant'una,
(a) hundred in France, in Turkey ninety-one,

ma, ma in Ispagna, son già mille
but, but in Spain, there-are already (a) thousand

e tre!
and three!

V'han fra queste contadine,
There-are among [these] (them) country-girls,

v'han Contesse, Baronesse, Marchesane, Principesse,
there-are countesses, baronesses, marchionesses, princesses,

e v'han donne d'ogni grado,
and there-are ladies of-every class,

d'ogni forma d'ogni età.
of-every figure, of-every age.

Nella bionda, egli ha l'usanza di lodar la gentilezza...
In-the blonde, he has the-habit of praising the gentility...
(With blondes,)

Nella bruna la costanza, nella bianca la dolcezza!
In-the brunette the constancy, in-the white the sweetness!
(With brunettes, the constancy; with pale ones the sweetness!)

Vuol d'inverno la grassotta,
He-wants in-winter the fat-one,

vuol d'estate la magrotta;
he-wants in-summer the lean-one;

e la grande, maestosa;
and the tall, majestic-one;

la piccina, ognor vezzosa.
the little-one, always delicate.

Delle vecchie fa conquista
Of-the old-ones he-makes conquest

per piacer di porle in lista:
for (the) pleasure of putting-them in list:
                              (on the list;)

sua passion predominante è la giovin principiante
his passion prevailing is the young beginner,
(his prevailing passion)

non si picca, se sia ricca
not himself he-picques, if she-is rich,
(it doesn't matter)

se sia brutta, se sia bella!
if she-is ugly, if she-is beautiful!

Purchè porti la gonnella,
Provided-that she-wears the skirt,

voi sapete quel che fa!
you know that which he-does!

Mozart MI TRADI
(Don Giovanni)

Recit. :
In quali eccessi, O Numi, in quai misfatti orribili,
In what excesses, O Gods, in what crimes horrible,
(that are horrible)

tremendi, è avvolto il sciagurato! Ah no,
tremendous, is wrapped-up the wicked-one! Ah, no,
(and tremendous, is the wicked one involved!)

non puote tardar l'ira del cielo,
not can be-late the-wrath of-[the] heaven,
(the wrath of heaven cannot be delayed,)

la giustizia tardar!
the justice be-late!
(and justice cannot be delayed!)

Sentir già parmi la fatale saetta
To-feel already it-seems-to-me the fatal flash-of-lightning
(Already I feel the fatal lightning)

che gli piomba sul capo!
that to-him falls on-the head!
(that will fall on his head!)

Aperto veggio il baratro mortal.
Open I-see the abyss mortal.
(I see the open abyss of hell.)

Misera Elvira, che contrasto d'affetti
Miserable Elvira, what (a) conflict of-emotions

in sen ti nasce!
in breast to-you is-born!
(there is in your breast!)

Perchè questi sospiri, e quest'ambascie?
Why these sighs, and these anxieties?

Aria:
Mi tradì quell'alma ingrata,
Me betrayed that-soul ungrateful,
(That ungrateful man betrayed me,)

247

infelice Oh Dio! mi fa!
unhappy, O God, me he-makes!

Ma, tradita e abbandonata,
But, betrayed and abandoned,

provo ancor per lui pietà.
I-experience still for him pity.

Quando sento il mio tormento,
When I-feel [the] my torment,

di vendetta il cor favella;
of vengeance the heart speaks;

ma se guardo il suo cimento,
but if I-perceive [the] his danger,
(but when I perceive that he is in danger,)

palpitando il cor mi va.
palpitating the heart to-me goes.
(my heart palpitates.)

Mozart NON MI DIR
(Don Giovanni)

Recit.:
Crudele? ah no, mio bene!
Cruel-one? Ah, no, my beloved!

Troppo mi spiace allontanarti un ben
Too-much me it-displeases to-withhold-from-you a blessing

che lungamente la nostr'alma desia...
that for-a-long-time [the] our-soul(s) desire...

ma il mondo...oh Dio!
but the world...oh, God!

Non sedur la costanza del sensibil mio core!
Not tempt the constancy of-[the] susceptible my heart!
(Do not tempt the constancy of my susceptible heart!)

Abbastanza per te mi parla amore.
Sufficiently for you to-me speaks love.

Aria:
Non mi dir, bell'idol mio,
Not to-me say, handsome-idol mine,

che son io crudel con te;
that am I cruel with you;

tu ben sai quant'io t'amai
you know well how-much-I you-(have always)-loved,

tu conosci la mia fè
you know [the] my faithfulness.

Calma, calma il tuo tormento,
Calm, calm [the] your torment,

se di duol non vuoi ch'io mora!
if of sorrow not you-wish that-I die!
(if you do not want me to die of sorrow!)

Forse un giorno il cielo ancora sentirà pietà di me!
Perhaps one day [the] heaven yet will-feel pity for me!

Mozart   OR SAI
                    (Don Giovanni)

Or sai chi l'onore rapir a me volse,
Now you-know who the-honor to-snatch-away to me wished,
(Now you know who tried to steal my honor,)

chi fu il traditore, ch'il padre mi tolse.
who was the traitor, who-the father from-me took-away.
                   (who took my father from me.)

Vendetta ti chieggo...la chiede il tuo cor.
Vengeance of-you I-ask...it demands [the] your heart.
                (your heart demands it.)

Rammenta la piaga del misero seno...
Remember the wound of-the wretched breast...
(Remember the wound in his poor breast...)

Rimira di sangue coperto il terreno,
Recall with blood covered the ground,
(Recall the ground covered with blood,)

se'l cor in te langue d'un giusto furor.
if-the heart in you grows-weak of-a just anger.
(if the just anger in your heart begins to diminish.)

Mozart   VEDRAI, CARINO
                       (Don Giovanni)

Vedrai, carino, se sei buonino,
You-will-see, dear-little-one, if you-are (a) good-little-one,

che bel remedio ti voglio dar.
what (a) beautiful remedy to-you I-wish to-give.

E naturale, non da disgusto,
It-is natural, not it-gives dislike,
           (it doesn't taste bad,)

e lo speziale non lo sa far, no.
and the apothecary not it knows-how to-make, no.

E un certo balsamo che porto addosso,
It-is a certain balsam that I-carry upon-me,

dare tel posso s'il vuoi provar!
to-give to-you-it I-can if-it you-wish to-try!
(I can give it to you if you'd like to try it!)

Saper vorresti dove mi sta?
To-know would-you-wish where to-me it-is?
(Would you like to know where I keep it?)

Sentilo battere, toccami quà!
Feel-it beating, touch-me here!

Mozart   A FORZA DI MARTELLI
                              (La Finta Gardiniera)

A forza di martelli il ferro si riduce
[To] (by the) force of hammers the iron itself reduces;
                              (iron is forged;)

a forza de scarpelli il marmo si lavora.
[to] (by the) force of chisels the marble itself works.
                              (marble is carved.)

Di donna il cor ognora nè ferro nè martello
Of woman the heart always neither iron nor marble
(The heart of woman, however, neither by iron nor marble)

nè amore tristarello la può ridurre a segno
nor love sad her can reduce to (the) mark,
(nor sad love can be made to obey,)

la può capacitar.
her can persuade.
(or can persuade her.)

Siam pazzi tutti quanti che andiam appresso a femmine;
We-are mad everyone that we-go near [to] women;
(How mad we all are)

si sprezzino, si faccino,
themselves let-be-despised, themselves let-be-cut-to-pieces,
(Let them be despised, let them be cut to pieces,)

si fugghino, si piantino,
themselves let-be-avoided, themselves let-be-abandoned,
(let them be avoided, let them be abandoned,)

si lascino crepar.
themselves let to-split.
(let them die.)

Mozart   CRUDELI, FERMATE, OH DIO!
                               (La Finta Giardiniera)

Crudeli, fermate, oh Dio! Qui sola mi lasciate...
Cruel-ones, stop; oh, God! Here alone me you-leave...

misera. Chi m'aiuta, soccorso chi mi da?
unhappy. Who me-helps? Aid who to-me gives?
          (Who will help me? Who will give me aid?)

Ah, Numi, son perduta, muovetevi a pietà.
Ah, Gods, I-am lost, move-yourselves to pity.

Dove son, che m'avvene!
Where am-I? What to-me-has-happened?

Dunque son qui condotta, infelice a morir!
Then I-am here led, unhappy, to die!

Numi pietosi, se vi muove il dolore, il pianto mio,
Gods merciful, if you moves [the] sadness, [the] weeping my,
(Merciful Gods, if my sadness and my weeping move you,)

deh, guidate i miei passi...
ah, guide [the] my steps...

Ma, oh Dio, per questi sassi,
But, O God, among these rocks,

non so dove m'inoltro...
not do-I-know where [myself]-to-proceed further...

Dovunque il guardo giro
Wherever [the] (my) glance I-turn,

altro non vedo che imagini d'orrore,
other not see-I but pictures of-horror,

e solo io sento le voci del mio duol,
and only I hear the utterances of-[the] my grief,

del mio tormento.
of-[the] my torment.

253

Mozart   GEME LA TORTORELLA
                          (La Finta Giardiniera)

Geme la tortorella lungi dalla campagna,
Laments the young-dove far from-the countryside,

del suo destin si lagna,
of-[the] its destiny [itself] it-complains,

e par che in sua favella
and it-seems that in its (own) [tongue] (language)

voglia destar pietà.
it-wishes to-arouse pity.

Mozart   UN MARITO, O DIO, VORRESTI
                          (La Finta Giardiniera)

Un marito, o Dio, vorresti,
A husband, oh, God, you-would-have,

amoroso e pien d'affetto:
loving and full of-affection:

ma un marito giovinetto,
but a husband very-youthful,

figlia mia, non fa per te.
girl my, not makes for you.
(my dear girl, is not for you.)

Mozart   NOI DONNE POVERINE
                              (La Finta Giardiniera)

Noi donne poverine, tapine, sfortunate,
We women poor-little, wretched, unfortunate,
(We poor little women,)

appena siamo nate che abbiamo da penar,
scarcely are-we born than we-have to suffer:

disgrazie da bambine, strapazzi grandicelle,
misfortunes as babies, abuses (as) old-people;

e dell'età nel fiore, o siamo brutte o belle,
and of-[the]-age in-the flower, either be-we ugly or beautiful,
(and in the flower of our age,)

il maledetto amore ci viene a tormentar,
the cursed love us comes to torment,
(cursed love comes to torment us;)

tapine, sfortunate, meglio sarà per noi
wretched, unfortunate, better it-will-be for us

non nascer o morir.
not to-be-born, or to-die.

Mozart   CON CERTE PERSONE
                          (La Finta Semplice)

Con certe persone vuol esser bastone
With certain people wishes to-be stick
(With certain people there needs to be a stick,)

e sia benedetta la bella ricetta,
and be blessed the beautiful recipe,

che tutte le donne dovrian adoprar.
that all [the] women ought to-make-use-of

Bastone, madama, con chi non vi ama,
(A) stick, madame, [with] (for) him-who not you loves,

con chi fa il geloso,
with him-who makes [the] jealous,
(for him who is jealous,)

con chi non vuol spendere
[with] (for) him-who not wishes to-spend,

ed osa pretendere farvi cascar.
and dares-to-aspire to-make-you fall.

257

Mozart   ELLA VUOLE ED IO TORREI
                          (La Finta Semplice)

Ella vuole ed io torrei,
She wishes and I would-draw-away,

Convenire non si può.
to-agree not one can.
(it is not possible to agree.)

Quando son vicino a lei,
When I-am near to her,

Vale a dir, solus cum sola, *
that-is-to-say, alone with alone,

a un occhiata, a una parola,
at one glance, at one word,

mi riscaldo, mi fo rosso,
[myself] I-grow-warm, [myself] I-make red,
                          (I blush,)

mi par ch'abbia il fuoco addosso
to-me it-seems that-I-have the fire about-me,

sento il sangue in ogni vena
I-feel the blood in each vein,

chi ribolle e fa blo, blo.
that boils and makes blo, blo.
(that boils and goes "blo, blo.")

Ma l'amor finisce poi
But [the]-love ends then

colla borsa e coll'anello.
with-the purse and with-the-ring.

Ed il sangue già bel bello
And the blood, formerly beautiful beautiful,
                          (formerly so wonderful,)

si rapprese, si gelò.
[itself] recovered, [itself] cooled-down

*Latin, meaning "he alone with her."

258

E son come un can carbone,
And I-am like a [dog] water-spaniel,

fra la carne, ed il bastone,
between the meat, and the stick;

Vorrei stender lo zampino
I-would-like to-stretch-out the little-paw

e al baston più m'avvicino
and to-the stick more [myself]-I-approach,
(and approaching the stick,)

e abbaiando, mugolando,
and barking, yelping,

piglio il porco e me ne vò.
I-seize the pig and myself from-there I-go.
(I would snatch the pig and run away.)

Mozart   UN MARITO, DONNE CARE
                              (La Finta Semplice)

Un marito, donne care, ci bisogna ritrovare,
A husband, ladies dear, for-us it-is-necessary to-find,

che non mangi, che non beva,
who not eats, who not drinks,

che da noi tutto riceva,
who from us everything accepts,

che a noi lascia commandar.
who [to] us lets command.

Se così non si ritrova,
If thus not himself discovers,
(If such a one cannot be found,)

nè si può farne di meno
nor one can-do-with-him of less,
(nor can one do without him,)

far con esso un patto almeno
make with him an agreement, at least,

ch'egli mangi, quando ha fame,
that-he eats, when he-has hunger,

ch'egli beva quando ha sete,
that-he drinks, when he-has thirst,

ma, ne lasci sole e chete
but [of]-us he-leaves alone and quiet
(but that he leaves us alone and quiet)

far noi pur quel che ne par.
to-do we only whatever to-us appears.
(to do whatever we like.)

Mozart   NON C'E AL MONDO ALTRO CHE DONNE
(La Finta Semplice)

Non c'è al mondo altro che donne,
Not there-is in-the world other than women,
(There is nothing in the world like women,)

ma sian belle, ma sian buone,
but (though) they-be beautiful, but (though) they-be good,

non mi voglio infeminire,
not myself I-wish to-become-womanized,

non mi vò matrimoniar,
not myself I-wish to-get-married.

Servitore, sì signore, sì, sì,
Servant, yes, sir, yes, yes;
(I would become a servant if I got married, yes, sir;)

sua sorella, l'ho con ella,
your sister, it-I-have with her;
            (I have had enough of her;)

vada altrove ad abitar.
let-her-go elsewhere to live.

Mozart   SENTI L'ECO OVE T'AGGIRI
                              (La Finta Semplice)

Senti l'eco ove t'aggiri
Listen-to the-echo where [yourself]-you-go,
(Listen to the echo wherever you go,)

sussurrar tra fiori e fiori
whispering among flowers and flowers;
        (between the flowers,)

ma se gridi o se sospiri
but if you-cry-out or if you-sigh,

quello sol l'eco risponde,
[that] only the-echo answers,

che ti sente a ragionar.
that you it-hears to discourse.
(which hears you talking.)

Così far dovrebbe ancora
Thus to-do one-must yet,
(yet one must do thus,)

cogli amanti e   questa e quella
with-[the] lovers, both this-one and that-one;

voler bene a chi l'adora,
wish well to him-who her-adores,
(love him who adores her,)

corbellar chi ne corbella,
joke who of-them jokes,
(joke with him who jokes,)

non dar niente a chi non dona,
[not] give nothing to him-who not gives;
(give nothing to him who does not give;)

che l'usanza è bella e buona,
for the-custom is beautiful and good,

di far quel, che gli altri fanno,
to do that which [the] others do,

e in amor non può fallar.
and in love not can-it fail.

Mozart TROPPA BRIGA A PRENDER MOGLIE
(La Finta Semplice)

Troppa briga a prender moglie,
Too-much trouble to take (a) wife,

troppa briga in verità,
too-much trouble in truth;

non è cosa da soldato
not it-is thing as soldier,
(it's not something for a soldier,)

che la vuole a buon mercato,
who her wishes at (a) good price,
(who wants one cheap,)

o di meno ancor ne fà,
or of less yet of-her does
(or even does without one.)

sì, sì, troppa briga.
yes, yes, too-much trouble.

Son le donne belle e buone,
Are the women beautiful and good,
(Women are beautiful and good,)

ma se tanto han da costar,
but if so-much they-have to cost,

per un sol mazzo di carte,
for a single pack of cards,

per un fiasco di buon vino,
for a flask of good wine,

per due pipe di tabacco,
for two pipes of tobacco,

ve le do tutte in un sacco
to-you them I-give all in a sack,

nè mi vò più maritar.
nor me I-wish longer to-get-married.
(nor do I wish to get married.)

Mozart   UBRIACO NON SON IO
                                (La Finta Semplice)

Ubriaco non son io, nò, nò,
Drunk not am I, no, no,

sono allegro un pocchettino,
I-am merry a very-little-bit,

ma l'annello è sempre mio,
but the-ring is still mine,

e lo posso dimandar.
and it I-can demand.

Perchè alfin se parla il vino,
Because at-last if speaks the wine,
(Even though the wine speaks for me,)

quel ch'è mio si lascia star.
that which-is mine itself leaves to-stay.
(what is mine stays mine.)

Mozart   VIENI, VIENI, O MIA NINETTA
                          (La Finta Semplice)

Vieni, vieni, o mia Ninetta,
Come, come, O my Ninetta,

che ho gran fretta di sposar.
that I-have great haste to get-married.
(for I am in great haste to marry.)

L'han giurato,
It-they-have sworn,

sì, l'han promesso,
yes, it-they-have promised,

son soldato e non è adesso
I-am soldier and not is now
(I am a soldier, and now there is not)

troppo tempo di tremar.
too-much time to [tremble] (hesitate).

Mozart   D'ORESTE, D'AJACE
                                 (Idomeneo)

Recit. :
Oh smania! Oh furie! Oh disperata Elettra!
O frenzy! O furies! O desperate Electra!

Vedrò Idamante alla rivale in braccio?
Shall-I-see Idamante to-the rival in arm?
(Shall I see Idamante in the arms of my rival?)

Ah, no, il germano Oreste ne' cupi abissi
Ah, no, the brother, Orestes, in-the dark abysses

io vuò seguir.
I wish to-follow.

Or'or compagna m'avrai là
Now, now (as) companion me-you-will-have there

nell'inferno,
in-the-inferno,

a sempiterni guai, al pianto eterno.
to everylasting woes (condemned), to-[the] weeping eternal.

Aria:
D'Oreste, d'Ajace ho in seno i tormenti,
Of-Orestes, of-Ajax I-have in (my) breast the torments,

D'Aletto la face già morte mi dà.
Of-Alecto the image already death to-me gives.
(The image of Alecto frightens me to death.)

Squarciate mi il core, ceraste, serpenti,
Tear [to-me] (my) [the] heart, horned-vipers, serpents,

O un ferro il dolore in me finirà.
Or a sword the pain in me will-end.

Mozart   FUOR DEL MAR
                           (Idomeneo)

Recit.:
Qual mi conturba i sensi equivoca favella!
What to-me disturbs the senses ambiguous speech!
(How that ambiguous speech disturbs me!)

Ne' suoi casi qual mostra a un tratto
In-[the] her cases what reveals suddenly
(In her situation, what suddenly does reveal)

in tempestiva gioja la Frigia principessa?
in timely joy the Phrygian princess?

Quei, ch'esprime teneri sentimenti per il prence,
Those, that-she-expresses, tender sentiments for the prince,

sarebber forse ahimè!... sentimenti d'amor, gioja,
could-they-be, perhaps, alas, sentiments of-love, joy,

di speme? Non m'inganno, reciproco è l'amore.
of hope? Not myself-do-I-deceive, mutual is the-love.
                                 (they love each other.)

Troppo, Idamante, a scior' quelle catene sollecito
Too-much, Idamante, to loosen those chains quick
(Too quick, Idamante, to loosen those chains)

tu fosti... Ecco il delitto,
you were... Here-is the crime,

che in te punisce il ciel...
that in you punishes the heaven...
(for which heaven punishes you.)

Sì, sì, a Nettuno, il figlio, il padre, ed Ilia,
Yes, yes, to Neptune, the son, the father, and Ilia,

tre vittime saran sull'ara istessa,
three victims will-be on-the-altar same,

Da egual dolor afflitte: una del ferro,
[From] (with) equal pain afflicted: one by-the sword,

E due dal duol trafitte.
And two by-[the] grief pierced.

267

Aria:
Fuor del mar ho un mar in seno,
Away from-the sea, I-have a sea in (my) breast,

Che del primo è più funesto,
That of-the first is more calamitous,
(Which is more calamitous than the real sea,)

E Nettuno ancor in questo
And Neptune, still in this (situation),

mai non cessa minacciar.
never [not] ceases to-menace.

Fiero Nume! dimmi almeno se al naufragio
Fierce God, tell-me at-least if to-[the] shipwreck

è si vicino il mio cor, qual rio destino
is so near [the] my heart, what wicked destiny

or gli vieta il naufragar.
now to-it prevents [the] ruin.
(now keeps it from ruin.)

Mozart   IDOL MIO
                                (Idomeneo)

Recit. :
Parto, e l'unico oggetto
I-leave, and the-one object

ch'amo ed adoro, o Dei!
whom-I-love and adore, O Gods,

meco s'en vien?
with-me himself-from-there comes?
(will he come with me?)

Ah, troppo angusto è il mio cor a tanta gioja!
Ah, too narrow is [the] my heart [to] (for) so-much joy!
(Ah, there is not room in my heart for such great joy!)

Lunge dalla rivale farò ben io,
Far from-the rival will-do well I,
(Far from my rival, I will succeed,)

con vezzi, e con lusinghe,
with charms, and with allurements,

che quel foco, che pria spegnere non potei,
that that fire, which before to-extinguish not I-could,
             (which I could not extinguish before,)

a quei lumi s'estingua
to those [lights] (eyes) [themselves]-go-out
(will not burn for her,)

e avvampi ai miei.
and blaze to-the mine.
(and instead will blaze for me.)

Aria:
Idol mio, se ritroso altro amante a me ti rende,
Idol mine, if adverse other love to me you gives-up,
(My idol, if your other love gives you up to me, though
      unwillingly,)

non m'offende rigoroso,
not myself-I-feel-offended severely,
(I am not offended,)

più m'alletta austero amor,
more me-attracts austere love.
(but rather attracted by restrained love.)

Scaccierà vicin ardore
Will-drive-away near ardor
(Love close at hand will drive away)

dal tuo sen l'ardor lontano;
from-[the] your breast the-ardor distant;
(love at a distance;)

più la mano può d'amore
more the hand is-able of love
(the power of love is greater)

s'è vicin l'amante cor.
if-is near the-loving heart.
(if the heart that gives it is near at hand.)

Mozart   SE IL PADRE PERDEI
                          (Idomeneo)

Se il padre perdei, la patria, il riposo
If the father I-(have)-lost, the homeland, the resting-place,
(If I have lost my father, my homeland, my abode,)

tu padre mi sei,
you father to-me are;

soggiorno amoroso è Creta per me.
residence loving is Crete for me.
(Crete is for me an abode of affection.)

Or più non rammento l'angoscie, gli affanni,
Now longer not-I-remember the-anguish[es], the anxieties,

or gioja e contento, compenso a miei danni
now joy and contentment, compensation for my injuries

il cielo mi diè.
[the] heaven to-me gave.

Mozart   SE IL TUO DUOL
                          (Idomeneo)

Se il tuo duol,
If [the] your sorrow,

se il mio desio se'nvolassero
if [the] my desire themselves-would disappear
(and if my desire)

del pari, a ubbidirti qual son io,
of-the same, to obey-you as am I,
(to serve you were the same, they would disappear;)

saria il duol pronto a fuggir.
would-be [the] sorrow promptly to flee.
(sorrow would be quick to flee.)

Quali al trono sian compagni,
Any to the throne would-be associates,
(Let those who may be near to the throne,)

chi l'ambisce or veda e impari.
who it-covets now let-him-see and learn.
(who covet it, now see and learn.)

Stia lontan, o non si lagni,
Let-him-be far-away, or not [himself] complain,
(Let him stay away, or not complain,)

se non trova che martir.
if not he-finds but suffering.
(if he finds nothing but suffering.)

Mozart   TORNA LA PACE AL CORE
                            (Idomeneo)

Recit.:
Popoli! A voi l'ultima legge impone Idomeneo qual rè.
People! To you the-last decree commands Idomeneo as king.
        (Idomeneo proclaims his last decree as king to you.)

Pace v'annunzio.
Peace to-you-I-announce.

Compiuto è il sacrifizio, e sciolto il voto.
Completed is the sacrifice, and unshackled the vow.
           (and the vow is rescinded.)

Nettuno e tutti i Numi a questo regno amici son.
Neptune and all the gods to this realm friends are.

Resta, che al cenno loro Idomeneo ora ubbidisca.
It-remains that to-[the] signal their Idomeneo now obeys.
(Idomeneo must obey their order.)

O quanto, o sommi Dei, m'è grato il cenno!
Oh, how-much, o supreme gods, to-me-is welcome the
    signal!
    (order!)

Eccovi un altro rè, un altro me stesso.
Here-is-for-you another king, another me myself.
                    (just like me.)

A Idamante mio figlio, al caro figlio,
To Idamante, my son, to-the dear son,

cedo il soglio di Creta e tutto insieme
I-cede the throne of Crete, and all at-the-same-time

il sovrano poter. I suoi comandi rispettate,
the sovereign power. [The] his commands respect,

eseguite ubbidienti, come i miei seguiste
execute (them) obediently, as [the] mine you-followed

e rispettaste, onde grato io vi son:
and respected, for-which grateful I to-you am:

questo è la legge. Eccovi la real sposa!
this is the decree. Here-is-for-you the regal bride!

Mirate in questa bella coppia un don
Look upon this beautiful couple (as) a gift

del cielo serbato a voi.
of-[the] heaven reserved to you.

Quanto a sperar vi lice!
How-much to hope to-you is-permitted!
(You have so much to hope for!)

O Creta fortunata! O me felice!
O Crete fortunate! O me happy!
                (Oh, how happy I am!)

Aria:
Torna la pace al core,
Returns [the] peace to-the heart,

torna lo spento ardore,
returns the spent ardor,
(my ardor is renewed,)

fiorisce in me l'età;
flourishes in me the-age;
(youth flourishes again in me;)

tal la stagion di Flora l'albero annoso infiora,
as the season of Flora the-tree old makes-bloom,
(as in spring the old tree blooms,)

nuovo vigor gli dà.
new vigor to-it gives.
(it is given new vigor.)

Mozart   TUTTE NEL COR VI SENTO
                           (Idomeneo)

Recit. :
Estinto è Idomeneo?
Dead is Idomeneo?

Tutto a miei danni, tutto conguira il ciel!
Everything to my harm[s], everything conjures the heaven!
(Heaven contrives everything to my harm!)

Può a suo talento Idamante disporre d'un impero,
Can to his power Idamante direct [of]-an empire,
(Idamante, with his power, can command an empire)

e del cor;
and [of]-the heart;

e a me non resta ombra di speme?
and to me not remains (a) shadow of hope?

O mio dispetto, ahi lassa!
O my anger, alas, unhappy-one!

Vedrò, vedrà la Grecia a suo gran scorno
I-will-see, will-see [the] Greece to its great shame
(I will see, Greece will see, to its great shame)

una schiava Trojana di quel soglio,
a slave Trojan of that throne,

e del talamo a parte...
and [of]-the nuptial-bed to share...

Invano Elettra ami l'ingrato...
In vain Electra let-love the-ingrate...
(Let Electra love the ingrate in vain...)

E soffre una figlia d'un rè,
And suffers a daughter of-a king,
(And does the daughter of a king permit,)

ch'ha rè vasalli,
she-who-has king(s) (as) vassals,

ch'una vil schiava aspiri al grand'acquisto?
that-a vile slave aspires to-[the] great-conquest?

O sdegno! O smanie! O duol! Più non resisto!
O wrath! O frenzies! O grief! More not I-endure!

Aria:
Tutte nel cor vi sento, furie del crudo averno,
All in-the heart of-you I-feel, furies of-the cruel hell,
(All of you I feel in my heart, cruel furies of hell,)

lunge a si gran tormento amor, mercè, pietà.
far [to] (from) such great torment (are) love, compassion, pity.

Chi mi rubò quel core,
The-one-who from-me stole that heart,

quel che tradito ha il mio,
that-one who betrayed has [the] mine,

provin' dal mio furore, vendetta e crudeltà
let-them-experience [from-the] my fury, vengeance and
   cruelty.

Mozart   ZEFFIRETTI LUSINGHIERI
                                    (Idomeneo)

Zeffiretti lusinghieri, deh volate al mio tesoro,
Little-breezes alluring, pray, fly to-[the] my treasure,

e gli dite, ch'io l'adoro,
and to-him say, that-I him-adore,

che mi serbi il cor fedel.
that to-me he-keep [the] (his) heart faithful.

E voi piante, e fior sinceri,
And you, plants, and flowers loyal,

che ora inaffia il pianto amaro,
that now drenches the weeping bitter,
(that my bitter weeping now drenches,)

dite a lui, che amor più raro
say to him, that love more rare

mai vedeste sotto al ciel.
never have-you-seen under [to-the] heaven.

Mozart   FRA I PENSIER
                          (Lucio Silla)

Frà i pensier più funesti di morte
Among the thoughts most baleful, of death,

veder parmi l'esangue consorte
to-see it-seems-to-me the-bloodless consort
(I seem to see the bloodless consort)

che con gelida mano, m'addita
who with icy hand, to-me-indicates

la fumante sanguigna ferita
the reeking, bloody wound,

e mi dice: che tardi a morir?
and to-me says: why delay to die?

Già vacillo, già manco, già moro,
Already I-waver, already I-am-failing, already I-die,

e l'estinto mio sposo che adoro
and [the]-dead my husband whom I-adore,

ombra fida m'affretto a seguir.
spectre faithful, [myself]-I hasten to follow.

Mozart   GUERRIER, CHE D'UN ACCIARO
                          (Lucio Silla)

Guerrier, che d'un acciaro impallidisce al lampo,
Warrior, who of-a sword pales at-the flash,
(A warrior, who at a sword's flash grows pale,)

a dar non vada in campo prove di sua viltà.
to give not let-go in field proofs of his cowardice.
(should not enter the field to show his cowardice.)

Se or cede a un vil timore,
If now he-yields to a vile fear,

se or cede alla speranza,
if now he-gives-up [to-the] hope,

e qual sarà incostanza
[and] what will-be [inconstancy] (cowardice),

se questo non sarà?
if this not will-be?
(if this is not?)

Mozart   PARTO, M'AFFRETTO
                          (Lucio Silla)

Recit.:
In un istante oh come s'accrebbe il mio timor!
In an instant, oh, how [itself]-increased [the] my fear!

Pur troppo è questo un presagio funesto
Moreover, too-much is this an omen fatal

delle sventure mie!
of-[the] misfortunes my!

L'incauto sposo più non è
The-audacious husband more not is,
(My audacious husband is no longer here,)

Forse ascoso al reo tiranno,
Perhaps hidden from-the king tyrannical,

a morte ei già lo condannò.
to death he already him condemned.

Fra i miei spaventi nel mio dolore estremo
Among [the] my terrors in-[the] my sorrow extreme,

che fò? Che penso mai? Misera io tremo!
what will-I-do? What think-I [ever]? Miserable, I tremble!

Ah no, più non si tardi.
Ah, no, longer not (let) one delay.
         (delay no longer.)

Il Senato mi vegga. Al di lui piede grazia
The Senate me let-see. At-the of him feet pardon
(Let the Senate see me. At its feet, pardon)

e pietà s'implori per lo sposo fedel.
and pity (let)-one-implore for the husband faithful.

S'ei me la nega, si chieda al Ciel.
If-it me it denies, (let) one ask [to- the] (of) heaven.
(If the Senate denies me, I will ask heaven.)

Se il Ciel l'ultimo fine
If [the] heaven the-final end

                          280

dell'adorato sposo oggi prescrisse,
of-the-adored husband today should-prescribe,

trafigga me chi l'idol mio trafisse.
let-pierce me he-who [the]-idol my pierced.
(let him who killed my idol kill me, too.)

Aria:
Parto, m'affretto,
I-leave, [myself]-I-hasten,

ma nel partire il cor si spezza,
but in-[the] leaving the heart itself breaks-[to-pieces],

mi manca l'anima, morir mi sento.
to-me lacks the-soul, to-die myself I-feel.
(my spirit is lacking; I feel I am dying.)

Nè so morir, e smanio,
Nor do-I-know-how to-die, and I-have-no-rest,

e gelo, e piango, e peno,
and I-freeze, and I-weep, and I-suffer,

ah se potessi almeno frà tanti spasimi, morir così.
ah, if I-could at-least among so-many torments, die thus.

Ma per maggior mio duolo verso un amante appressa
But for greater to-me sorrow [toward] a lover near
(But for my greater sorrow, near a lover,)

divien la morte istessa pietosa in questo dì.
becomes [the] death itself merciful in this day.
(death becomes merciful this day.)

Mozart   PUPILLE AMATE
                               (Lucio Silla)

Pupille amate, non lagrimate,
Eyes beloved, (do) not weep,

morir mi fate, pria di morir.
to-die me you-make, sooner than to-die.
(you make me die prematurely.)

Quest'alma fida a voi
This-soul, (so) faithful to you,

d'intorno farà ritorno,
all-around (you) will-[make] return,

sciolta in sospir.
dissolved in sighs.

Mozart   GIA DAGLI OCCHI
                           (Mitridate, Re di Ponto)

Già dagli occhi il velo è tolto,
Already from-the eyes the veil is removed,

vili affetti io v'abbandono:
vile desires, I you-abandon.

son pentito, e non ascolto
I-am penitent, and not do-I-hear

che i latrati del mio cor.
but the [barkings] (urgings) of-[the] my heart.

Tempo è omai, che al primo impero
Time is now, that to-the first command
(Now the time has come)

la ragione in me ritorni.
the reason in me returns.

Già ricalco il bel sentiero
Already I-tread-again the beautiful path

della gloria, e dell'onor.
of-[the] glory, and of-[the]-honor.

Mozart   PARTO: NEL GRAN CIMENTO
                                (Mitridate, Re di Ponto)

Parto: nel gran cimento sarò germano e figlio
I go: in-the great test I-will-be brother and son;

eguale al tuo periglio la sorte mia sarà.
equal to-[the] your peril [the] fate my will-be.

T'adopra a tuo talento;
[You] make-use of your power;

nè in me mancar già mai
nor in me to-lack truly never
(never lacking in me)

vedrai la fedeltà.
will-you-see [the] faithfulness.

SON REO: L'ERROR CONFESSO
(Mitridate, Re di Ponto)

Son reo: l'error confesso;
I-am guilty; the-error I-confess;

e degno del tuo sdegno
and deserving of-[the] your anger,

non chiedo a te pietà.
not ask-I [to] (of) you pity.

Ma reo di me peggiore
But guilty than me worse,
(But more guilty than I,)

il tuo rivale, è questo,
[the] your rival, is this-one,
(is this one, your rival,)

che meritò l'amore della fatal beltà.
who earned the-love of-the deadly beauty.

Nel mio dolor funesto
In-[the] my affliction baleful

gemer ancor tu dei;
to-moan yet you must;
(you must still moan;)

ridere a danni miei Sifare non potrà, no.
to-laugh at injuries my Sifare not will-be-able, no.
(Sifare will not be able to laugh at my injuries, no!)

285

Mozart   **TU SAI PER CHI M'ACCESE**
                           (Mitridate, Re di Ponto)

Tu sai per chi m'accese
You know for whom me-he-inflamed,

quanto sopporto anch'io
how-much endure also-I,

e pur l'affanno mio non cangiasi in furor.
and yet [the]-pain my not changes-itself into anger.
(and yet my pain does not turn to anger.)

Potrei punirlo, è vero, ma tollero le offese
I-could punish-him, it-is true, but I-endure the injuries

e ancora non dispero di vincere quel cor.
and still not despair-I of conquering that heart.

Mozart   VA, L'ERROR MIO PALESA
(Mitridate, Re di Ponto)

Va, l'error mio palesa
Go, [the]-mistake my disclose

e la mia pena affretta,
and [the] my punishment hasten,

ma forse la vendetta cara ti costerà.
but perhaps [the] revenge dear(ly) [to]-you will-cost.

Quando sì lieve offesa
When so slight (an) offense

punita in me vedrai,
punished in me you-will-see,

te stessa accuserai di troppa crudeltà.
you yourself will-accuse of too-much cruelty.
(you will accuse yourself of too much cruelty.)

Mozart   VENGA PUR, MINACCI E FREMA
                          (Mitridate, Re di Ponto)

Venga pur, minacci e frema,
(Let-him) come then, threaten and roar,

l'implacabil genitore;
the-implacable father;

al suo sdegno, al suo furore
to-[the] his wrath, to-[the] his fury

questo cor non cederà.
this heart not will-yield.

Roma in me rispetti e tema,
Rome, in me, let-(him)-respect and fear;

men feroce e men severo,
less ferocious and less severe (let him be),

o più barbaro, o più fiero
or more savage, or more fierce

l'ira sua mi renderà.
[the]-wrath his me will-render.
(his wrath will make me.)

Mozart   APRITE UN PO' QUEGLI OCCHI
                            (Le Nozze di Figaro)

Recit. :
Tutto è disposto; l'ora dovrebbe esser vicina;
Everything is prepared; the-hour must be near;

io sento gente... è dessa! Non è alcun.
I hear people... it-is she! Not it-is someone.
                              (No, there is no one.)

Buia è la notte, ed io comincio omai a fare
Dark is the night, and I begin now to play

il scimunito mestiere di marito. Ingrata!
the silly occupation of husband. Ungrateful-woman!

Nel momento della mia cerimonia
[In]-(at)-the moment of-[the] my ceremony
(During our wedding ceremony)

ei godeva leggendo,
he was-enjoying reading (Susanna's note),

e nel vederlo io rideva di me
and in-[the] seeing-him I was-laughing [of] (at) myself

senza saperlo. Ah, Susanna! Quanta pena mi costi!
without knowing-it. Ah, Susanna! How-much pain me you-cost!
                              (How much pain you cost me!)

Con quell' ingenua faccia, con quegli occhi innocenti,
With that ingenuous face, with those eyes innocent,

chi creduto l'avria? Ah!
who believed it-would-have? Ah!
(who would have believed it?)

Che il fidarsi a donna è ognor follia.
[That the] trusting-oneself to (a) woman is always folly.

Aria:
Aprite un po' quegli occhi, uomini incauti e sciocchi;
Open a bit those eyes, men imprudent and foolish;

guardate queste femmine, guardate cosa son!
behold these females, look-at (what) [thing] they-are!

289

Queste chiamate dee dagli ingannati sensi,
These you-call goddesses, [from]-(with)-the deceived senses,

a cui tributa incensi la debole ragion.
to whom offers flattery the weak reason.
(to whom weak reason offers flattery.)

Son streghe che incantano per farci penar,
They-are witches that enchant to make-us suffer,

sirene che cantano per farci affogar,
sirens that sing to make-us drown,

civette che allettano per trarci le piume,
coquettes that ensnare to pull-(from)-us the feathers,

comete che brillano per toglierci il lume.
comets that glitter to take-away-(from)-us the light.

Son rose spinose, son volpi vezzose,
They-are roses thorny, they-are foxes graceful,

son orse benigne, colombe maligne,
they-are she-bears benign, doves evil,

maestre d'inganni, amiche d'affanni,
mistresses of-deceit, friends of-anguish[es],

che fingono, mentono, amore non senton,
that pretend, lie; love not do-they-feel,

non senton pietà. No, no, no, no.
not do-they-feel pity. No, no, no, no.

Il resto nol dico, già ognuno lo sa.
The rest not-it I-say, already everyone it knows.
(I do not say the rest because everyone already knows it.)

Mozart DEH VIENI, NON TARDAR
(Le Nozze di Figaro)

Recit. :
Giunse alfin il momento
Arrived-has finally the moment

che godrò senza affanno in braccio all'idol mio.
that I-will-enjoy without uneasiness in arms to-the-idol my.
(in the arms of my idol.)

Timide cure, uscite dal mio petto,
Timid fears, leave [from-the] my breast,

a turbar non venite il mio diletto.
to disturb not come the my delight.
(do not come to disturb my delight.)

Oh, come par che all' amoroso foco
Oh, how it-seems that to-the amorous fire

l'amenità del loco, la terra e il ciel risponda,
the-pleasantness of-the place, the earth and the sky respond,

come la notte i furti miei seconda!
as the night [the] deceptions my assists!
(as the night assists my deceptions!)

Aria:
Deh vieni, non tardar, o gioia bella,
Ah, come, (do) not delay, O joy beautiful,

vieni ove amore per goder t'appella
come where love to enjoy you-summons,
(come where for pleasure love summons you,)

finchè non splendi in ciel notturna face,
as-long-as not shines in sky nocturnal torch,
(while the moon does not yet shine in the sky,)

finchè l'aria è ancor bruna, e il mondo tace.
as-long-as the-air is still dark, and the world is-still.
(while it is still dark,)

Qui mormora il ruscel, qui scherza l'aura
Here murmurs the brook, here plays the breeze

291

che col dolce sussurro il cor ristaura;
that with-the sweet whisper the heart restores;

qui ridono i fioretti e l'erba è fresca,
here smile the little-flowers, and the-grass is fresh;

ai piaceri d'amor qui tutto adesca.
to-the pleasures of-love here everything entices.

Vieni, ben mio, tra queste piante ascose,
Come, darling my, among these trees hidden,

vieni, vieni! ti vo' la fronte
come, come! [To-you] I-wish [the] (your) forehead

incoronar di rose.
to-crown with roses.

Mozart   DOVE SONO I BEI MOMENTI
                          (Le Nozze di Figaro)

Recit.:
E Susanna non vien?
And Susanna not comes?

Sono ansiosa di saper come il conte accolse la proposta.
I-am anxious to know how the count received the proposal.

Alquanto ardito il progetto mi par...
Rather daring the project to-me seems...

ad uno sposo si vivace e geloso...
to a husband so full-of-spirit and jealous...

Ma che mal c'è?
But what harm there-is?

Cangiando i miei vestiti con quelli di Susanna,
Changing [the] my clothes with those of Susanna,

e i suoi co' miei al favor della notte...
and [the] hers with mine to-the protection of-the night...
                          (under cover of night...)

Oh cielo! a qual umil stato fatale
Oh, heaven! to what lowly condition unfortunate

io son ridotta da un consorte crudel!...
I am reduced by a consort cruel!...

che dopo avermi con un misto inaudito
who after having-me with a mixture unheard-of
(who, with an incredible mixture)

d'infedeltà, di gelosia, di sdegno...
of-faithlessness, of jealousy, of disdain...

prima amata, indi offesa, e alfin tradita...
first loved, then offended, and finally betrayed...
(having first loved, then offended, and finally betrayed me)

fammi or cercar da una mia serva aita!
makes-me now seek from [a] my servant help!

                          293

Aria:
Dove sono i bei momenti di dolcezza e di piacer?
Where are the beautiful moments of sweetness and of pleasure?

Dove andaron i giuramenti di quel labbro menzogner?
Where have-gone the promises of that lip lying?
                              (of those deceitful lips?)

Perchè mai, se in pianti e in pene
Why ever, if in tears and in grief[s]
(Why, if into tears and grief)

per me tutto si cangiò,
for me everything [itself] has-changed,

la memoria di quel bene
the memory of that goodness
(has the memory of that sweet past)

dal mio sen non trapassò?
from-[the] my breast not disappeared?
(not left my memory?)

Ah! se almen la mia costanza
Ah, if only [the] my constancy,

nel languire amando ognor
in-the languishing loving always
(while I am languishing but still loving,)

mi portasse una speranza
to-me might-bring a hope

di cangiar l'ingrato cor!
of changing the-ungrateful heart!
          (his)

Mozart   NON PIU ANDRAI
                        (Le Nozze di Figaro)

Non più andrai, farfallone amoroso
No longer will-you-go, butterfly amorous,

notte e giorno, d'intorno girando;
night and day, all-around roaming;

delle belle turbando il riposo
of-the beautiful-ones disturbing the sleep,

Narcisetto, Adoncino d'amor.
Little-Narcissus, little-Adonis of-love.

Non più avrai questi bei pennacchini,
No longer will-you-have these beautiful feathers,

quel cappello, leggero e galante,
that cap, light and gallant,

quella chioma, quell'aria brillante,
that head-of-hair, that air clever,

quel vermiglio donnesco color. Fra guerrieri, poffar Bacco!
that scarlet womanly color. Among soldiers, by Bacchus,

gran mustacchi, stretto sacco,
great mustache, narrow pack,

schioppo in spalla, sciabla al fianco,
musket on shoulder, saber at-the side,

collo dritto, muso franco,
neck straight, face frank,

o un gran casco o un gran turbante,
either a great helmet or a large turban,

molto onor, poco contante.
much honor, little cash.

Ed in vece del fandango, una marcia per il fango,
And instead of-the fandango, a march through the mud,

per montagne, per valloni,
through mountains, through valleys,

colle nevi e i sollioni,
with-the snow and the dog-days,

al concerto di tromboni, di bombarde, di cannoni,
to-the harmony of blunderbusses, of mortars, of cannon,

che le palle in tutti i tuoni
which the bullets in all the keys

all'orecchio fan fischiar.
to-the-ear make whistle.
(which make the bullets whistle past the ears in all the keys.)

Cherubino alla vittoria, alla gloria militar.
Cherubino to-the victory, to-the glory military.
(Cherubino, on to victory and to military glory.)

Mozart   NON SO PIU COSA SON, COSA FACCIO
                    (Le Nozze di Figaro)

Non so più cosa son, cosa faccio.
Not know-I more what I-am, what I-do.
(I know no longer what I am, what I am doing.)

Or di foco, ora sono di ghiaccio.
Now of fire, now I-am of ice,
(First I'm like fire, then I'm like ice.)

Ogni donna cangiar di colore, ogni donna mi fa palpitar.
Each woman to-change of color, each woman me makes
     palpitate.
(Every woman makes me blush; every woman makes me
     tremble.)

Solo ai nomi d'amore di diletto,
Only at-the names of-love, of delight,
(Even at the mention of love, with delight)

mi si turba, mi s'altera il petto,
me itself disturbs, me itself-alters the breast,
(I am disturbed, and my heart pounds,)

e a parlare mi sforza d'amore,
and to speak me obliges of love,
(And I am forced to speak of love)

un desio ch'io non posso spiegar.
a desire that-I not can explain.
(by a desire that I cannot explain.)

Parlo d'amor vegliando, parlo d'amor sognando,
I-speak of-love while-waking, I-speak of-love while-
     dreaming,

all'acqua, all'ombra, ai monti,
to-the-water, to-the-shadow, to-the mountains,

ai fiori, all'erbe ai fonti,
to-the flowers, to-the-grass, to-the fountains,

all'eco, all'aria, ai venti,
to-the-echo, to-the-air, to-the-winds,

297

che il suon de' vani accenti portano via con se.
which the sound of-[the] useless words carry away with them.
(which carry away with them the sound of my futile words.)

E se non ho chi m'oda,
And if not I-have (one) who me-hears,

parlo d'amor con me.
I-speak of-love with myself.

Mozart   PORGI AMOR
                       (Le Nozze di Figaro)

Porgi amor qualche ristoro
Bestow, love, some consolation

al mio duolo, a' miei sospir!
[to-the] (on) my sorrow [to-the] (on) my sighs!

O mi rendi il mio tesoro,
Either to-me restore [the] my treasure,

o mi lascia almen morir.
or me allow at-least to-die.

Mozart   SE VUOL BALLARE
                          (Le Nozze di Figaro)

Recit.:
Bravo, signor padrone!
Bravo, [sir] master!

Ora incomincio a capire il mistero
Now I-begin to understand the mystery

e a veder schietto tutto il vostro progetto.
and to see plainly all [the] your plan.

A Londra, è vero? Voi ministro, io corriero,
To London, is-it true? You (as) minister, I (as) courier,

e la Susanna... segreta ambasciatrice.
and [the] Susanna... secret ambassadress.

Non sarà, Figaro il dice.
Not it-will-be, Figaro it says.

Aria:
Se vuol ballare, signor Contino,
If you-wish to-dance, sir, little-Count,
                    (my dear little Count,)

il chitarrino le suonerò, sì.
the little-guitar for-you I-will-play, yes.

Se vuol venire nella mia scuola,
If you-wish to-come into-[the] my school,

la capriola le insegnerò, sì.
the capriola (dance step) to-you I-will-teach, yes.

Saprò... ma piano, piano...
I-will-know...but quietly, quietly...

meglio ogni arcano dissimulando scoprir potrò.
better each secret dissembling to-discover I-will-be-able.
(I will be able to discover each secret better by pretending.)

L'arte schermendo, l'arte adoprando,
[The]-cunning parrying, [the]-cunning using,
(Parrying with cunning, using cunning,)

300

di quà pungendo, di là scherzando,
from here pricking, from there joking,

tutte le macchine rovescierò.
all [the] (your) stratagems I-will-overturn.

Mozart   VEDRO MENTR'IO SOSPIRO
(Le Nozze di Figaro)

Recit.:
Hai già vinta la causa! Cosa sento!
You-have already won the suit! (What) [thing] do-I-hear?

In qual laccio cadea? Perfidi!
In what snare did-I-fall? Perfidious-ones!

Io voglio di tal modo punirvi;
I wish of such manner to-punish-you;
(How I will punish you!)

a piacer mio la sentenza sarà.
to pleasure my the sentence will-be.

Ma s'ei pagasse la vecchia pretendente?
But if-he might-pay the old claimant?

Pagarla! In qual maniera?
Pay-her! In what manner?
      (How can he?)

E poi v'è Antonio che all'incognito Figaro
And then there-is Antonio who to-the-unknown Figaro

ricusa di dare una nipote in matrimonio.
refuses to give [a] (his) niece in matrimony.

Coltivando l'orgoglio di questo mentecatto...
Exploiting the-pride of this idiot...

tutto giova a un raggiro...il colpo è fatto.
all is-useful to [a] (my) scheme... the blow is done.
          (I have decided!)

Aria:
Vedrò mentr'io sospiro, felice un servo mio!
Shall-I-see, while-I sigh, happy a servant (of) mine?

E un ben che invan desio, ei posseder dovrà?
And a good-thing that in-vain I-desire, he to-possess must?
(And must he possess something that I in vain desire?)

Vedrò per man d'amore unita a un vile oggetto
Shall-I-see by (the) hand of-love united to a vile object

che in me destò un affetto che per me poi non ha?
she-who in me awoke an affection that for me then not she-has?
(she who awoke a desire in me that she does not return?)

Ah, no! Lasciarti in pace non vo' questo contento,
Ah, no! To-leave-for-you in peace not I-wish this contentment,
(I do not wish to leave this happiness for you,)

tu non nascesti, audace, per dare a mie tormento,
you not were-born, audacious-one, to give to me torment,

e forse ancor per ridere di mia infelicità.
and perhaps yet to laugh [of] (at) my unhappiness.

Già la speranza sola delle vendette mie
Already the hope only of-[the] vengeance[s] my
(Already only the hope of vengeance)

quest'anima consola, e giubilar mi fa.
this-soul consoles, and to-rejoice me makes.
(consoles my soul and makes me rejoice.)

Mozart   LA VENDETTA
                          (Le Nozze di Figaro)

La vendetta, oh, la vendetta
[The] vengeance, oh, [the] vengeance

è un piacer serbato ai saggi.
is a pleasure reserved to-the wise.

L'obliar l'onte,
The-forgetting (of) [the] shame, (and)

gli oltraggi è bassezza, è ognor viltà.
[the] outrage[s] is baseness, is always cowardice.

Coll' astuzia, coll' arguzia,
With-[the] craftiness, with-[the] quick-wittedness,

col giudizio, col criterio
with-[the] judgment, with-[the] discernment

si potrebbe, il fatto e serio;
one could (do it, though) the matter is [serious] (difficult);

ma credete si farà.
but believe (me), it will-be-done.

Se tutto il codice dovessi volgere,
If all the statute-book(s) I-must change,

se tutto l'indice dovessi leggere,
if all the-list(s) I-must read,

con un equivoco, con un sinonimo,
with an equivocation, with a synonym,
(with equivocation or ambiguity,)

qualche garbuglio si troverà.
some entanglement itself will-find
(I'll find some way to confuse,)

Tutta Siviglia conosce Bartolo,
All (of) Seville knows Bartolo,

il birbo Figaro vinto sarà.
the knave Figaro vanquished will-be.

304

Mozart   VENITE INGINOCCHIATEVI
        (Le Nozze di Figaro)

Venite inginocchiatevi, restate fermo lî.
Come, kneel-down-[yourself], remain still there.

Pian piano or via giratevi. Bravo!
Very slowly now away turn-yourself. Bravo!

Va ben cosî. La faccia ora volgetemi.
It-goes well thus. The face now turn-to-me.

Olà, quegli occhi a me.
There, those eyes (turn) to me.

Drittissimo guardatemi, madama qui non è!
As-straight-as-possible look-at-me, my-lady here not is!

La faccia ora volgetemi... restate fermo lî,
The face now turn-to-me... remain still there,

or via giratevi, guardatemi, bravo!
now away turn-yourself, look-at-me, bravo!

Più alto quel colletto. Quel ciglio un po' più basso,
More high that collar. That brow a little more low,

le mani sotto il petto,
the hands under the bosom,

vedremo poscia il passo,
we-shall-see then the walk,

quando sarete in piè.
when you-will-be [in] (on your) feet.

Mirate il bricconcello, mirate quanto è bello,
Look-at the little-rascal, see how-much he-is handsome,

che furba guardatura, che vezzo, che figura.
what (a) sly appearance, what charm, what (a) figure.

Se l'amano le femmine,
If him-love the ladies,

hanno certo il lor perchè.
they-have certainly [the] their reason-why.

Mozart   VOI CHE SAPETE
                                 (Le Nozze di Figaro)

Voi che sapete che cosa è amor,
You that know what [thing] is love,

donne, vedete s'io l'ho nel cor.
ladies, see if-I it-have in-the heart.
(ladies, see if I have it in my heart.)

Quello ch'io provo vi ridirò.
That which-I experience, to-you I-will-repeat.

E per me nuovo, capir nol so.
It-is for me new, to-understand not-it I-know-how.
(It's new to me; I don't understand it.)

Sento un affetto pien di desir,
I-feel a longing full of desire,

ch'ora è diletto, ch'ora è martir.
that-now is delight, that-now is suffering.

Gelo, e poi sento l'alma avvampar
I-freeze, and then I-feel the-soul burst-into-flame,

e in un momento torno a gelar;
and in a moment I-go-back to freezing;

ricerco un bene fuori di me,
I-search-for a blessing outside of me,

non so ch'il tiene, non so cos'è.
not know-I who-it holds, not know-I what-it-is.
(I don't know who holds it; I don't know what it is.)

Sospiro e gemo senza voler,
I-sigh and moan without wishing-to,

palpito e tremo senza saper.
I-throb and tremble without knowing (that I do).

Non trovo pace notte ne dî,
Not find-I peace night nor day,

ma pur mi piace languir cosî.
but yet me it-pleases to-pine thus.

Mozart   L'AMERO, SARO COSTANTE
                          (Il Re Pastore)

L'amerò, sarò costante:
You-will-I-love, I-will-be constant:

fido sposo, e fido amante
faithful spouse, and faithful lover,

sol per lei sospirerò!
only for you will-I-sigh!

In sì caro, e dolce oggetto
In (one) so dear, and (so) sweet (an) object

la mia gioia, il mio diletto,
[the] my joy, [the] my delight,

la mia pace io troverò.
[the] my peace I will-find.

Io ti lascio, o cara addio,
I you leave, O dear-one, goodbye,

vivi più felice e scordati di me.
live more happy and forget-[yourself of] me.

Strappa, pur dal tuo bel core
Tear-out, then from-[the] your beautiful heart

quell'affetto, quell'amore;
that-affection, that-love;

pensa che a te non lice
think that to you not it-is-permitted

il ricordar si di me.
to remember-[yourself of] me.

Ti lascio, addio!
You I-leave, goodbye!

Ridente la calma nell'alma si desti,
Smiling [the] calm in-the-soul itself let-awaken,
(Let smiling calm be awakened in the soul,)

ne resti un segno di sdegno e timor.
nor let-there-remain a trace of anger and fear.

Tu vieni frattanto a stringer, mio bene,
You come meanwhile to tighten, my beloved,

le dolce catene si grate al mio cor.
the sweet chains so welcome to-[the] my heart.

Mozart   UN MOTO DI GIOIA

Un moto di gioia mi sento nel petto,
An impulse of joy [myself] I-feel in-the breast,
(An emotion of joy I feel in my breast,)

che annunzia diletto in mezzo il timor!
that predicts delight in (the) middle (of) [the] fear!

speriam che in contento finisca l'affanno,
let-us-hope that in contentment may-finish [the]-anguish,

non sempre è tiranno il fato ed amor.
not always is tyrant [the] fate and love.
(not always are fate and love a tyrant.)

Paisiello   CHI VUOL LA ZINGARELLA

Chi vuol la zingarella, graziosa, accorta e bella?
Who wants the gypsy-girl, graceful, cunning and beautiful?

Signori, eccola quà.
Gentlemen, behold-her here.

Le donne sul balcone
The women on-the balcony,

so bene indovinar,
I-know-how well to-tell-their-fortunes,

i giovani al cantone
the young-men at-the corner

so meglio stuzzicar.
I-know-how better [to-stir up] (how to excite.)

A vecchi innamorati
[To] (of) old-men enamoured

scaldar fo le cervella;
heat-up I-make the brains;
(I fire the imagination;)

chi vuol la zingarella?
who wants the gypsy-girl?

Signori, eccola quà.
Gentlemen, behold-her here.

Il mio ben quando verrà
[The] my treasure, when he-will-come

a veder la mesta amica
to see the sad sweetheart,

di bei fior s'ammanterà la spiaggia aprica.
with beautiful flowers itself-will-cover the beach sunny.
(the sunny beach will be covered with beautiful flowers.)

Ma nol vedo, no, il mio ben,
But not-him I-see, no, [the] my beloved,

il mio bene, ahimè non vien.
[the] my beloved, alas, (does) not come.

Mentre all'aure spiegherà
While to-the-breezes he-will-spread

la sua fiamma, i suoi lamenti,
[the] his flame, [the] his complaints,

miti augei, v'insegnerà più dolci accenti.
gentle birds, to-you-he-will-teach more sweet accents.

Ma non l'odo.   E chi l'udì?
But not him-do-I-hear.   And who him-heard?

Il mio bene ammutolì.
[The] my beloved became-silent.

Tu cui stanca omai già fè,
You to-whom tired now already made,
(You who have been made tired by)

il mio pianto, eco pietosa,
[the] my weeping, echo compassionate,

ei ritorna e dolce a te
he returns and sweetly of you

chiede la sposa.
[seeks] (asks-for) the wife.

Pian, mi chiama, piano ahimè!
Soft(ly) me he-calls, softly, alas!

No, non chiama, O Dio, non c'è.
No, not he-calls, O God, not there-he-is.

Nel cor più non mi sento
In-the heart more not myself I-feel
(I no longer feel in my heart)

brillar la gioventù;
sparkle [the] youth;

cagion del mio tormento,
cause of-[the] my torment,

amor, sei colpa tu.
love, you-are (the) guilty (one) [you].

Mi pizzichi, mi stuzzichi,
Me you-pinch, me you-excite,

mi pungichi, mi mastichi;
me you-prick, me you-bite;

che cosa è questo, ahimè?
what thing is this, alas?

Pietà, pietà, pietà!
Pity, pity, pity!

Amore è un certo che
Love is a certain something

che disperar mi fa!
which despair me makes!
(which is driving me crazy!)

Si vuol saper chi sono,
[One wants] (they want) to-know who I-am,

chi sono or si saprà!
who I-am now one will-know!

Talvolta son di Plauto la sostenuta attrice;
Sometimes I-am of Plautus the sustained actress;

talvolta Euridice de'regni dell'orror.
sometimes Euridice of-the-Kingdoms of-[the]-horror.

Son pastorella amante,
I-am (a) shepherdess loving,

che al suon di dolci avene
who to-the sound of sweet shepherd's-pipes

accanto al caro bene
beside [to]-the dear beloved

si spassa a far l'amor.
herself amuses to make [the]-love,

Son furia, che se m'altero,
I-am (a) fury, who if myself-I-excite,

sconquasso, abbatto, e fulmino,
I-crush, I-overthrow, and I-strike-lightning,

qual foco sbalzo in aria, nessun mi può frenar.
like fire I-jump into (the) air; no-one me can restrain.

Questa son io, temetemi, se no vi fò tremar.
This am I; fear-me; if not you I-(will)-make tremble.

O pargoletto arciero, non esser più sî fiero
O [little-boy archer] (Cupid), (do) not be [more] so cruel,

abbi pietà del cor.
have pity [of-the] (on my) heart.

Se vero nume sei, tiranno esser non dei,
If (a) true divinity you-are, tyrant be not you-must,
                                (you must not be a tyrant)

ne sempre feritor.
nor always (a) wounder.
(nor inflict wounds.)

317

Quanto è folle quell'amante,
How is stupid that-lover,

che penando si dispera;
who suffering [himself] despairs;

la Fortuna, ch'è incostante,
[the] fortune, which-is inconstant,

varia aspetto e cangia sfera.
changes aspect and changes [spheres] (stars).

Con speranza di mercede,
With (the) hope of reward,

ostinato negli amori alla mia superba Clori
obstinate in-[the] love[s] to-[the] my proud Cloris

ho giurato eterna fede.
I-have sworn eternal faith.

Verdi tronchi, annose piante,
Green trunks, ancient trees,

fosco asil d'ombre secrete,
dark refuge of-shadows secret,

per pietà qui raccogliete
in pity here receive

del dolore un'ombra errante!
of [the] sorrow a-shade wandering!
(a shade wandering in sorrow!)

Sì che lungi dal mio sole
Indeed [that] far from-[the] my sun

ombra mesta il duol mi rende;
shade sad [the] sorrow me renders;
(sorrow makes me become a sad spectre;)

ma quel sol, che arder mi vuole,
but that sun, which to-burn me wants,
                    (which wishes to burn me,)

è sparito e pur m'accende.
is disappeared and yet me-kindles.
(has disappeared, and yet it kindles me.)

Ogni pena più spietata
Every punishment more bitter

soffriria quest'alma afflitta desolata,
would-endure this-soul afflicted (and) desolate,

se godesse la speranza
if it-could-enjoy the hope

di potersi consolar.
of being-able-itself to-console.

Ma ohimè, cade ogni speme,
But alas, fails every hope,

non c'è luogo, non c'è vita,
not there-is place, not there-is life,
(there is no place, there is no life,)

non c'è modo di sperar.
not there-is (a) way to hope.
(there is no way to hope.)

Pergolesi   SE CERCA, SE DICE

Se cerca, se dice:
If she-seeks, if she-says:

l'amico dov'è?
[the-friend] (my beloved) where-is-he?

L'amico infelice, rispondi, morì!
[The]-(my)-lover unfortunate, reply, he-died!

Ah, no! Sì gran duolo non darle per me!
Ah, no! Such great sorrow (do) not give-her for me!

Rispondi, ma solo: piangendo partì!
Reply, but only: weeping he-left!

Che abisso di pene
What (an) abyss of suffering[s]

lasciare il suo bene,
to-leave [the] one's treasure,

lasciarlo per sempre, lasciarlo così!
to-leave-it for ever, to -leave-it thus!

Pergolesi   SE TU M'AMI

Se tu m'ami, se tu sospiri sol per me,
If you me-love, if you sigh only for me,

gentil pastor,
kind shepherd,

ho dolor dei tuoi martiri,
I-have sorrow [of]-(for)-[the] your suffering[s],

ho diletto del tuo amor.
I-have pleasure [of-the] (in) your love.

Ma se pensi che soletto io ti debba riamar,
But if-you-think that alone I you must love-(in-return),
                    (that I must love only you,)

pastorello, sei soggetto
little-shepherd, you-are subject

facilmente a t'ingannar.
easily to [yourself-deceive] (being deceived).

Bella rosa porporina oggi Silvia sceglierà;
Beautiful rose red today Silvia will-choose;

con la scusa della spina
with the excuse of-the thorn
(because the thorn pricks her finger)

doman poi la sprezzerà.
tomorrow then it she-will-despise.

Ma degli uomini il consiglio
But of-[the] men the advice

io per me non seguirò.
I for myself not will-follow.

Non perchè mi piace il giglio
Not because to-me pleases the lily
(Just because I like the lily)

gli altri fiori sprezzerò.
the other flowers will-I-despise.
(I do not have to despise other flowers.)

322

Pergolesi   STIZZOSO, MIO STIZZOSO
                                       (La Serva Padrona)

Stizzoso, mio stizzoso, voi fate il borioso
Angry-one, my angry-one, you act (like) the proud-one,

ma non vi può giovare.
but not you it-can help.
(but it cannot help you.)

Bisogna al mio divieto
It-is-necessary at-[the] my forbidding

star cheto e non parlare.
to-remain silent and not to-speak.

Serpina vuol così.
Serpina wants (it) thus.

Cred'io che m'intendete
I-believe that me-you-understand,
(I believe that you understand me,)

dacchè mi conoscete son molti e molti dì.
since me you-know [there-are] (since) many and many days.
(since you have known me a long time.)

Pergolesi (?) TRE GIORNI SON (NINA)

Tre giorni son che Nina
Three days there-are that Nina
(It has been three days)

in letto se ne sta.
in bed [herself from-there] stays.
(that Nina has stayed in bed.)

Pifferi, timpani, cembali,
Fifes, drums, cymbals,

svegliate mia Ninetta
awaken my little-Nina

acciò non dorma più
so-that not she-may-sleep more.
(so that she will sleep no longer.)

Peri GIOITE AL CANTO MIO (INVOCAZIONE DI ORFEO)
(Euridice)

Gioite al canto mio, selve frondose.
Rejoice at-[the] singing my, woods leafy.

Gioite, amati colli, e d'ogn'intorno
Rejoice, beloved hills, and from-everywhere-around

eco rimbombi dalle valli ascose.
(let the) echo resound from-the valleys hidden.

Risorto è il mio bel sol di raggi adorno,
Risen-again is [the] my beautiful sun with rays adorned,

e coi begli occhi,
and with-[the] beautiful eyes,

onde fa scorno a Delo,
with-which it-makes scorn to Delos,

raddoppia fuoco all'alme e luce al giorno
redoubles fire to-[the]-souls and light ,to-the day

e fa servi d'amor
and makes (into) servants of-love

la terra e il cielo.
[the] earth and [the] heaven.

Nel puro ardor della più bella stella
In-the pure ardor of-the most beautiful star

aurea facella di bel foco accendi
(a) golden torch of beautiful fire you-kindle,

e qui discendi su l'aurate piume,
and here you-descend upon [the]-golden wings,

giocondo Nume, e di celeste fiamma l'anime infiamma.
happy God, and with celestial flame the-souls animate.

Lieto Imeneo, d'alta dolcezza un nembo
Joyous Hymen, of-high sweetness a tempest

trabocca in grembo a fortunati amanti,
pour-out in (the) lap [to] (of the) happy lovers,

e tra bei canti di soavi amori
and amid beautiful songs of sweet love[s]

sveglia nei cori una dolce aura,
awaken in-the hearts a gentle aura,

un riso di Paradiso!
a smile of Paradise!

Begli occhi, io non mi pento,
Beautiful eyes, I do-not [myself] repent,

d'avervi offerto il sen.
of-having-to-you offered [the] (my) bosom.

Anzi, se le mie pene fossero senza spene,
On-the-contrary, if [the] my pains were without hope,

l'anima sul cimento vorrei portare almen.
[the]-(my)-soul to-the test I-would [carry] (put) at-least.
(at least I would put my soul to the test.)

Io son zitella ma sono scaltra,
I am (a) young-girl, but I-am [cunning] (shrewd),

e tanto scaltra che la so tutta.
and so cunning that [it] I-know all.
                    (that I know everything.)

Quando un amante con te favella,
When a lover with you speaks,

tu sei la cara, tu sei la bella.
you are the dear-one, you are the beautiful-one.

Se da te parte e va da un'altra,
If from you he-departs and goes to another,

la vaga è quella, tu sei le brutta!
the attractive-one is that-one; you are the ugly-one!

Ponchielli   AH! PESCATOR
                             (La Gioconda)

Ah! pescator, affonda l'esca, a te l'onda sia fedel;
Ah, fisherman, sink the-bait, to you the wave be faithful;
(Ah, fisherman, cast your bait, may the sea reward you;)

lieta sera e buona pesca ti
happy evening and good fishing to-you

promette il mare, il ciel.
promises the sea, the sky.
(are promised by the sea and the sky.)

Va, tranquilla cantilena, per l'azzurra immensità. Ah!
Go, quiet song, through the-blue immensity. Ah!

Una placida sirena nella rete cascherà.
A placid siren in-the net will-fall.

Spia coi fulminei tuoi sguardi accorti,
Watch with-[the] lightning your glances keen,
(Watch with your keen, lightning glances,)

e fra le tenebre conta i tuoi morti.
and in the darkness count [the] your dead.

Sì, da quest'isola deserta e bruna
Yes, from this-island, deserted and dark,

or deve sorgere la tua fortuna.
now must arise [the] your fortune.

Sta in guardia! e il rapido sospetto svia,
Be [in] (on) guard! And [the] quick suspicion divert,

e ridi, e vigila, e canta, e spia.
and laugh, and be-vigilant, and sing, and keep-watch.

E canta, e spia, ridi! canta!
And sing, and keep-watch, laugh! sing!

Ah, brilla Venere serena in un ciel di voluttà.
Ah, shines Venus serene in a heaven of delight.

Una fulgida sirena nella rete cascherà.
A dazzling siren in-the net will-fall.

                             329

Ponchielli   CIELO E MAR!
                                  (La Gioconda)

Cielo e mar! l'etereo velo
Sky and sea! The-ethereal veil

splende come un santo altar.
shines like a holy altar.

L'angiol mio verrà dal cielo?
[The]-angel my will-come from-the sky?
(Will my angel come from the sky?)

L'angiol mio verrà dal mare?
[The]-angel my will-come from-the sea?
(Will my angel come from the sea?)

Qui l'attendo ardente spira
Here her-I-await, ardently blows

oggi il vento dell' amor.
today the wind of-[the] love.

Ah, quell'uom che vi sospira
Ah, that-man that for-you sighs

vi conquide, o sogni d'or!
you conquers, O dreams of-gold!
(Conquers you,)

Per l'aura fonda
Through the-air deep
(Through the distant space)

non appar nè suol, nè monte
[not] appears neither soil, nor mountain;

l'orizzonte bacia l'onda,
the-horizon kisses the-wave,

l'onda bacia l'orizzonte!
the-wave kisses the-horizon!

Qui nell' ombra ov'io mi giacio
Here in-the shadow where-I myself lie

coll'anelito del cor,
with-the-panting of-the heart

vieni, o donna, vieni al bacio
come, O (my) lady, come to-the kiss

della vita e dell' amor.
of-[the] life and of-[the] love.

Ponchielli LA TURBINI E FARNETICHI
(La Gioconda)

Recit.:
Sì! morir ella de'!
Yes, die she must!

Sul nome mio scritta l'infamia impunemente avrà?
On-[the] name my written [the]-infamy unpunished will-have?
(Will infamy be written on my name with impunity?)

Chi un Badoer tradì non può sperar pietà!
She-who a Badoer betrayed not can hope-for pity!

Se ier non la ghermì
If yesterday not her caught
(If yesterday she was not caught)

nell'isola fatal questa mia man,
in-the-island fateful this my hand,
(On the fateful island by my hand,)

l'espiazion non fia tremenda meno!
the-expiation not will-be terrible less!
(the expiation will not be less terrible!)

Ieri un pugnal le avria squarciato il seno;
Yesterday a dagger to-her would-have rent the breast;
(Yesterday a dagger would have pierced her breast;)

oggi... un ferro non è... sarà un veleno!
today... a sword not it-is... it-will-be a poison!
(today, no dagger..a poison it shall be!)

Aria:
Là turbini e farnetichi la gaia baraonda,
There let-whirl and grow-delirious the merry confusion,

dell'agonia col gemito la festa si confonda,
of-[the] agony with-the moan the merry-making itself let-mix,
(let the moan of agony mingle with the merry-making,)

ombre di mia prosapia, non arrossite ancora!
shades of my lineage, (do) not blush yet!
                  (ancestors)

Tutto la morte vendica, anche il tradito onor!
All [the] death vindicates, even [the] betrayed honor!
(Death vindicates all, even honor betrayed!)

332

Colà farnetichi la gaia baraonda!
There let-grow-delirious the merry confusion!

Dell'agonia col gemito la festa si confonda,
Of-[the]-agony with-the moan the merry-making itself let-mix!
(Let the moan of agony mingle with the merry-making!)

là del patrizio veneto s'adempia
there of-the nobility Venetian let-one-fulfill
(there let the Venetian nobility enjoy)

al largo invito.
to-the broad invitation.
(my hospitality.)

Quivi il feral marito provveda al proprio onore!
Here the deadly husband let-provide to-the own honor!
(Here let the avenging husband satisfy his own honor!)

Fremete, oh danze, oh cantici!
Roar, O dances, O singing!
(On with the dancing and singing!)

E una infedel che muor!
It-is an unfaithful-one that dies!

Ponchielli   STELLA DEL MARINAR!
         (La Gioconda)

Recit.:
Ho il cuor gonfio di lagrime.
I-have the heart swollen with tears.
(My heart is filled with tears.)

Quel lume! Ah! una Madonna!
That light! Ah, a Madonna!

Aria:
Stella del marinar! Vergine Santa,
Star of-the mariner! Virgin holy,

tu mi difendi in quest'ora suprema;
[you] me defend in this-hour supreme;
(defend me in this last hour;)

tu vedi quanta passione e quanta fede
you see how-much passion and how-much faith

mi trasse a tale audacia estrema!
me moved to such boldness extreme!
(have moved me to such extreme boldness!)

Sotto il tuo velo che i prostrati ammanta
Under [the] your veil that the prostrate-ones cloaks
        (that cloaks the prostrate ones)

ricovera costei che prega e trema.
save her that prays and trembles.

Ah, scenda per questa fervida orazione
Ah, let-descend through this fervent prayer

sul capo mio, Madonna del perdona,
on-[the] head my, Madonna of-[the] pardon,

scenda sul capo mio una benedizion.
let-descend on-[the] head my a benediction.

Oh, Vergin, su me discenda la tua benedizione.
Oh, Virgin, on me let-descend [the] your benediction.

334

Ponchielli   SUICIDIO!
                             (La Gioconda)

Suicidio! In questi fieri momenti to sol mi resti,
Suicide! In these fierce moments you alone to-me remain,

e il cor mi tenti...
and the heart to-me you-tempt...
(and you tempt my heart...)

ultima voce del mio destino,
final voice of-[the] my destiny,

ultima croce del mio cammin.
final cross of-[the] my road.

E un dì leggiadre volavan l'ore,
And one day charming flew the-hours,
(The hours used to fly charmingly in the past;)

perdei la madre, perdei l'amore,
I-have-lost [the] (my) mother; I-have-lost [the]-(my)-love;

vinsi l'infausta gelosa febbre!
I-conquered the-unfortunate jealous fever!

Or piombo esausta fra le tenebre!
Now I-fall exhausted among the shadows!

Tocco alla meta...
I-touch to-the goal...
(I reach my goal...)

Domando al ciel di dormir queta dentro l'avel.
I-ask [to-the] heaven to sleep quietly within the-tomb.

335

Ponchielli   VOCE DI DONNA
                          (La Gioconda)

Voce di donna o d'angelo le mie catene ha sciolto;
Voice of woman or of-angel [the] my chains has loosened;
(The voice of a woman or an angel has loosened my chains;)

mi vietan le mie tenebre di quella santa il volto.
to-me forbid [the] my shadows of that blessed-one the face.
(My blindness prevents me from seeing the face of that blessed
    one.)

Pure da me non partasi, senza un pietoso don, no, no!
Yet from me not let-one-part, without a pious gift, no, no!

A te questo rosario, che le preghiere aduna,
To you this rosary, that the prayers brings-together,
                          (that brings prayers together.)

io te lo porgo, accettalo, ti porterà fortuna.
I to-you it offer, accept-it, to-you it-will-bring fortune.

Sulla tua testa vigili la mia benedizion.
On-[the] your head let-watch [the] my blessing.
(Let my blessing watch over your head.)

336

Puccini   CHE GELIDA MANINA
                                 (La Bohème)

Che gelida manina, se la lasci riscaldar.
What (a) frozen little-hand, itself it let warm.
                       (let me warm it.)

Cercar che giova? Al buio non si trova.
To-look what is-the-use? In-the dark not itself it-finds.
(What's the use of looking? We won't find it in the dark.)

Ma per fortuna è una notte di luna,
But through luck it-is a night of moon,
                       (it is a moonlit night)

e qui la luna l'abbiamo vicina.
and here the moon [it]-we-have near.
                       (is close.)

Aspetti signorina, le dirò con due parole
Wait, little-miss, to-you I-will-say with two words

chi son, e che faccio, come vivo. Vuole?
who I-am, and what I-do, how I-live. Do-you-wish?
                            (Do you want me to?)

Chi son? Sono un poeta. Che cosa faccio? Scrivo.
Who am-I? I-am a poet. What [thing] do-I-do? I-write.

E come vivo? Vivo. In povertà mia lieta
And how do-I-live? I-live. In poverty my happy
                       (In my happy poverty)

scialo da gran signore rime e inni d'amore.
I-squander like (a) great lord rhymes and hymns of-love.

Per sogni e per chimere e per castelli in aria,
For dreams and for fancies, and for castles in (the) air,

l'anima ho milionaria.
the-spirit I-have (of a) millionaire.

Talor dal mio forziere
Sometimes from-[the] my strongbox

ruban tutti i gioielli due ladri: gli occhi belli.
steal all the jewels two thieves: the eyes beautiful.
(two thieves--beautiful eyes--steal all the jewels.)

337

V'entrar con voi pur ora,
Here-they-entered with you just now,

ed i miei sogni usati e i bei sogni miei
and ⌊the⌋ my dreams customary, and ⌊the⌋ beautiful dreams my

tosto si dileguar!
suddenly [themselves] disappeared!

Ma il furto non m'accora poichè...
But the theft not me-grieves because...

poichè v'ha preso stanza la speranza.
because there-has taken residence [the] hope.
(because hope has taken their place.)

Or che mi conoscete parlate voi, deh! parlate.
Now that me you-know, speak [you], please speak.

Chi siete? Vi piaccia dir!
Who are-you? To-you let-it-please to-say!
            (Let it please you to say!)

Puccini   DONDE LIETA
                            (La Bohème)

Donde lieta uscî al tuo grido d'amore,
From-whence happy she-left at-[the] your call-of-love,

torna sola Mimi al solitario nido.
returns alone Mimi to-[the] (her) solitary nest.

Ritorna un'altra volta a intesser finti fior!
She-returns another time to weave artificial flowers!

Addio, senza rancor.   Ascolta, ascolta,
Goodbye, without bitterness.   Listen, listen,

le poche robe aduna che lasciai sparse.
the few things gather that I-left scattered.

Nel mio cassetto stan chiusi quel cerchietto d'or
In-[the] my drawer remain [shut] that little-ring of-gold

e il libro di preghiere.
and the book of prayers.
(and my prayer-book.)

Involgi tutto quanto in un grembiale
Wrap everything in an apron

e manderò il portiere.
and I-will-send the concierge.

Bada, sotto il guanciale c'è la cuffietta rosa.
Wait, under the pillow there-is the little-bonnet pink.

Se vuoi... se vuoi serbarla a ricordo d'amor...
If you-wish... if you-wish to-keep-it as (a) keepsake of-love...

Addio, senza rancor.
Goodbye, without bitterness.

Puccini   QUANDO ME'N VO
                           (La Bohème)

Quando me'n vo...
When [me-from-there] I-go...

Quando me'n vo soletta per la via
When [me-from-there] I-go alone through the street

la gente sosta e mira, e la belezza mia
the people stop and look, and [the] beauty my

tutta ricerca in me, ricerca in me da capo a piè...
all seek in me, seek in me from head to foot...
(they all look me over from head to foot...)

ed assaporo allor la bramosia sottil
and I-savor then the desire subtle

che da gl'occhi traspira
that from the-eyes comes-out

e dai palesi vezzi intender sa
and from-the evident charms to-appreciate knows-how
(and that knows how to appreciate)

alle occulte beltà.
[to]-the hidden beauties.

Così l'effluvio del desio tutta m'aggira,
Thus the-aura of-[the] yearning completely me-surrounds;

felice mi fa.
happy me it-makes.

E tu che sai, che memori e ti struggi,
And you that know, that remember and yourself destroy,

da me tanto rifuggi?
from me so-much do-you-run-away?
(why do you run away from me?)

So ben: le angoscie tue non le vuoi dir,
I-know well: the anguish[es] your not them you-wish to-say,
            (you do not wish to tell me of your suffering,)

340

non le vuoi dir, so ben,
not them you-wish to-say, I-know well,
(you don't want to tell me, I know very well,)

ma ti senti morir.
but yourself you-feel to-die.
(but you're dying from it.)

Puccini   SI, MI CHIAMANO MIMI
                                 (La Bohème)

Sì, mi chiamano Mimì, ma il mio nome è Lucia.
Yes, me they-call Mimi, but [the] my name is Lucia.

La storia mia è breve.
[The] story my is brief.

A tela o a seta ricamo in casa e fuori.
On linen or on silk I-embroider at home and outside.

Son tranquilla e lieta
I-am tranquil and happy

ed è mio svago far gigli e rose.
and it-is my recreation to-make lilies and roses.

Mi piaccion quelle cose che han si dolce malìa,
Me please those things that have such sweet enchantment,
(Those things that have such sweet enchantment please me,)

che parlano di sogni e di chimere,
that speak of dreams and of fancies,

quelle cose che han nome poesia. Lei m'intende?
those things that have name poetry. You me-understand?
(those things that are called poetry. Do you understand me?)

Mi chiamano Mimì, il perchè non so.
Me they-call Mimi, the reason not I-know.

Sola, mi fo il pranzo da me stessa.
Alone, [for-myself] I-make [the] dinner by [me] myself.

Non vado sempre a messa ma prego assai il Signor.
Not go-I always to mass but I-pray often (to) the Lord.

Vivo sola, soletta, là in una bianca cameretta,
I-live alone, all-alone; there in a white little-room,

guardo sui tetti e in cielo,
I-look-out on-the roofs and into (the) sky,

ma quando vien lo sgelo il primo sole è mio,
but when comes the thaw, the first sun is mine,

il primo bacio dell' aprile è mio.
the first kiss of-[the] April is mine.

Il primo sole è mio. Germoglia in un vaso una rosa...
The first sun is mine. (There) grows in a vase a rose...

Foglia a foglia la spio!
Leaf by leaf it I-observe!

Così gentil il profumo d'un fior!
How pleasing the perfume of-a flower!

Ma i fior ch'io faccio, ahimè, non hanno odore!
But the flowers that-I make, alas, (do) not have fragrance!

Altro di me non le saprei narrare;
Other of myself not to-you would-I-know to-tell;
(I wouldn't know what else to tell you about myself;)

sono la sua vicina
I-am [the] your neighbor

che la vien fuori d'ora a importunare.
who you comes outside of-hour to bother.
(who comes at the wrong hour to bother you.)

Puccini   VECCHIA ZIMARRA, SENTI
                           (La Bohème)

Vecchia zimarra, senti, io resto al pian,
Old coat, listen, I remain at-the level,
                (I remain here below,)

tu ascendere il sacro monte or devi.
you ascend the "sacred mountain" now must.
(you must go to the pawnshop.)

Le mie grazie ricevi.
[The] my thanks receive.

Mai non curvasti il logoro dorso
Never [not] you-bent [the] (your) worn-out back

ai ricchi ed ai potenti.
to-the rich and to-the mighty.

Passar nelle tue tasche come in antri tranquilli
Have-passed in-[the] your pockets, as in caves tranquil,

filosofi e poeti.
philosophers and poets.

Ora che i giorni lieti fuggir, ti dico addio,
Now that the days happy have-fled, to-you I-say goodbye,

fedele amico mio.   Addio, addio.
faithful friend my.   Goodbye, goodbye.

Puccini   FIRENZE E COME UN ALBERO FIORITO
                 (Gianni Schicchi)

Recit.:
Avete torto! E fine!...astuto...
You-have wrong! He's fine!...astute...
(You are wrong!)

Ogni malizia di leggi e codici
Every cunning-trick of law and legal-codes

conosce e sa.   Motteggiatore! Beffeggiatore!
he-comprehends and knows. Jester! Banterer!

C'è di fare una beffa nuova e rara?
There-is to make a jest new and rare?
(Is there a new and rare joke to be played?)

E Gianni Schicchi che la prepara!
It-is Gianni Schicchi that it prepares!
                          (that prepares it!)

Gli occhi furbi gli illuminan di riso
The eyes shrewd to-him light-up with laughter,
(His shrewd eyes light up with laughter,)

lo strano viso, ombreggiato da quel suo gran nasone
the strange face, shaded by [that] his great huge-nose

che pare un torracchione par cosî!
which looks-like a big-ugly-tower, as so!
                          (like this!)

Vien dal contado? Ebbene?
He-comes from-the country? Well?

E che vuol dire?
And what does-it-wish to-say?
(And what does that mean?)

Basta con queste ubbie grette e piccine!
Enough [with] (of) these superstitions stingy and small!

Aria:
Firenze è come un albero fiorito,
Florence is like a tree flowering,

345

che in piazza dei Signori ha tronco e fronde,
that in (the) square of-the Signori has trunk and branches,

ma le radici forze nuove apportano
but the roots strength new carry
(but the roots bring new strength)

dalle convalli limpide e feconde;
from-the valleys limpid and fruitful;

e firenze germoglia ed alle stelle
and Florence grows, and to-the stars

salgon palagi saldi e torri snelle!
ascend palaces staunch and towers slender!

L'Arno prima di correre alla foce
The-Arno, before running to-the river-mouth,

canta, baciando piazza Santa Croce
sings, kissing (the) square (of) Santa Croce,

e il suo canto è sì dolce e si sonoro
and [the] its song is so sweet and so sonorous

che a lui son scesi i ruscelletti in coro!
that to it are descended the little-brooks in chorus!

Così scendano i dotti in arti e scienze
Thus let-descend the learned-ones in (the) arts and sciences

a far più ricca e splendida Firenze!
to make more rich and splendid Florence!

E di Val d'Elsa giù dalle castella
And from Val d'Elsa down from-the castles

ben venga Arnolfo a far la torre bella!
welcome Arnolfo to make the tower beautiful!

E venga Giotto del Mugel selvoso
And comes Giotto from-the Mugel wooded
(And let Giotto come from the wooded Mugel)

e il Medici mercante coraggioso!
and the Medici merchant courageous!

Basta con gli odi gretti e coi ripicchi!
Enough [with] (of) the hatreds stingy and with-the retorts!
(Enough of snobbish remarks!)

Viva la gente nuova e Gianni Schicchi!
Long-live the people new and Gianni Schicchi!
                    ("new" people)

Puccini   O MIO BABBINO CARO
                           (Gianni Schicchi)

O mio babbino caro, mi piace, è bello, bello;
O my daddy dear, me he-pleases, he-is handsome, handsome;

vo' andare in Porta Rossa a comperar l'anello!
I-want to-go to Porta Rossa to buy the-ring!

Sì, sì, ci voglio andare!
Yes, yes, there I-wish to-go!

E se l'amassi indarno,
And if him-I-should-love in-vain,

andrei sul Ponte Vecchio
I-would-go on-the Ponte Vecchio

ma per buttarmi in Arno!
but [for] to-throw-myself into (the) Arno!

Mi struggo e mi tormento!
[Myself] I-pine-away and myself I-torment!

O Dio, vorrei morir!
O God, I-would-like to-die!

Babbo, pietà, pietà!
Daddy, (have) pity, pity!

Puccini ADDIO FIORITO ASIL
(Madama Butterfly)

Addio fiorito asil di letizia e d'amor.
Goodbye, flowered refuge of happiness and of-love.

Sempre il mite suo sembiante
Always [the] gentle her face
(Always her gentle face)

con strazio atroce vedrò...
with torment atrocious I-will-see...
(with terrible torment I will see before me.)

Addio fiorito asil...
Goodbye, flowered refuge...

Non reggo al tuo squallor, ah!
Not (can) I-bear [to-the] your [squalidness] (misery), ah!

Fuggo, son vil!
I-flee, I-am cowardly!

Addio, non reggo al tuo squallor,
Goodbye, not (can) I-bear [to-the] your [squalidness] (misery),

ah! son vil!
ah, I-am cowardly!

349

Puccini   AMORE O GRILLO
                          (Madama Butterfly)

Amore o grillo, dir non saprei.
Love or whim, to-say not I-would-know.
                    (I couldn't say.)

Certo costei m'ha coll' ingenue arti invescato.
Certainly she me-has with-the ingenuous arts snared.
(Certainly she has ensnared me with her ingenuous arts.)

Lieve qual tenue vetro soffiato,
Light as thin glass blown,

alla statura, al portamento
[to-the] (in) stature, [to-the] (in) manner

sembra figura da paravento.
she-seems (a) figure from (a) screen.

Ma dal suo lucido fondo di lacca
But from its bright depth of lacquer,

come con subito moto si stacca,
how, with (a) sudden movement herself she-detaches,

qual farfalletta svolazza e posa
like (a) butterfly she-flutters and rests

con tal grazietta silenzïosa
with such gracefulness silent

che di rincorrerla furor m'assale
that [of] to-pursue-her fury me-assails
(that a fury to pursue her assails me)

se pure infrangerne dovessi l'ale.
if even to-break-of-her I-should the-wing(s).
(even if I should break her wings.)

350

Puccini

UN BEL DI
(Madama Butterfly)

Un bel dì,
One beautiful day,

Vedremo levarsi un fil di fumo
we-shall-see [raise-itself] a thread of smoke (rising)

sull'estremo confin del mare.
on-the-farthest edge of-the ocean.

E poi la nave appare.
And then the ship appears.

Poi la nave bianca entra nel porto,
Then the ship white enters in-the port,

romba il suo saluto. Vedi? E venuto!
thunders [the] its salute. You-see? He's come!

Io non gli scendo incontro. Io no.
I not to-him go-down towards, I not.
(I do not go down to meet him, not I.)

Mi metto là sul ciglio del colle e aspetto,
Myself I-place there on-the brow of-the hill and I-wait,

e aspetto gran tempo e non mi pesa,
and I-wait (a) long time and not (on) me (it) weighs,

la lunga attesa. E... uscito dalla folla cittadina
the long waiting. And... gone-out from-the crowd city,
                        (leaving the crowd of the city,)

un uomo, un picciol punto s'avvia per la collina.
a man, a tiny speck [himself]-starts up the hill.

Chi sarà? E come sarà giunto che dirà?
Who will-it-be? And when he-will-be arrived, what will-he-say?
                        (And when he has arrived,)

Chiamerà Butterfly dalla lontana.
He-will-call, "Butterfly," from-the distance.

Io senza dar risposta me ne starò nascosta
I without giving answer [myself] from-him will-stay hidden,

351

un po' per celia e un po' per non morir
a little for (a) joke and a little in-order not to-die

al primo incontro, ed egli alquanto in pena
at-the first meeting, and he, somewhat [in pain] (worried),

chiamerà, chiamerà: Piccina mogliettina, olezzo di verbena,
will-call, will-call: "Tiny little-wife, perfume of verbena,"

i nomi che mi dava al suo venire.
the names that to-me he-gave at-[the] his coming.

Tutto questo avverrà, te lo prometto.
All this will-happen, to-you it I-promise.

Tienti la tua paura, io con sicura fede l'aspetto.
Keep [you the] your fear, I with firm faith him-await.

Puccini   DONNA NON VIDI MAI
                           (Manon Lescaut)

Donna non vidi mai simile a questa!
Woman not I-saw never like to this-one!
(Never have I seen a woman like this!)

A dirle: io t'amo,
To tell-her: you I-love,

a nuova vita l'alma mia si desta.
to new life [the]-soul my itself awakens.
(my soul is awakened to new life.)

"Manon Lescaut mi chiamo."
"Manon Lescaut myself I-call."
("My name is Manon Lescaut.")

Come queste parole profumate mi vagan nello spirto
How these words fragrant to-me wander in-the spirit
(How these fragrant words wander in my spirit)

e ascose fibre vanno a carezzare.
and hidden fibers they-go to caress.
(and caress my quivering heart.)

O sussurro gentil, deh! non cessare!
O murmur gentle, ah, (do) not cease!

"Manon Lescaut mi chiamo."
"Manon Lescaut myself I-call."
("My name is Manon Lescaut.")

Susurro gentil, deh! non cessar!
Murmur gentle, ah, (do) not cease!

                            353

Puccini   IN QUELLE TRINE MORBIDE
                           (Manon Lescaut)

In quelle trine morbide, nell'alcova dorata,
In those laces soft, in-the-alcove gilded,

v'è un silenzio, un gelido mortal..
there-is a silence, a chill mortal...

un freddo che m'agghiaccia!
a coldness that me-freezes!

Ed io che m'ero avvezza a una carezza voluttuosa
And I, who [myself]-was accustomed to a caress voluptuous

di labbra ardenti e d'infuocate braccia
of lips ardent and of-fiery embrace,

or ho tutt'altra cosa!
now have (an) entirely-different thing!

O mia dimora umile, tu mi ritorni innanzi...
O my abode humble, you to-me return before...
                        (you return before my eyes...)

gaia, isolata, bianca,
gay, isolated, white,

come un sogno gentile e di pace e d'amor!
like a dream gentle both of peace and of-love!
                        (of both peace and love!)

Puccini   SENZA MAMMA, BIMBO, TU SEI MORTO!
               (Suor Angelica)

Senza mamma, bimbo, tu sei morto!
Without (your) mother, baby, you are dead!
                        (you died!)

Le tue labbra senza i baci miei,
[The] your lips without [the] kisses my,

scoloriron fredde, fredde!
grew-pale, cold, cold!

E chiudesti, bimbo, gli occhi belli!
And you-closed, baby, [the] (your) eyes beautiful!

Non potendo carezzarmi,
Not being-able to-caress-me,

le manine componesti in croce!
the little-hands you-arranged in (a) cross!
(you crossed your little hands on your breast!)

E tu sei morto senza sapere
And you are dead without knowing

quanto t'amava questa tua mamma!
how-much you-loved this your mother!
(how much your mother loved you!)

Ora che tutto sai, angelo bello, dimmi
Now that everything you-know, angel beautiful, tell-me

quando potrò volar con te nel cielo?
when I-will-be-able to-fly with you into-[the] heaven?

Quando potrò vederti? Dimmi! Dimmi!
When will-I-be-able to-see-you? Tell-me! Tell-me!

Quando potrò baciarti?
When will-I-be-able to-kiss-you?

Baciarti! Amor mio santo!
To-kiss-you! Love my sacred!
                (My sacred love!)

Puccini   E LUCEVAN LE STELLE
                              (Tosca)

E lucevan le stelle e olezzava la terra,
And were-shining the stars and gave-forth-perfume the earth,

stridea l'uscio dell'orto e un passo sfiorava la rena.
creaked the-gate of-the-garden, and a step grazed the sand.

Entrava ella, fragrante, mi cadea fra le braccia...
Entered she, fragrant, to-me she-fell into the arms...
                          (she fell into my arms...)

O dolci baci, o languide carezze, mentr'io fremente
O sweet kisses, O languid caresses, while-I, trembling,

le belle forme disciogliea dai veli!
the beautiful forms loosened from-the veils!
(undid the garments of the beautiful one!)

Svanì per sempre il sogno mio d'amore...
Vanished forever [the] dream my of-love...

L'ora è fuggita...e muoio disperato..
The-hour is fled... and I-die desperate...

E non ho amato mai tanto la vita, tanto la vita.
And [not] have-I loved never so-much [the] life, so-much
    [the] life.
(And never have I loved life so much!)

                           356

Puccini   RECONDITA ARMONIA
                                 (Tosca)

Recondita armonia di bellezze diverse!
Hidden harmony of beauties diverse!

E bruna Floria, l'ardente amante mia,
Is dark Floria, [the]-ardent love my,
(Floria, my ardent love, is dark,)

e te, beltade ignota... cinta di chiome bionde!
and you, beauty unknown... girded with hair blonde!

Tu azzurro hai l'occhio... Tosca ha l'occhio nero!
You blue have [the]-eye(s)... Tosca has [the]-eye(s) dark!
(You have blue eyes, Tosca's are dark!)

L'arte nel suo mistero
[The] art in-[the] its mystery

le diverse bellezze insiem confonde.
the diverse beauties together confuses.

Ma nel ritrar costei il mio solo pensiero,
But in-the portraying (of) this-one [the] my only thought,

ah, il mio sol pensier sei tu! Tosca sei tu!
ah, [the] my only thought is you, Tosca, is you!

Puccini   VISSI D'ARTE, VISSI D'AMORE
                           (Tosca)

Vissi d'arte, vissi d'amore,
I-lived for art, I-lived for-love,

non feci mai male ad anima viva!
not did-I never evil to soul living!
(never did I harm a living soul!)

Con man furtiva quante miserie conobbi, aiutai...
With hand secret how-many miseries I-knew, I-relieved...
(Secretly I relieved many miseries,)

Sempre con fè sincera,
Always with faith sincere,

la mia preghiera ai santi tabernacoli salì.
[the] my prayers in-[the holy tabernacles] (church) arose.

Sempre con fè sincera, diedi fiori agli altar.
Always with faith sincere, I-gave flowers for-the altars.

Nell'ora del dolore perchè, perchè, Signore,
In-the-hour of-[the] sorrow, why, why, Lord,

perchè me ne rimuneri così?
why me for-it do-you-reward thus?

Diedi gioielli della Madonna al manto,
I-gave jewels of-the Madonna to-the mantle,
(I gave jewels for the mantle of the Madonna,)

e diedi il canto agli astri, al ciel,
and I-gave [the] (my) singing to-the stars, to-the heavens,

che ne ridean più belli...
which because-of-it smiled more beautifully...

Nell'ora del dolor perchè, perchè, Signor, ah...
In-the-hour of-[the] suffering, why, why, Lord, ah...

perchè me ne rimuneri così?
why me for-it do-you-reward thus?

Puccini   IN QUESTA REGGIA
             (Turandot)

In questa reggia, or son mill'anni e mille,
In this palace, now are thousand years and thousand,
            (a thousand and a thousand years ago,)

un grido disperato risonò.
a cry desperate sounded.

E quel grido, traverso stirpe e stirpe,
And that cry, crossing offspring and offspring,
            (through descendant after descendant,)

qui nell'anima mia si rifugiò!
here in-[the]-soul my [itself] took-refuge!

Principessa Lo-u-Ling, ava dolce e serena,
Princess Lo-u-Ling, grandmother sweet and serene,

che regnavi nel tuo cupo silenzio, in gioia pura,
who ruled in-[the] your dark silence, in joy pure,

e sfidasti inflessibile e sicura, l'aspro dominio,
and defied, inflexible and sure, the-harsh domination,

oggi revivi in me!
today you-live-again in me!

Pure, nel tempo che ciascun ricorda,
Still, in-the time that everyone remembers,

fu sgomento e terrore e rombo d'armi!
there-was alarm and terror and rumble of-arms!

Il regno vinto! E Lo-u-Ling, la mia ava,
The kingdom defeated! And Lo-u-Ling, [the] my grandmother,

trascinata da un uomo come te, come te, straniero,
dragged by a man like you, like you, foreigner,

là nella notte atroce,
there in-the night atrocious,

dove si spense la sua fresca voce!
where [itself] was-extinguished [the] her fresh voice!

359

O Principi che a lunghe carovane
O Princes, who [to] (in) long caravans

d'ogni parte del mondo
from-every part of-the world

qui venite a gettar la vostra sorte,
here come to try [the] your fate,

io vendico su voi, su voi quella purezza,
I avenge on you, on you that purity,

quel grido e quella morte!
that cry and that death!

Mai nessun m'avrà! Mai nessun, nessun m'avrà!
Never no-one me-will-have! Never no-one, no-one me-will-
    have!
(No one will ever possess me, never, no one!)

L'orror di chi l'uccise vivo nel cor mi sta!
The-horror of him-who her-killed alive in-the heart to-me is!
(The horror of him who killed her lives in my heart!)

No, no! Mai nessun m'avrà!
No, no! Never no-one me-will-have!
        (No one will ever possess me!)

Ah, rinasce in me l'orgoglio di tanta purità!
Ah, is-reborn in me the-pride of such purity!

Straniero! Non tentar la fortuna!
Foreigner! (Do) not tempt [the] fate!

"Gli enigmi sono tre, la morte è una!" No, no!
"The enigmas are three, [the] death is one!" No, no!

Puccini   NESSUN DORMA
                           (Turandot)

Nessun dorma! Tu pure, O Principessa,
(Let) no-one sleep! You, likewise, O Princess,

nella tua fredda stanza guardi le stelle
in-[the] your cold room are-looking-at the stars

che tremano d'amore e di speranza!
that tremble with-love and with hope!

Ma il mio mistero è chiuso in me,
But [the] my mystery is shut-up within me,

il nome mio nessun saprà!
[the] name my no-one will-know!

No, no, sulla tua bocca lo dirò
No, no, on-[the] your mouth it I-will-say

quando la luce splenderà!
when the light will-shine!

Ed il mio bacio scioglierà il silenzio
And [the] my kiss will-undo the silence

che ti fa mia!
that you makes mine!
(that makes you mine!)

Dilegua, o notte...! Tramontate, stelle!
Disappear, O night...! Set, stars!

All'alba vincerò!
At-[the]-dawn I-will-win!

Puccini NON PIANGERE, LIU
(Turandot)

Non piangere, Liù! Se in un lontano giorno
(Do) not cry, Liù! If [in] (on) one far-off day

io t'ho sorriso, per quel sorriso, dolce mia fanciulla,
I at-you-have smiled, for that smile, sweet my child,

m'asolta: Il tuo Signore sarà domani
to-me-listen: [The] your master will-be, tomorrow,

forse solo al mondo...
perhaps alone in-the world...

Non lo lasciare, portalo via con te!
(Do) not him leave, take-him away with you!

Dell'esilio addolcisci a lui le strade!
Of-the-exile alleviate to him the roads!
(Make the roads of exile easy for him!)

Questo...o mia povera Liù,
This... O my poor Liù,

al tuo piccolo cuore che non cade
to-(of)-[the] your little heart that not falls
(of your little heart that does not fail)

chiede colui che non sorride più..!
asks that-one who (does) not smile (any) longer..!

362

Puccini   SIGNORE, ASCOLTA
                           (Turandot)

Signore, ascolta! Ah, Signore, ascolta!
My-lord, listen! Ah, my-lord, listen!

Liù non regge più!
Liù (can) not bear more!

Si spezza il cuor! Ahimè, quanto cammino
Itself breaks the heart! Alas, how-long (a) journey
(Her heart is breaking!)

col tuo nome nell'anima
with-[the] your name in-[the]-(my)-soul,

col nome tuo sulle labbra!
with-[the] name your on-[the] (my) lips!

Ma se il tuo destino doman sarà deciso,
But if [the] your destiny tomorrow will-be decided,

noi morrem sulla strada dell'esilio!
we will-die on-the road of-[the]-exile!

Ei perderà suo figlio...Io l'ombra d'un sorriso!
He will-lose his son... I the-shadow of-a smile!

Liù non regge più! Ah, pietà!
Liù (can) not bear more! Ah, (have) pity!

Italian text copyright © 1926, 1929 by G. Ricordi & Co., Milan.
English text copyright © 1972 by G. Ricordi & Co., Milan.

363

Puccini   TU CHE DI GEL SEI CINTA
                           (Turandot)

Tu che di gel sei cinta, da tanta fiamma vinta,
You that with frost are girded, by such flame overcome,

l'amerai anche tu!
him-you-will-love also [you]!

Prima di questa aurora io chiudo stanca gli occhi,
Before [of] this dawn I close weari(ly) [the] (my) eyes,

perchè egli vinca ancora...
so-that he may-win again...

per non...per non vederlo più!
to not...to not see-him (any) more!

Prima di questa aurora, di questa aurora
Before [of] this dawn, [of] this dawn

io chiudo stanca gli occhi per non vederlo più!
I close weari(ly) [the] (my) eyes to not see-him (any) more!

Apra il suo verde seno
Let-open [the] its verdant bosom

ogni bel prato ameno!
every beautiful meadow [pleasing]!

Lieta e vezzosa esca la rosa,
Happy and charming let-blossom the rose,

spiri ogni fiore aure d'amore,
let-breathe-out every flower breezes of-love,
(let every flower give off fragrance of love,)

a salutar accinto
to greet [prepared] (appropriately)

nova ninfa d'Amor, nova Giacinto!
(a) new nymph of-love, (a) new Hyacinth!

Corran dagli alti monti chiari cristalli e fonti!
Let-run from-the high mountains clear crystals and
    fountains!

Aure odorate, or v'accordate
Breezes fragrant, now yourselves-harmonize

col mormorare dell'aque chiare,
with-the murmuring of-the-waters clear,

or che tra fiori e fronde
now that among flowers and branches

nova Ninfa d'Amor esce dall'onde!
(a) new nymph of-love comes-forth from-the-waves!

Voi vaghi e pinti augelli,
You lovely and [painted] (colored) birds,

amorosetti e snelli,
charming and swift,

nel verde prato col canto amato
in-the green meadow with-the song beloved,

destate il giorno vago ed adorno,
awaken the day lovely and radiant,

or che già spunta fuora
now that already blossoms forth

nova Ninfa d'Amor, novella Aurora!
(a) new nymph of-love, (a) new Dawn!

Caldi sospiri, che uscite dal core,
Hot sighs that come from-[the] (my) heart,

gite volando nel seno al mio amore;
go flying into-the bosom [to-the] (of) my love;

dite alla crude ch'io l'amo e l'adoro,
say to-the cruel-one that-I her-love and her-adore,

che miri ch'io moro fra tanti martiri,
that she-should-see that-I die among so-many tortures,

o caldi sospiri.
O hot sighs.

Caldi sospiri, correte da Clori,
Hot sighs, run to Cloris,

pungete il bel petto, temprate i miei ardori
sting the beautiful bosom, temper [the] my ardors

e poi felici cangiatemi incanto.
and then [happy] (happily) change-for-me (the) spell.

E gioia il mio pianto se cangia desiri,
Is joy [the] my weeping if she-changes desires,
(My weeping is turned to joy if she changes desires,)

o caldi sospiri
O hot sighs.

Or ch'io non seguo più il dispietato Amor
Now that-I (do) not follow (any) more [the] pitiless Love,

non sento più dolor.
not do-I-feel [more] (any longer) pain.

E il cor, che in doglia fu,
And the heart, which in grief was,

allegro sta, che vive in libertà.
happy remains, since it-lives in liberty.

Or ch'io non amo piu colei, che mi ferî,
Now that-I (do) not love (any) more her, who me wounded,

felice passo i dî.
happy I-pass the days.

Or ch'io non veggio più quel viso lusinghier
Now that-I (do) not see (any) more that face alluring,

non vivo prigionier.
not do-I-live (as a) prisoner.

Or ch'io non sento più i finti suoi sospir
Now that-I (do) not hear (any) more [the] false her sighs,

non posso più morir.
not can-I (any) more die.

Se bel rio, se bell'auretta
If (a) beautiful brooklet, if (a) lovely-breeze

tra l'erbetta sul mattin mormorando erra,
amid the-grass in-the morning murmuring wanders,

se di fiori un praticello si fa bello,
if with flowers a meadow itself makes beautiful,

noi diciam, ride la terra.
we say, laughs the earth.

Quando avvien che un zeffiretto per diletto
When it-happens that a little-breeze for pleasure

bagni il pie nell'onde chiare
bathes the foot in-the-waves clear

sì che l'acqua su l'arena scherzi a pena
so that the-water on the-sand plays scarcely

noi diciam che ride il mare.
we say that laughs the sea.

Se già mai tra fior vermigli
If [now] ever among flowers vermilion

se tra gigli veste l'alba un aureo velo
if among lilies dresses the-dawn a golden veil

e su rote di zaffiro move in giro,
and upon circles of sapphire moves in turn,

noi diciamo che ride il cielo.
we say that laughs the sky.

Ben è ver; quando è giocondo ride il mondo;
Indeed it-is true; when it-is happy laughs the world;

ride il ciel quando è gioioso;
laughs the sky when it-is joyful;

ben è ver, ma non san poi come voi
indeed it-is true, but not do-they-know-how then like you

fare un riso grazioso.
to-make a smile lovely.

(When a brooklet murmurs in the morning
    we say the earth laughs,
When a breeze blows along the shores
    we say that the sea laughs,
If the flowers are beautiful beneath the radiant sky
    we say that the sky laughs,
But they cannot — like you —
    make a lovely smile.)

Selve, voi che le speranze
Woods, you that [the] (my) hopes

al gioir liete serbate,
[to-the] (for) joy happy preserve,

del piacer siete le stanze
of-[the] pleasure you-are the rooms
(you are the rooms of pleasure)

ove passar degg'io l'ore beate!
where pass must-I the-hours blessed!
(where I must pass the blessed hours!)

Rosa   STAR VICINO

Star vicino al bell'idol che s'ama
To-be near to-the beautiful-idol that one-loves

è il più vago diletto d'amor!
is the most attractive joy of-love!

Star lontan da colei che si brama
To-be far from her whom one desires

è d'amor il più mesto dolor!
is of-love the most sad sorrow!

Vado ben spesso cangiando loco;
I-go very often changing place;
                    (from place to place;)

ma non so mai cangiar desio.
but not I-know-how ever to-change desire.
(I don't know how to change my longing.)

Sempre l'istesso sarà il mio foco
Always the-same will-be ⌊the⌋ my fire,

e sarò sempre l'istesso anch'io.
and I-shall-be always the-same [also-I].
(and I, too, shall always be the same.)

Non la volete intendere,
Not it do-you-wish to-understand,

ostinati pensieri,
obstinate thoughts,

a due begli occhi neri
(that) to two beautiful eyes [black] (dark)

sî che mi voglio rendere.
indeed [that] myself I-want to-surrender.

Ho combattuto assai: io non ne posso più.
I-have fought enough: I not of-it can more.

Amore, tu m'avrai, qualora che vuoi tu!
Love, you me-will-have, whenever [that] wish you!
(You will have me whenever you wish!)

O cara servitù! O catena gradita!
O dear slavery! O chain welcome!

Chi mi sostiene in vita mi premia con l'offendere.
She-who me sustains in life me rewards with [the] offending.

Quegli, che al mondo tutto l'arti tutte insegnò,
That-one, who to-the world entire the-arts all taught,

con ciglio non asciutto la piaghe sue mirò,
with eye-lash not dry [the] wounds his admired.
(with tears admired his wounds)

Beltà, quanto mai può,
Beauty, how-much ever can-it-do,
(How powerful she is,)

quanto è dolce tiranna!
how-much she-is (a) sweet tyrant!
(what a sweet tyrant she is!)

I più sagaci inganna
The most wise she-deceives,

quand'altri sa riprendere.
while-others she-knows-how to-rebuke.

Se mi toglie ria sventura,
If from-me takes bad misfortune,
(If misfortune takes from me,)

chi le faci al cor mi desta
the-one-who the torches to-the heart me awakens
(the one who awakens my heart)

l'alte mura cangerò
the-high walls I-will-change
(I will leave town)

con la foresta. (Eco) Resta!
with the forest.   (Echo) Remain!
(and take refuge in the forest!)

Or ch'io prendo altro sentiero,
Now that-I take (an)other path,

udir parmi il suono istesso
to-hear it-seems-to-me the sound same
(I seem to hear the voice)

del guerriero, che nel seno
of-the warrior, which in-the bosom

io porto impresso. (eco) Esso!
I carry imprinted. (Echo) He!

L'aspre pene ormai consolo
The-bitter pains now I-console,

attendendo i dì sereni,
awaiting the days serene,

se nel duolo, fido amante,
if in-[the] (my) sorrow, faithful lover,

a me sovvieni. (Eco) Vieni!
to me you-remember. (Echo) Come!
(you remember me.)

Rossini   A UN DOTTOR DELLA MIA SORTE
                         (Il barbiere di Siviglia)

A un dottor della mia sorte queste scuse, signorina!
To a doctor of-[the] my class these excuses, young-lady!

Vi consiglio, mia carina,
You I-advise, my little-dear-(one),

un po' meglio a imposturar,
a bit better to deceive,
(you'll have to do better if you're going to deceive me,)

meglio, sì!
better, yes!

I confetti alla ragazza!
The candies to-the little-girl!

Il ricamo sul tamburo!
The embroidery on-the drum!
(The embroidery on its frame!)

Vi scottaste: eh via!
You burned-yourself: come now!

Ci vuol altro, figlia mia,
Here it-needs something-else, daughter my

per potermi corbellar, altro.
to be-able-me to-make-fun-of, something else.

Perchè manca là quel foglio?
Why is-missing there that sheet-of-paper?

Sono inutili le smorfie;
Are useless the wry-faces;

ferma là, non mi toccate! No!
stay there, (do) not me touch! No!

Figlia mia, non sperate
Daughter my, (do) not hope

ch'io mi lasci infinocchiar. No, no!
that-I myself let to-be-circumvented. No, no!

Via carina, confessate;
Come-now, dear-little-one, confess;

son disposto a perdonar.
I-am disposed to pardon (you).

Non parlate? Vi ostinate?
Not you-speak? You are-obstinate?

So ben io quel che ho da far.
Know well I that which I-have to do.

Signorina, un'altra volta quando Bartolo andrà fuori
Young-lady, another time when Bartolo will-go outside,

la consegna ai servitori,
her he-consigns to-the servants,
(he'll leave you in the hands of the servants,)

a suo modo far saprà.
to his way to-do he-will-know.
(he will know how to do things his way.)

Faccia pur la gatta morta, faccia pure,
Make then (like) the cat dead, make then,

faccia pur la gatta morta. Cospetton!
make then (like) the cat dead. Plague-on-it!
(making like a dead cat won't do you any good.)

Per quella porta nemmen l'aria entrar potrà,
Through that door not-even the-air to-enter will-be-able,

e Rosina innocentina, sconsolata, disperata...
and Rosina, little-innocent-one, disconsolate, desperate...

in sua camera serrata,
in her room shut,

fin ch'io voglio star dovrà,
until [that]-I wish to-remain she-will-have-to,
(as long as I want her to remain there,)

sì, sì, sì, sì.
yes, yes, yes, yes.

377

Rossini   LA CALUNNIA
                            (Il barbiere di Siviglia)

La calunnia è un venticello, un'auretta assai gentile,
[The] slander is a little-breeze, a-little-zephyr so gentle,

che insensibile, sottile, leggermente, dolcemente,
that gradually, subtly, lightly, sweetly,

incomincia a sussurrar; piano, piano, terra terra,
begins to murmur; softly, softly, ground ground
                                (along the ground,)

sotto voce sibilando, e va scorrendo, e va ronzando,
under voice, hissing, and goes rolling, and goes buzzing,
(in a low voice)

nell' orecchie della gente,
in-the ears of-the people;

s'introduce destramente,
itself-(it)-introduces dexterously,

e le teste ed i cervelli
and the heads and the brains

fa stordire e fa gonfiar.
it-makes to-stun and makes to-swell-up.

Dalla bocca fuori uscendo
From-the mouth out going,

lo schiamazzo va crescendo,
the noise goes increasing,

prende forza a poco a poco,
takes force little by little,

vola già di loco in loco;
flies now from place to place;

sembra il tuono, la tempesta,
it-resembles the thunder, the tempest,

che nel sen della foresta
that in-the depth of-the forest

378

va fischiando, brontolando e ti fa d'orror gelar.
goes whistling, rumbling and you makes of-horror freeze.
                              (and makes you freeze with horror.)

Alla fin trabocca e scoppia,
At-[the] last it-boils-over and explodes,

si propaga, si raddoppia
[itself] breeds, [itself] redoubles,

e produce un'esplosione come un colpo di cannone,
and produces an explosion like a shot from (a) cannon,

un tremuoto, un temporale che fa l'aria rimbombar.
an earthquake, a storm that makes the-air reverberate.

E il meschino calunniato, avvilito, calpestato,
And the wretched slandered-one, degraded, trampled-on

sotto il pubblico flagello per gran sorte va a crepar.
under the public scourge by great chance goes to die.
(under public scrutiny more often than not gives up the
    ghost.)

Sì, va a crepar.
Yes, he-goes to die.

Rossini   ECCO RIDENTE IN CIELO
                          (Il barbiere di Siviglia)

Ecco ridente in cielo spunta la bella aurora,
Lo, smiling in (the) sky, breaks-forth the beautiful dawn,

e tu non sorgi ancora? E puoi dormir cosî? Ah!
and you (do) not rise yet? And can-you sleep thus? Ah!

Sorgi, mia dolce speme, vieni, bell' idol mio;
Rise, my sweet hope; come, beautiful idol mine;

rendi men crudo, oh Dio, lo stral che mi ferî.
render less cruel, O God, the arrow that me wounded.
                                    (that wounded me.)

Oh sorte! già veggo quel caro sembiante:
O fortune, already I-see that dear countenance:

quest'anima amante ottenne pietà!
this-soul loving obtained pity!

Oh istante d'amore! Felice momento!
Oh, moment of-love! Happy moment!

Oh dolce contento che egual, no, non ha!
Oh, sweet contentment that equal, no, not has!
                                    (that has no equal!)

                              380

Rossini   LARGO AL FACTOTUM
                          (Il barbiere di Siviglia)

La la la le ra, la la le ra, la ran la le ra, la ran la la.
(Nonsense syllables, as "la, la, la" in English)

Largo al factotum della città,
Make-room [to]-(for)-the factotum of-the city,

largo! La ran la, etc.
make-room! la la la, etc.

Presto a bottega,
Quickly to-the shop,

che l'alba è già, presto! la la ran, etc.
because [the]-dawn is already (here), quickly! la la la, etc.

Ah, che bel vivere,
Ah, what (a) beautiful life,

che bel piacere per un barbiere di qualità!
what beautiful pleasure for a barber of quality!

Ah bravo Figaro, bravo bravissimo, bravo! la ran la, etc.
Ah, bravo, Figaro, bravo, bravissimo, bravo! la la la, etc.

Fortunatissimo per verità, bravo, la ra la, etc.
Luckiest (one) indeed, bravo, la la la, etc.

Pronto a far tutto, la notte il giorno,
Ready to do everything, [the] night (and) [the] day,

sempre d'intorno in giro sta.
always around in motion he-is.
(everywhere, he's on the go.)

Miglior cuccagna per un barbiere,
Better abundance for a barber,
(A better livelihood,)

vita più nobile, no, non si dà. La le ran la.
(a) life more noble, no, not itself gives. La la la la.
(a nobler life, is not to be had.)

Rasori e pettini, lancette e forbici,
Razors and combs, lancets and scissors,

                          381

al mio comando tutto qui sta.
at-[the] my command everything here is.

V'è la risorsa poi del mestiere
There-is the resource then of-[the] business
(There are matters of discretion)

colla donnetta, col cavaliere,
with-the young-lady, with-the gentleman,
(with young ladies and gentlemen)

tutti mi chiedono, tutti mi vogliono,
they-all me ask-for, they-all me want,

donne, ragazzi, vecchi, fanciulle.
ladies, boys, old-men, young-girls.

Qua la parrucca...presto la barba...
Here the wig... quickly the beard...

qua la sanguigna, presto il biglietto...
here the blood-letting, quickly the note...

Figaro! Ahimè! che furia! Ahimè! che folla!
Figaro! Alas! What (a) frenzy! Alas! What (a) crowd!

Uno alla volta, per carità!
One at-[the]-(a) time, for heaven's-sake!

Figaro...son quà.   Ehi, Figaro...son quà.
Figaro...I'm here. Hey, Figaro...I'm here.

Figaro quà, Figaro là, Figaro su, Figaro giù.
Figaro here, Figaro there, Figaro up, Figaro down.

Pronto prontissimo son come il fulmine:
Ready, ready-as-can-be, I-am like the lightning:

sono il factotum della città.
I-am the factotum of-the city.

Ah bravo Figaro! Bravo, bravissimo!
Ah, bravo, Figaro! Bravo, bravissimo!

A te fortuna non mancherà.
[To] (for) you fortune not will-be-lacking.

Rossini IL VECCHIOTTO CERCA MOGLIE
(Il barbiere di Siviglia)

Il vecchiotto cerca moglie,
The old-man seeks (a) wife,

vuol marito la ragazza;
wishes (a) husband the young-girl;
(the young girl wants a husband;)

Quello freme questa è pazza.
That-one trembles (with passion), this-one is crazy.

Tutti e due son da legar.
All and two are to tie.
(Both are fit to be tied.)

Sì, sì, tutti e due son da legar.
Yes, yes, all and two are to tie.
          (both are fit to be tied.)

Ma che cosa è questo amore che fa tutti delirar?
But what [thing] is this love that makes everyone rave?

Egli è un male universale, una smania,
It is an ill universal, a frenzy,

un pizzicore, un solletico, un tormento...
an itch, a tickling, a torment...

Poverina, anch'io lo sento, nè so come finirà.
Poor-little-one, even-I it feel, nor know-I how it-will-end.

Oh, vecchiaia maledetta! Son da tutti disprezzata
Oh, old-age accursed! I-am by everyone despised,

e vecchietta disperata
and (an) old-woman desperate

mi convien così morir,
for-me it-is-necessary thus to-die;

sì, sì, mi convien così morir.
yes, yes, for-me it-is-necessary thus-to-die.

383

Rossini UNA VOCE POCO FA
(Il barbiere di Siviglia)

Una voce poco fa qui nel cor mi risuonò.
A voice (a) while ago here in-the heart to-me resounded.
(resounded here in my heart.)

Il mio cor ferito è già,
[The] my heart wounded is already,

e Lindoro fu che il piagò.
and Lindoro it-was who it wounded.
(and it was Lindoro who wounded it.)

Si, Lindoro mio sarà, lo giurai, la vincerò.
Yes, Lindoro mine shall-be, it I-swore, [it] I-shall-win.

Il tutor ricuserà, io l'ingegno aguzzerò,
[The] (my) guardian will-refuse, I the-cunning will-sharpen,
(I will sharpen my wits,)

alla fin s'accheterà
at-the end [himself]-he will-quiet-down,

e contenta io resterò.
and happy I shall-be.

Io sono docile, son rispettosa,
I am docile, I-am respectful,

sono obbediente, dolce, amorosa,
I-am obedient, sweet, loving.

Mi lascio reggere, mi fo guidar.
Myself I-allow to-be-ruled, myself I-make to-be-led.
(I can be led.)

Ma se mi toccano dov'è il mio debole,
But if me they-touch where-is [the] my weakness,

sarò una vipera, sarò.
I-will-be a viper, I-will-be.

E cento trappole prima di cedere farò giocar!
And hundred traps before to give-in I-shall-make to-play!
(And I shall spring a hundred traps before I give in!)

384

Rossini   NON PIU MESTA
                           (La Cenerentola)

Recit.:
Nacqui all' affanno e al pianto,
I-was-born to-[the] anguish and to-[the] tears,

soffrî tacendo il core;
suffered silently the heart;

ma per soave incanto dell'età mia nel fiore,
but through (a) sweet spell of-the-age my in-the flower,
                           (in the flower of my youth)

come un baleno rapido la sorte mia cangiò.
as a lightning-flash swift, [the] fate my changed.

No, no, no, no, tergete il ciglio;
No, no, no, no, wipe-dry the [brow] (tears);

perchè tremar, perchè?
why tremble, why?

A questo sen volate figlia, sorella, amica,
To this breast fly--daughter, sister, friend,

tutto, tutto, tutto, tutto trovate in me.
all, all, all, all, you find in me.

Aria:
Non più mesta accanto al fuoco
Not longer sad near [to]-the fire

starò sola a gorgheggiar, no,
I-will be alone to sing, no,

ah, fu un lampo, un sogno, un giuoco il mio lungo palpitar.
ah, was a flash, a dream, a game [the] my long palpitation.
(ah, my long distress was but a flash, a dream, a game.)

385

Rossini   LA DANZA

Già la luna è in mezzo al mare
Now the moon is in-the middle [to-the] (of-the) sea,

mamma mia si salterà;
mother mine, [one] (we) will-dance;

l'ora è bella per danzare,
the-hour is beautiful for dancing,

chi è in amor non mancherà.
whoever is in love not will-lack.
                    (will be there.)

Presto in danza a tondo a tondo,
Quickly in dance [in circle, in circle] (round and round),

donne mie venite quà,
women mine, come here,

un garzon bello e giocondo a ciascuna toccherà.
a boy, handsome and gay, to each-one will-belong.

Finchè in ciel brilla una stella
As-long-as in (the) sky shines a star,

e la luna splenderà
and the moon will-shine,

il più bel con la più bella
the most handsome with the most beautiful

tutta notte danzerà.
all night will-dance.

Salta, salta, gira, gira, ogni coppia a cerchio va,
Skip, skip, turn, turn, each couple in (a) circle goes,

già s'avanza, si ritira,
now [one]-(we)-advance[s], [one] (we) retreat[s],

e all'assalto tornerà.
and to-the attack will-return

Serra, serra colla bionda,
Clinch, clinch with-the blonde,
(hold tight)
                  386

colla bruna va quà e là,
with-the brunette go here and there,

colla rossa va a seconda,
with-the red-head go to second (place),

colla smorta fermo sta.
with-the pale-one still stand.
     (stand still.)

Viva il ballo a tondo a tondo,
Long-live the dance [in circle in circle] (round and round),

sono un Rè, sono un Bascià;
I-am a King, I-am a Pasha;

è il più bel piacer del mondo,
it-is the most beautiful pleasure [of]-(in)-the world,

la più cara voluttà.
the most dear satisfaction.

Frinche, frinche, frinche, frinche (nonsense syllables)

mamma mia,* si salterà.
mother mine, we will-dance.

*Mamma mia--colloquial

Rossini   IN SI BARBARA SCIAGURA
(Semiramide)

In sî barbara sciagura
In such barbarous misfortune

m'apri tu le braccia almeno,
to-me-open [you the] (your) arms at-least,

Lascia a te ch'io versi
Let to you that-I pour-out
(Let me pour out)

in seno il mio pianto, il mio dolor.
in breast [the] my weeping, [the] my sorrow.
(on your breast my weeping and sorrow.)

A quest'anima smarrita porgi tu conforto, aita.
To this-soul lost give [you] comfort, aid.

Di mie pene al crudo eccesso
Of my sufferings to-the cruel excess

langue oppresso in petto il cor.
languishes oppressed in breast the heart.
(Oppressed by the cruel excess of my suffering, my
    heart languishes in my breast.)

Sî, sî, vendetta! Porgi omai!
Yes, yes, vengeance! Give (it to me) now!

Sacro acciar del genitore,
Sacred sword of-[the] (my) father,

Tu ridesti il mio valore,
You awake-again [the] my courage,

Già di me maggior mi sento.
Already than myself greater myself I-feel.
(Already I feel more worthy.)

Sî, del ciel nel fier cimento
Yes, of-[the] heaven in-the fierce test

il voler si compirà.
the will itself will-accomplish.
(Yes, in my fierce test the will of heaven will be .done.)

Ah! ella è mia madre. Al mio pianto forse
Ah, she is my mother. To-[the] my weeping perhaps
                    (Because of my weeping, perhaps,)

il padre perdonarle ancor vorrà.
the father to-pardon-her yet will-wish.
(my father will wish to pardon her.)

Sì, vendicato il genitore,
Yes, avenged [the] (my) father,

a lui svenato il traditor,
for him opened-the-veins (of) the traitor,
(the traitor slain for him;)

pace quest'anima sperar potrà, sì.
peace this-soul to-hope will-be-able, yes.
(then this soul will be able to hope for peace, yes.)

Ai dolce palpiti di gioia e amore
To-the sweet beatings of joy and love

felice il core ritornerà, sì.
happy the heart will-return, yes.

Sì! al gran cimento m'affretto ardito.
Yes, to-the great test [myself]-I-hasten bold(ly).

Si, l'Assiria respirerà.
Yes, [the]-Assyria will-breathe (again).

Sen corre l'agnelletta
[Itself-from-there] runs the-little-lamb
(The little lamb runs)

al cenno del pastor
at-the command of-the shepherd,

nè sa da lui partir.
nor knows-it from him to-depart.

Quel labbro che m'alletta
That lip which me-entices
(Those lips which entice me)

dispor può del mio cor
[dispose] (command) can [of-the] my heart
(can command my heart)

a vivere, a morir.
to live, (or) to die.

Tace il labro e geme il core
Remain[s]-silent the lip(s) and moans the heart,

che in amore si consuma e nol può dir.
which in love itself consumes and not-it can say.
(which consumes itself in love and cannot speak.)

Vieni, o Dio, deh vieni, o morte,
Come, O God, then come, O death,

se la sorte rende muto il mio languir.
if [the] fate renders mute [the] my languishing.

Lungi dal caro bene vivere non poss'io.
Far from-the dear beloved live not can-I.

Sono in un mar di pene;
I-am in an ocean of suffering;

lungi dal caro bene sento mancarmi il cor.
far from-the dear beloved I-feel to-fail-me the heart.
       (my heart fails me.)

Un dolce estremo sonno
A sweet last slumber,
(In a sweet last slumber,)

se lei mirar non ponno
if her look-upon not they-can
(if they cannot look upon her,)

mi chiuda i lumi ancor.
to-me may-it-close the eyes [yet].
(may death close my eyes.)

Oh, che umore stravagante
Oh, what (a) disposition capricious

ch'è colei, che servo ognora;
[that-is] (has) she, whom I-serve always;

or mi sprezza, ora m'adora,
now me she-despises, now me-she-adores,

ha un pensier sempre volante.
she-has a mind always fickle.

Un giorno mi giura
One day to-me she-swears

ch'io solo ho il suo core
that-I alone have [the] her heart

e che a ogni altro ardore eccede il mio foco,
and that [to] every other ardor surpasses [the] my fire,
(that my fire surpasses all others,)

e poi di lì a poco,
and then [from there] a little (later),

parlando con me, mi dice che affè
talking with me, to-me she-says that-in-faith

quel dì veduto ancor non ha il suo amante.
that day seen yet not has-she [the] her lover.
(she has not yet seen her lover that day.)

Infatti è bizzarra
In-fact she-is strange

e se per fortuna in capo ha la luna
and if by chance in (her) head she-has the moon
     (she is in a bad mood)

mi sfida a battaglia.
me she-challenges to battle.

Ma è foco di paglia, io bene lo so,
But it-is fire of straw, I well it know,
(I know that it is short-lived,)

393

che durar non può
that last not can,
(it cannot last,)

perchè vuole e non vuole in un istante.
because she-wants and not wants in an instant.
(because she wants and doesn't want at the same time.)

All'acquisto di gloria e di fama tra belliche schiere
To-the-winning of glory and of fame among warlike troops,

di trombe guerriere mi chiama il fragor.
of trumpets martial me calls the noise.
(the sound of martial trumpets calls me to glory.)

Ma portando del caro mio bene
But carrying of-[the] dear my treasure

fisse all'alma le gravi sventure
fixed in-the-soul the heavy disasters
(but remembering the misfortunes of my beloved,)

avrò sempre dure le pene nel cor.
I-shall-have always cruel [the] pains in-[the] (my) heart.

Scarlatti, A.   CALDO SANGUE

Caldo sangue,
Hot blood,

che bagnando il sen mi vai
which bathing the bosom to-me you-go
(which goes bathing my bosom)

e d'amore
and of-love

fai gran fede al genitore,
you-make great faith to-the father,
(you do honor to the parent,)

fuggi pur, fuggi da me,
flee then, flee from me,

ch'io già moro e resto esangue!
for-I already die and remain bloodless!

Forse un dì risorgerai
Perhaps one day you-will-rise-up-again

per vendetta
for revenge

della man, che mi saetta;
[of]-(on)-the hand, which me strikes-down;

e il vigor, che in me già manca,
and the energy, which in me already is-lacking,

caldo sangue,
hot blood,

passerà più saldo in te.
will-pass more solid in you.
(will-pass, more courageous, into you.)

396

Scarlatti, A.　　　　　　CARA, CARA E DOLCE

Cara, cara e dolce libertà,
Dear, dear and sweet liberty,

l'alma mia consoli tu;
[the]-soul my console [you];
(console my spirit;)

più non vive in servitù
more not it-lives in servitude
(it no longer lives in servitude)

s'il mio cor sciolto s'en va.
if-[the] my heart free [itself-from-there] goes.

Vola, fuggi pure sola, fuggi pur da me,
Fly, flee then alone, flee then from me,

fa retrato Dio d'amor.
make retreat (the) God of-love.

E già libero il mio cor
Is already free [the] my heart

se più lacci il piè non ha.
if more snares the foot not has.
(if the foot has no more snares.)

Scarlatti, A.   CHI VUOLE INNAMORARSI

Chi vuole innamorarsi, ci deve ben pensar!
He-who wants to-fall-in-love, on-it must well think!

Amore è un certo foco,
Love is a certain fire,

che, se s'accende un poco,
which, if [itself]-it-takes-fire a little,

eterno suol durar.
forever is-accustomed to-last.

Non è lieve tormento,
Not is-it light torment,

aver piagato il cor!
to-have wounded the heart!
(to have a wounded heart!)

Soggetta ogni volere
He-submits every wish

a due pupille arciere,
to two eyes archer,
(to Cupid's two eyes,)

chi serve al dio d'amor.
[he]-who serves [to]-the god of-love.

Scarlatti, A.   ELITROPIO D'AMOR

Recit. :
Elitropio d'amor sempre m'aggiro
Heliotrope of-love, always [myself]-I-turn

a vagheggiarti o mio bel sole altero,
to admire-you, O my beautiful sun proud,

tu quanto vago più tanto severo
you (the) more lovely (the) more [so-much] severe,
(the more lovely you are, the more severe,)

mi rendi per amor doglia e martiro.
to-me you-offer for love pain and martyrdom.
(you offer me pain and martyrdom in exchange for love.)

Aria:
Belle chiome inanellate, molli guancie imporporate,
Beautiful tresses curled, soft cheeks blushing,

io vi voglio idolatrar.
I you want to-worship.

Coll'armarvi di rigore,
With-[the]-arming-yourself with severity,
(By arming yourself with severity,)

di fierezza e di furore
with pride and with fury,

assai più vi fate amar.
much more yourself you-make to-be-loved.
(you make yourself loved much more.)

Recit. :
Bell'idol mio d'Amore, non esser si ritroso,
Beautiful-idol my of-love, (do) not be so stubborn,

non ti mostrar sdegnoso
(do) not yourself show disdainful

con chi t'offerse in olocausto il core.
with him-who to-you-offered in sacrifice [the] (his) heart.

Care fila in cui d'amore son cifrate
Dear threads in which of-love are spelled

le catene, sempre mai v'adorerò.*
the chains, always forever you-I-will-adore.

Quanto più legate il core e accrescete
[How-much] (the) more you-bind [the] (my) heart and
    increase

le mie pene, più fedele v'amerò.
[the] my pains, (the) more faithful you-I-will-love.

*text variant: sempre mai v'adornerò.
              forever [ever] you-I-will-adorn.

Scarlatti, A.   ERGITI, AMOR
                             (Scipione nelle Spagne)

Ergiti, amor, sui vanni
Raise-yourself, love, upon-[the] wings

e prendi ardito il volo
and take daring [the] flight

senz'abbassarti più.
without-lowering-yourself more.

Perchè con nuovi inganni
So-that with new mistakes

tu non ricada al suolo,
you not may-fall to-the ground,

lo sosterrà virtù.
it will-sustain virtue.
(Virtue will sustain your flight.)

401

Recit.:
Fermate omai fermate,
Stop now, stop,

candide mie colombe il volo errante,
white my doves, [the] (your) flight wandering,

e sciolte dal rigor d'aurato freno,
and released from-the rigor of-golden restraint,

libere trascorrete di Cnido
free fly-over of Cnidus

il suol più verdeggiante e ameno.
the ground more green and pleasant.

Per atterrar l'orgoglio d'una bellezza altera,
To humble the-pride of-a beauty proud,

dalla più vaga sfera
from-the most lovely sphere

ch'il terzo Ciel di bella luce indore,
which-the third Heaven with beautiful light gilds,

guidato dallo sdegno, or giunge Amore.
guided by-[the] indignation, now arrives Love.

Aria:
Se, quando di pace Cupido è foriero,
If, since of peace Cupid is (the) quartermaster,

sì ardente ha la face, lo strale ha sì fiero,
so burning has the torch, the arrow he-has so fierce,
(he has the burning torch and the fierce arrow,)

che sarà quando a far guerra scende in terra
what will-[be] (happen) when to make war descends on earth

Nume irato e Dio e Dio guerriero?
Divinity enraged, both God and God warrior?

Recit.:
Dunque di sua beltà tanto presumi,
Then of her beauty so-much do-you-presume,

402

Psiche, che di bellezza è un ombra sola
Psyche, who of beauty is a shadow only

che alla madre d'amore,
who [to]-(from)-the mother of-love,

al più bel Nume gl'incensi usurpa,
from-the most beautiful God the-incense[s] usurps,

e gl'olocausti invola.
and the-sacrifices steals.

Aria:
Fieri dardi, acuti strali,
Fierce darts, sharp arrows,

a ferir v'invita un cor
to wound you-invites a heart
(a heart invites you to cause wounds,)

ma con piaghe aspre e mortali
but with wounds, bitter and mortal,

di fierezza e non d'amor.
of daring and not of-love.

Benchè d'oro, il dardo mio
Although of-gold, [the] dart my

gran ferite apre in un sen;
great wounds opens in a bosom;

son fanciullo è ver, ma Dio.
I-am (a) boy, it-is true, but (also a) god.

Spargo nettare e velen.
I-spread nectar and poison.

Già il sole dal Gange
Already the sun [from]-(over)-the Ganges

più chiaro sfavilla
more bright(ly) sparkles

e terge ogni stilla dell'alba, che piange.
and dries every drop of-the-dawn, which weeps.

Col raggio dorato
With-[the] (a) ray gilded

ingemma ogni stelo
it-adorns (with gems) every blade (of grass)

e gli astri del cielo
and the stars of-the sky

dipinge nel prato.
it-paints in-the field.

Scarlatti, A.   HO UN'ALMA
                  (Gerone tiranno di Siracusa)

Ho un'alma, o mio nume,
I-have a-soul, O my idol,

per voi tutt'ardor.
for you all-ardor.

Per legarmi a voi, Cupido
To tie-me to you, Cupid

la sua benda si slacciò,
[the] his blind-fold [himself] untied,

nè mai può, no, no, no, quel laccio fido
nor ever can, no, no, no, that bond faithful

separarvi dal mio cor.
separate-you from-[the] my heart.

405

Io morirei contento
I would-die happy

se il mio caro tesoro,
if [the] my dear [treasure] (beloved),

se l'idol mio potesse con sue luci istesse
if [the]-idol my could with her eyes same
                   (with her own eyes)

veder la fedeltà con cui mi moro.
see the fidelity with which [myself] I-die.

Potrebbe allor sicura viver l'anima mia
Could then [secure] (free) live [the]-soul my

dall'empia gelosia e deporre ogni cura
from-the-inhuman jealousy and put-aside every care

di timor, di sospetto e di tormento.
of fear, of suspicion and of torment.

S'ogni fiamma spargesse faville,
If-every flame scattered sparks,

s'ogni bella vedesse l'ardor,
if-every beautiful-one saw the-ardor,

voi sapreste, adorate pupille,
you would-know, adored eyes,

quanto v'ama l'acceso mio cor.
how-much you-loves [the]-burning my heart.
(how much my burning heart loves you.)

S'ogni amante con salde catene
If-every lover with firm chains

dasse avvinta la sua libertà
gave bound-up [the] his liberty

voi sapreste, adorato mio bene,
you would-know, adored my beloved,

quanto è grande la mia fedeltà.
how-much is great [the] my faithfulness.
(how great my faithfulness is.)

Recit. :
Ma sia quanto si voglia aspra la via
But let-it-be as-much-as one wishes rough the road

ch'al Ciel d'Amor conduce, sempre nel petto mio
that-to-the heaven of-love leads, always in-[the] bosom my

cresce e germoglia più fervido il desire
grows and sprouts more fervent the desire

d'intrepido seguire per faticoso calle,
of-dauntless(ly) following, by difficult path,

incerta luce, e soffrendo e sperando,
uncertain light, both suffering and hoping,

nel colmo del piacer viver penando.
in-the height of-[the] pleasure to-live suffering.

Aria:
S'armi pur d'empio veleno
(Though)-[it-be]-armed even with-bitter poison

quel bel seno,
that beautiful bosom,

sempre tuo, bella, sarò.
always yours, beautiful-one, I-will-be.

Mi vedrai più fido amante
Me you-will-see (a) more faithful lover

più costante sarò morto, morto e t'amerò.
more constant I-will-be dead, dead, and you-I-will-love.
(though I were dead, I would still love you.)

Aria II:
Vibri pur lingua mendace, la sua face,
Let-vibrate moreover tongue lying, [the] its torch
(Though lying tongues)

407

per dar vita al mio martir,
to give life to-[the] my suffering,
(may increase my suffering,)

chiede sol per sua mercede
asks only for its reward

la mia fede dirti o cara
[the] my faith to-declare-to-you, O dear-one,

e poi morir.
and then to-die.

Recit.:
Sì, sì, fido mio core
Yes, yes, faithful my heart

di severa bellezza l'ostinato rigore mercè
of severe beauty [the]-obstinate rigor thanks
(thanks to the rigor of a severe beauty)

d'alta speranza trofeo rimirerai
of-high hope (a) trophy you-will-see

di tua costanza.
of your constancy.
(in your constancy.)

Scarlatti, A. MOSTRI DELL'EREBO
(La fede riconosciuta)

Mostri dell'Erebo, furie terribili,
Monsters of-[the]-Erebus, furies terrible,

di sdegno armatemi, in sen spiratemi
with indignation arm-me, in (my) bosom breathe-[to-me]

ira e furor.
wrath and fury.

Dorinda è morta ed io vivrò?
Dorinda is dead and I shall-live?

Non voglio, no. Morir degg'io,
Not do-I-want, no. Die must-I,
(I do not want that, no. I must die.)

iniquo e perfido ingannator.
evil and perfidious deceiver.

Scarlatti, A.　　　　　　　　NELL'ASPRO MIO DOLOR
　　　　　　　　　　　　　　　(Griselda)

Nell'aspro mio dolor
In-[the]-bitter my pain

non ti lusinghi il cor vana speranza.
(let) not [to-you] flatter [the] (your) heart vain hope.
(let vain hope not flatter your heart.)

Vedrai ch'io son più forte
You-will-see that-I am more strong

della crudel mia sorte;
than-[the] cruel my fate;
(than my cruel fate;)

vedrai che amor mi diede
you-will-see that love to-me gave

per anima la fede e la costanza.
for (a) breast-plate [the] faith and [the] constancy.

Scarlatti, A. NON MI SPREZZAR
(La caduta dei decemviri)

Non mi sprezzar, crudele,
(Do) not me despise, cruel-one,

non mi sprezzar così,
(do) not me despise thus,

io son la tua fedele,
I am [the] your faithful-one,

ch'agli occhi tuoi fui bella
who-to-[the] eyes your was beautiful

e chi ti piacqui un di.
and who you pleased one day.
(and who pleased you once.)

Crudele, sono quella,
Cruel-one, I-am that-one,

crudele, fui bella
cruel-one, I-was beautiful

e che ti piacqui un dì.
and who you pleased one day.
(and I pleased you once.)

Scarlatti, A.   NON VI VORREI CONOSCERE
                                 (Griselda)

Non vi vorrei conoscere,
Not you would-I-want to-know,

begli occhi lusinghieri
beautiful eyes flattering,

per non penar cosî.
in-order not to-suffer so.

Ma già che peno tanto
But since [that] I-suffer so-much

non vi mostrate alteri;
(do) not yourself show proud;

non mi tradite voi
(do) not me betray [you]

se il fato mi tradî.
if [the] fate me has-betrayed.

Non vogl'io se non vederti
Not want-I if not to-see-you
(I do not want to see you)

men crudel, mio ben, con me.
less cruel, my beloved, with me.
(if you are not less cruel with me.)

Ti prometto compiacerti
[You] I-promise to-please-you

e donarmi tutto a te!
and give-myself all to you!

Bramo sol di rimirarti,
I-desire only to see-again-you,

bella mia, con men rigor.
beautiful-one mine, with less severity.

Mi contento d'adorarti
Myself I-satisfy with-adoring-you

anco a costo del mio cor.
even at (the) cost of-[the] my heart.

O dolcissima speranza,
O sweetest hope,

sei il ristoro del mio sen;
you-are the comfort of-[the] my bosom;

per estinguer il velen,
to [extinguish] (counteract) the poison,

vieni, e assisti a mia costanza.
come, and be-witness to my constancy.

Scarlatti, A.   QUAL MIA COLPA, O SVENTURA

Qual mia colpa, o sventura,
What my fault, O misfortune,
(What sin of mine, O misfortune,)

m'ha rapito il mio ben, l'idolo mio?
from-me-has stolen [the] my treasure, [the]-idol my?
(has stolen from me my treasure, my idol?)

Dimmi o caro infedel, che t'ho fatt'io?
Tell-me O dear unfaithful-one, what to-you-have done-I?
(Tell me, O dear unfaithful one, what have I done to you?)

Se delitto è l'adorarti
If (a) crime it-is [the]-to-adore-you

io son rea d'un grande error.
I am guilty of-a great error.

Tu, signor de' miei voleri
You, lord of-[the] my wishes

e tiranno di pensieri,
and tyrant of (my) thoughts,

altra colpa che l'amarti
other sin than [the]-loving-you

non ritrovo nel mio cor.
not I-find in-[the] my heart.

415

Recit.:
Quando amor vuol ferirmi
When love wants to-wound-me

si cela il traditore
himself he-hides, the traitor,

sotto il tuo ciglio,
under [the] your eye-lash,

o bella e mi saetta il core.
O beautiful-one, and to-me he-darts-at the heart.
                    (and he shoots darts at my heart.)

Ma perchè mi ferisce col tuo dardo
But because me he-wounds with-[the] your dart

adoro la ferita e bacio il dardo.
I-adore the wound and I-kiss the dart.

Aria:
Voi mi date la vita
You to-me [you]-give [the] life

con sì dolce ferita, o luci belle.
with such (a) sweet wound, O eyes beautiful.

Ecco al vostro rigore
Behold, to-[the] your severity

consacro questo core, o care stelle.
I-consecrate this heart, O dear stars.

Recit.:
All'or che io vi vedo,
When [that] I you see,

o pupille adorate, parmi di stare
O eyes adored, it-seems-to-me to be

a fosca notte in seno;
in dark night in (my) bosom;
(in the midst of a dark night;)

ma se vi guardo, poi voi m'abbagliate.
but if you I-look-at, then you me-blind.

Ah, che ben io m'avveggio
Ah, [that] well I [myself]-perceive (that)

vedervi è male e non vedervi è peggio.
to-see-you is bad, and not to-see-you is worse.

S'io sto vicin di tua bellezza i rai,
If-I stand near of your beauty the rays,
(When I am near the rays of your beauty,)

mi struggo a quell'ardore.
myself I-consume with that-ardor.
(I am consumed with ardor.)

E se lungi ti sto, anima mia,
And if far from-you I-am, soul my,

tiranna gelosia mi gela il core.
tyrannical jealousy [to-me] freezes [the] (my) heart.

Aria:
Sol di mirarvi, mie luci care,
Only [of] (in) looking-at-you, my eyes dear,

gode ogni istante l'amante cor.
is-happy (at) every moment [the]-(my)-loving heart.

E se in amarvi deggio penare,
And if in loving-you I-must suffer,

sarò costante nel mio dolor.
I-shall-be faithful in-[the] my pain.

Scarlatti, A.   RUGIADOSE, ODOROSE (LE VIOLETTE)

Rugiadose, odorose violette graziose,
Dewy, fragrant violets graceful,

voi vi state vergognose,
you there stand modest(ly),

mezzo ascose tra le foglie
half hidden among the leaves,

e sgridate le mie voglie
and you-rebuke [the] my desires

che son troppo ambiziose.
which are too ambitious.

Se delitto è l'essere amante,
If (a) crime it-is [the]-to-be (a) lover,

costante i martiri son pronto a soffrir.
constant the sufferings I-am ready to suffer.

Ma se colpa la sorte a miei danni
But if is-at-fault [the] fate to my damage[s]
(But if fate is to blame,)

affanni e tormenti non devo patir.
pains and torments not I-must suffer.

Se adorando, soffrendo in amor
If adoring, suffering in love
(Suffering in love, while adoring,)

è troppo rigore bambino crudel,
is too-much severity, child cruel,

se la sempre tu paghi d'affanno
if it always you repay with-anguish,
(if you always repay it with anguish,)

tiranno sì fiero d'un alma fedel.
tyrant so fierce of-a soul faithful.
(fierce tyrant over a faithful soul.)

Scarlatti, A.   SE FLORINDO E FEDELE

Se Florindo è fedele io m'innamorerò.
If Florindo is faithful, I [myself]-will-fall-in-love.

Potrà ben l'arco tendere il faretrato arcier,
Will-be-able well the-bow to-draw the quivered archer,
(Cupid can well draw his bow,)

ch'io mi saprò difendere
for-I myself will-know-how to-defend

d'un guardo lusinghier.
from-a glance flattering.

Preghi, pianti e querele io non ascolterò,
Pleas, tears and arguments I not will-[hear] (listen-to),

ma se sarà fedele
but if he-will-be faithful

io m'innamorerò.
I [myself]-will-fall-in-love.

(In some editions the name appears as Florinda, which would
be appropriate if sung by a man.)

Se tu della mia morte a questa destra forte
If you of-[the] my death to this right-arm strong

la gloria non vuoi dar, dalla ai tuoi lumi,
the glory not want to-give, give-it to-[the] your eyes,

e il dardo del tuo sguardo
and the dart of-[the] your glance,

sia quello che m'uccida e mi consumi.
let-it-be that which me-kills and me consumes.

(If you do not wish to give the glory of my death
to this strong right arm, give it to your eyes,
and let the arrow of your glance be that
which kills and consumes me.)

Scarlatti, A.   SE VUOI CH'IO VIVA
                                        (L'amor generoso)

Se vuoi ch'io viva,
If you-wish that-I should-live,

cara mia diva, non disprezzarmi
dear my goddess, (do) not despise-me

ch'io viverò.
(so) that-I shall-live.

Ma tutto, tutto sdegno
But all, all (the) scorn

d'un vile, vile indegno
of-a base, base unworthy-one
(of an unworthy rival)

ben vendicarmi allor saprò.
[well] to-avenge-[myself] then I-will-know-how.
(I will know how to avenge.)

Sento nel core certo dolore
I-feel in-the heart (a) certain pain

che la mia pace turbando va.
which [the] my peace disturbing goes.
(that disturbs my peace.)

Splende una face,
(There) shines a torch,

che l'alma accende;
which the-soul kindles;
(which kindles the soul)

se non è amore, amor sarà.
it not it-is love, love it-will-be.

Scarlatti, A.   SON TUTTA DUOLO

Son tutta duolo, non ho che affanni
I-am all sadness, not I-have but worries

e mi dà morte pena crudel:
and to-me gives death suffering cruel:
(and cruel suffering brings me death)

e per me solo sono tiranni
and for me alone are tyrants

gli astri, la sorte, i numi, il ciel.
the stars, [the] fate, the gods, [the] heaven.
(the stars, the gods, fate, and heaven are tyrants for me alone.)

Sono unite a tormentarmi,
They-are united to torment-me,

fiera sorte e crudo amor.
fierce fate and cruel love.

Con lusinghe e non con l'armi
With allurements and not with [the]-weapons,

fanno guerra a questo cor.
they-make war on this heart.

Scarlatti, A.   SPERANZE MIE

Recit. :
Speranze mie addio io v'abbandono
Hopes mine, goodbye; I you-abandon

fra il son di crudi marmi
amid the sound of crude [marble] (stones),

all'ingiurie de'tempi
to-the-injuries of-the-weather
(in spite of the rigors of the weather),

a pianger rie aventure io mi deporto
to weep wretched misfortunes I myself take-away

a scegliere fra rupi un bel conforto.
to choose among rocks a gentle consolation.

Aria:
Così vuol della mia sorte
Thus wants [of-the] (for) my destiny

l'empio fato darmi morte
[the] inhuman fate to-give-me death

per ch'il cor non goda più
so that-the heart not may-be-happy more

di felice sventurata.
of (a) happy unfortunate-one.

Alma, gemi abbandonata in sì cruda servitù.
Soul, moan abandoned in such cruel slavery.

Di donzelle infedeli l'insidiosi sospiri
Of young-girls unfaithful the-insidious sighs
(The insidious sighs of young, unfaithful girls)

non udirai mai più, mio cor tradito.
[not] you-will-hear never more, my heart betrayed.

Assai fosti schernito,
Enough were-you scorned,

un viso lusinghier più non si miri,
a face flattering more not (let) one admire,

e per non disamar un dì infelice,
and to not fall-out-of-love one day unhappy,

s'astenga ogn'un d'amar troppo felice.
[himself]-let-abstain everyone from-loving too happy.

Miei affetti, statene in pace,
My affections, rest-[from there] in peace,

già per voi pietà non v'è,
now for you pity not there-is,

che a quel sen che a più d'un piace,
for to that bosom which [to] more than-one pleases,
(to that heart which pleases more than one lover,)

più dar fede non si dè.
longer give faith not one must.
(one must no longer give faith.)

Scarlatti, A.   SU, VENITE A CONSIGLIO

L'autore: (The author)
Su, venite a consiglio, o pensieri.
Up, come to counsel, O thoughts.

Com'esser mai può ch'io serva a Semira
How-be ever can-it that-I serve [to] Semira

che scopo è dell'ira di chi m'infiammo?
who (the) object is of-the-wrath with which myself I-inflame?

I pensieri: (His thoughts)
E meglio soffrire, penare, morire,
It-is better to-endure, to-suffer, to-die,

che mai rimirare oggetti si fieri.
than ever to-see-again object[s] so cruel.
                              (a woman so cruel.)

L'autore:
Eh, lasciate i consigli, o pensieri!
Oh, leave-off the advice, o thoughts!

L'autore:
No, tornate a consiglio, o pensieri.
No, return to counsel, O thoughts.

Chi il seno m'aprì con dolce ferita
She-who the bosom to-me-opened with sweet wound
(She who opened my bosom with a sweet wound)

vedrà che è schernita sua fede così.
will-see that is despised her faith thus.

I pensieri:
Il cielo permetta men grave vendetta!
(May) [the] heaven permit (a) less heavy revenge!

Destin più soave è forza ch'io speri.
(A) destiny more sweet it-is necessary that-I hope (for.)

L'autore:
Oh, lasciate i consigli, o pensieri!
Oh, leave-off the advice, O thoughts!

Scarlatti, A.   SUSURRANDO IL VENTICELLO
                                  (Tigrane)

Susurrando il venticello
Murmuring the breeze

par che dica, "è caro, è bello
seems that it-says, "it-is dear, it-is beautiful
(seems to say)

il morire per amor."
[the] to-die for love."

Purchè viva il mio diletto
Provided-that lives [the] my beloved;
(Provided that my beloved lives;)

della morte il fiero aspetto
of-[the] death the fierce aspect
(the fierce aspect of death)

sarà gioia a questo cor.
will-be joy to this heart.

Toglietemi la vita ancor crudeli cieli,
Take-away-from-me [the] (my) life [even], cruel heavens,

se mi volete rapire il cor.
if from-me you-wish to-steal the heart.

Negatemi i rai del dì, severe sfere,
Deny-to-me the [rays] (light) of-[the] day, severe stars,

se vaghe siete del mio dolor.
if glad you-are of-[the] my sorrow.
(if you are happy over my sorrow.)

Vengo a stringerti, dolce mia vita,
I-come to embrace-you, sweet my life,

vengo, o cara, il tuo labbro a baciar!
I-come, O dear-one, [the] your lip(s) to kiss!

La pupilla, che l'alma ha ferita,
The eye, which the-soul has wounded,
(The eyes, which have wounded the soul,)

potrà ancora la piaga sanar.
will-be-able yet the wound to-heal.

Scarlatti, A.   VI CREDO, O NO
                                 (Attilio Regolo)

Vi credo, o no, speranze amate;
You I-believe, or [no] (not), hopes beloved;

che m'ingannate, ancor paventa nel petto il cor.
that me-you-deceive still fears in-the bosom the heart.
(my heart still fears that you deceive me.)

Goder non so,
To-be-happy not do-I-know-how,

che se gradite, spera mi dite,
for if you-are-pleasing, hope to-me you-say,
                         (you tell me to hope)

pur mi tormenta freddo timor.
nevertheless me torments cold fear.
(nevertheless cold fear torments me.)

Scarlatti, A.   VINTO SONO
                                 (La Statira)

Vinto sono, e del nume bendato
Conquered I-am, and of-the god blind-folded (Cupid)

bagio l'arco et adoro gli strali,
I-kiss the-bow and I-adore the arrows,

che temprati nel volto adorato di Statira
which tempered in-the face adored of Statira

fan piaghe mortali.
make wounds mortal.

Scarlatti, A.   VOGLIO AMAR

Voglio amar chi mi disprezza
I-want to-love (the) one-who me despises

senza speme di mercè.
without hope of reward.

La costanza di mia fè
The constancy of my faith

stancherà la tua fierezza.
will-wear-down [the] your pride.

Chi mi fugge io vuò seguire,
Her-who from-me flees I want to-follow,

fin che spirto in sen avrò.
as-long-as breath in (my) bosom I-shall-have.

Se un tuo sguardo m'allettò,
If [a] your glance me-enticed

un tuo stral m'ha da ferire.
[a] your arrow me-has to wound.
(your arrow must wound me.)

434

Consolati e spera!
Console-yourself and hope!

Potrai d'altro oggetto più lieto goder.
You-will-be-able [of]-another object more happy to-enjoy.
(You will be able to love another.)

La stella più fiera, se cangia d'aspetto
The star most severe, if it-changes [of]-aspect,

può ancora l'affanno mutare in piacer.
can still [the]-anxiety change into pleasure.
(can change anguish into pleasure.)

Scarlatti, D.   QUAL FARFALLETTA AMANTE

Qual farfalletta amante
As (a) butterfly loving

io volo a quella fiamma
I fly to that flame

che in petto il cor m'infiamma
which in (my) bosom [the] (my) heart to-me-kindles
(which kindles my heart in my bosom)

e morte non mi dà, ah, no.
and death not to-me gives, ah, no.
(but does not kill me.)

Il vago tuo sembiante,
[The] lovely your image,

se accresce in me l'ardore,
if it-increases in me the-ardor,

a quest'afflitto core
to this-afflicted heart

ristoro pur darà.
comfort nevertheless will-give.

Da quel sembiante appresi a sospirar d'amore,
From that face I-learned to sigh with-love,

sempre per quel sembiante sospirerò d'amore.
always for that face I-shall-sigh with-love.

La face a cui m'accesi
The torch at which myself-I-kindled

solo m'alletta e piace,
alone me-lures and pleases,
(Only the torch from which I first took fire pleases me;)

è fredda ogn'altra face per riscaldarmi il cuore.
is cold every-other torch to warm-[to-me] [the] (my) heart.
(every other torch that attempts to warm my heart is cold.

Guarda, che bianca luna, guarda, che notte azzurra,
See, what (a) white moon, see, what (a) night blue,

un aura non susurra, non tremola uno stel.
a breeze not whispers, not trembles a blade (of grass).

L'usignoletto solo
The-little-nightingale alone

va dalla siepe all'orno,
goes from-the hedge to-the-ash-tree,

e sospirando intorno chiama la sua fedel.
and sighing around calls [the] his faithful (mate).

Ella, che il sente appena vien di fronda in fronda
She, who him hears scarcely, comes from branch to branch

e pare che gli dica, no,
and it-seems that to-him she-says, no,

non piangere, son qui,
(do) not weep, I-am here.

Che gemiti son questi, che dolci pianti,
What moans are these, what sweet complaints,

Irene, son questi?
Irene, are these?

Tu mai non me sapesti rispondere così.
You never [not] (to) me knew-how to reply thus.

Da voi, cari lumi dipende il mio stato,
[From] (on) you, dear eyes depends [the] my condition,

voi siete i miei Numi, voi siete il mio fato.
you are [the] my Gods, you are [the] my fate.

A vostro talento mi sento cangiar.
At your wish myself I-feel change.

Ardir m'inspirate se lieti splendete,
To-dare me-you-inspire if happy you-shine,
(You inspire me to dare if you shine happily,)

se torbidi siete, mi fate tremar.
if troubled you-are, me you-make tremble.
(if you are troubled, you make me tremble.)

Schubert   MIO BEN RICORDATI

Mio ben ricordati
My beloved, remember-[yourself],

se avvien ch'io mora,
if it-comes-to-pass that-I die,

quanto quest'anima fedel t'amò.
how-much this-soul faithful you-loved.
(how much this faithful soul loved you.)

E se pur amano le fredde ceneri,
And if moreover love [the] cold ashes,
(And if cold ashes can love,)

nell'urna ancora t'adorerò.
in-the-urn still you-I-will-love.
(I shall still love you after death.)

Or su! non ci pensiamo,
Now then! not-of-it let-us-think,
(Let-us not worry about it,)

coraggio e concludiamo;
(have) courage and let-us-finish;

al fin s'io prendo moglie so ben perchè lo fo.
finally if-I take (a) wife, I-know well why it I-do.

Lo fo per pagar i debiti,
It I-do to pay [the] (my) debts,

la prendo per contanti di dirlo e di repeterlo,
her I-take for cash, to say-it and to repeat-it,

difficoltà non ho.
difficulty not do-I-have.

Fra tanti modi e tanti di prender moglie al mondo,
Among so-many ways and so-many to take a wife in-the world,
(Among so many, so many ways)

un modo più giocondo del mio trovar
a way more happy than-[the] mine to-find

non so.
not do-I-know-how.

Si prende per affetto,
One takes (them) through affection,

si prende per rispetto,
one takes (them) through respect,

si prende per consiglio
one takes (them) through advice

si prende per puntiglio,
one takes (them) through obstinacy,

si prende per capriccio, è vero, sì o no?
one takes (them) through caprice, is-it-true, yes or no?

Ed io per medicina di tutti i mali miei
And I for medicine [of] (for) all [the] ills my
(And as medicine for all my ills)

un poco di sposina prendere non potrò?
a bit of wife take not can-I?
(can't I take a little-wife?)

Ho detto e'l ridico lo fò per li contanti,
I-have said (it) and-it I-say-again: it I-do for [the] cash,

lo fanno tanti e tanti anch'io lo farò.
it they-do so-many, [and] so-many, also-I it will-do.
(so many, so many do it; so will I).

Non t'accostar all'urna
(Do) not [yourself]-approach [to]-the-urn

che l'ossa mie rinserra.
which [the]-bones my encloses.
(which holds my bones.)

Questa pietosa terra è sacra al mio dolor.
This sad ground is sacred to-[the] my sorrow.

Ricuso i tuoi giacinti,
I-refuse [the] your hyacinths,

non voglio i pianti tuoi;
not do-I-want [the] weeping[s] your;

che giovan agli estinti due lagrime, due fior?
what use-are to-the dead two tears, two flowers?

Empia, dovevi allor porgermi
Inhuman-one, you-should-have then offered-me

un fil d'aita,
a thread of-aid,

quando traea la vita
when I-dragged-out [the] (my) life

in grembo dei sospir.
in (the) lap of-[the] sighs.

Ah, che d'inutil pianto assordi la foresta?
Ah, why with-useless weeping do-you-deafen the forest?

Rispetta un ombra mesta e lasciala dormir.
Respect a spectre sad, and let-it sleep.

LA PASTORELLA

La pastorella al prato contenta se ne va,
The shepherdess in-the field happy [herself thence] goes,

coll'agnellino a lato, cantando in libertà.
with-the-little-lamb at (her) side, singing in liberty.

Se l'innocente amore gradisce il suo pastore,
If [the] (her) innocent love pleases [the] (her) shepherd,

la bella pastorella contenta ognor sarà.
the beautiful shepherdess happy always will-be.

Pensa, che questo istante del tuo destin decide,
Think, that this moment [of-the] your destiny decides,

ch'oggi rinasce Alcide per la futura età!
that-today is-reborn Alcide for the future age!

Pensa che adulto sei,
Think that adult you-are,

che sei di Giove un figlio,
that you-are of Jove a son,

che merto e non consiglio la scelta tua sarà.
that merit and not advice [the] choice your will-be.

Schubert   IL TRADITOR DELUSO

Ahimè, io tremo!
Alas, I tremble!

Io sento tutto inondarmi il seno di gelido sudor!
I feel all inundate-myself the bosom with cold sweat!
(My chest is damp with cold sweat!)

Fugga si, Ah quale, qual'è la via?
Let-flee one, ah, which, which-is the way?
(I'll run away,)

Chi me l'addita? o Dio!
Who to-me it-points-out? O God!

Che ascoltai? Che n'avenne?
What did-I-hear? What [of-it]-happened?

O Dio! Ove son io?
O God! Where am I?

Ah, l'aria d'intorno lampeggia,
Ah, the-air around (me) is-filled-with-lightning-flashes,

sfavilla, ondeggia, vacilla l'infido terren.
sparkles, waves, trembles the-treacherous earth.
(the treacherous earth sparkles, waves, and trembles.)

Qual notte profonda d'orror mi circonda,
What (a) night profound of-horror me surrounds,

che larve funeste, che smanie son queste,
what ghosts sad, what frenzies are these,

che fiero spavento mi sento nel sen!
what fierce terror [to-myself] I-feel in-[the] (my) bosom!

446

Lungi dal caro bene vivere non poss'io.
Far from-the dear beloved live not can-I.

Sono in un mar di pene;
I-am in an ocean of suffering;

lungi dal caro bene sento mancarmi il cor.
far from-the dear beloved I-feel to-fail-me the heart.
                              (my heart fails me.)

Un dolce estremo sonno
A sweet last slumber,
(In a sweet last slumber,)

se lei mirar non ponno
if her look-upon not they-can,
(if they cannot look upon her,)

mi chiuda i lumi ancor.
to-me may-it-close the eyes [yet].
(may death close my eyes.)

Io consolo i cori amanti,
I console the hearts loving,

ma per me non v'è pietà.
but for me not there-is pity.

Per domar l'alme sprezzanti,
To tame the-souls disdainful,

han più forza degl'incanti le malie della beltà.
have more power than-[the]-magic the charms of-[the] beauty.
(the charms of beauty have more power than magic spells.)

Così, Amor, mi fai languir!
Thus, Love, me you-make languish!

Non è mio quel che desio;
Not is mine that which I-desire;

chi mi fugge seguir deggio,
(the) one-who me avoids follow must-I,
(I must follow the one who avoids me,)

e chi si strugge del mio foco
and (the) one-who is consumed [of-the] (by) my fire
(and the one who is consumed by my fire)

ho da fuggir!
I-have to flee!
(I must flee!)

Così, Amor, mi fai penar!
Thus, Love, me you-make suffer!

Non mi dai chi tanto amai;
Not to-me do-you-give (the) one-whom so-much I-loved;

il mio bene scacciar deggio,
[the] my beloved drive-away must-I,
(I must drive away my beloved,)

e mi conviene chi non amo pure amar!
and to-me it-is-necessary one-whom not I-love yet to-love!
(and I must love one whom I do not love!)

Stradella   DORMITE, OCCHI, DORMITE!
                                   (Giasone)

Dormite, occhi, dormite!
Sleep, eyes, sleep!

E voi, noiose cure, nascondetevi pure
And you, annoying cares, hide-yourselves also

nel centro del mio seno,
in-the center of-[the] my bosom,

che non vedrete almeno
so-that not you-will-see at-least

tutte le furie a tormentarvi unite!
all the furies to torment-you united!
                (united to torment you!)

Dormite, occhi, dormite! Fuggite, occhi, fuggite
Sleep, eyes, sleep! Flee, eyes, flee

in più fosco soggiorno gli odiosi rai del giorno!
in (a) more dark dwelling the hateful rays of-the day!
(from the light of day to a darkened room!)

E se l'interna guerra talora vi disserra,
And if the-internal warfare sometimes you unlocks,
(And if your heart-ache unlocks the door,)

al pianto sol l'egre pupille aprite!
to-[the] weeping only the-sick eyes open!
(Open your eyes only to weeping!)

Dormite, occhi, dormite!
Sleep, eyes, sleep!

Per pietà, deh, torna a me!
In pity, ah, return to me!

Amor mio, e dove sei?
Beloved my, [and] where are-you?

Son dolenti i lumi miei,
Are sad [the] eyes my,
(My eyes are sad,)

non san viver senza te.
not they-know-how to-live without you.
(they do not know how to live without you.)

Col mio sangue comprarei quella vita a me si cara,
With [the] my blood I-would-buy that life to me so dear,

se a una perdita si amara son due fiumi gli occhi miei.
if to be a loss so bitter are two streams [the] eyes mine.
(if my eyes are two streams from a loss so bitter.)

Recit. :
Rendetemi il mio bene
Give-back-to-me [the] my beloved,

empie squadre nemiche,
inhuman squadrons enemy,

ch'ogni altra offesa fatta al regio trono,
for-every other offense [made] to-the royal throne,

se Feraspe rendete, io vi perdono.
if Feraspe you-give-back, I [to]-you pardon.

Aria:
Per pietà, deh torna a me,
[for] (in) pity, then return to me,

Ah Feraspe, e dove sei?
Ah, Feraspe, [and] where are-you?

Se dolenti i lumi miei,
If sad [the] eyes my,

non san viver senza te!
not they-know-how to-live without you!
(they do not know how to live without you!)

Pietà, Signore, di me dolente!
Pity, Lord, [of] (on) me sorrowing!

Se a te giunge il mio pregar
If to you arrives [the] my ⌜praying⌝ (prayer)

non mi punisca il tuo rigor.
not me let-punish [the] your rigor.
(Let your severity not punish me.)

Meno severi, clementi ognora,
Less severe, merciful always,

volgi i tuoi sguardi sopra di me.
turn [the] your glances upon [of] me.

Non fia mai che nell'inferno
Not let-it-be ever that in-[the]-inferno

sia dannato nel fuoco eterno.
I-may-be damned in-the fire eternal.

Ragion sempre addita ad alma gentile
Reason always indicates to (a) soul genteel

che amata o schernita,
that, loved or despised,

lo stabil suo stile non cangi, no, no.
[the] fixed her custom not should-change, no, no.
(her customary manner must not change.)

Io pur seguirò;
I too will-continue (thus):

che sciogliere il piè dai lacci di fè
for to-loosen the foot from-the ties of [faith] (fidelity)
(for to escape from the bonds of fidelity)

non tento, non vò.
not I-attempt, not I-wish.
(I shall not try, nor do I want to.)

Se amor m'annoda il piede
If love to-me-ties the foot
(If love binds me)

come dunque fuggirò?
how then will-I-flee?

Da quel cor che non ha fede
From that heart which not has faith

libertà non spero, no.
liberty not do-I-hope, no.
(I do not hope for liberty.)

Sian pur dure le catene,
Let-be nevertheless cruel [the] (my) chains,
(Let my chains be cruel,)

che in servitù costante
for in servitude constant

gode ognora languendo un core amante.
is-happy forever languishing a heart loving.

Lo stral, che porto al core
The arrow, which I-carry-in-[the] (my) heart

d'un bel guardo colpo fu.
of-a beautiful glance blow was.
(was hurled by a beautiful glance.)

Più non curo il mio dolore;
More not-I-care-for [the] my pain;
(I disregard my pain;)

vivo lieto in servitù.
I-live happy in servitude.

Se nel ben sempre incostante
If in-the good always inconstant
(If on good luck, capricious)

fortune vagante di farsi stabile uso non ha,
fortune wandering to make-itself fixed custom not has,
(fortune does not remain fixed,)

anco mutabile nel mal sarà.
also changeable in-the bad will-be.
(so bad luck is changeable too.)

So ben, che mi saettano,
I-know well, that to-me strike-lightning,

che mi trafiggono e che m'uccidono
that me pierce and that me-kill

gli sguardi del mio ben.
the glances of-[the] my beloved.
(The glances of my beloved strike, pierce and kill me.)

Ma tanto mi dilettano
But so-much me they-delight,

ch'io lieta vengo men,
that-I happy [come less] (faint),

Amor, se lo puoi cingere,
Love, if him you-can [enclose] (catch),

il piede leggagli ed incatenalo,
the foot tie-to-him and chain-him,
(tie his feet and chain him,)

perchè non parta più;
so-that not he-may-depart [more] (again);

già che mi stringere
since [that] myself I-feel-bound

in dolce servitù.
in sweet servitude.

Strozzi   AMOR DORMIGLIONE

Amor* non dormir più!
Love, (do) not sleep longer!

Su, svegliati, omai!
Up, wake-yourself, now!

Che mentre dormi tu, dormon le gioie mie!
For while sleep you, sleep [the] joys my!

Vegliano i guai.
Remain-awake [the] (my) misfortunes.

Non esser Amor dappoco.
(Do) not be Love worthless.
(Do not be an idle Cupid.)

Strali foco!
Arrows, fire!

O pigro, o tardo, tu non hai senso!
O lazy-one, O slow-one, you (do) not have sense!
                          (you have no sense!)

Amor melenso, Amor codardo!
Love stupid, Love cowardly!

Quale, io resto che nel mio ardore tu dorma,
What, I remain for in-[the] my ardor you should-sleep,
(That I should remain here and burn while you sleep,)

Amore, mancava questo!
Love, it-lacked (only) this!
(Love, that's all I needed!)

*Cupid, or the god of Love

458

BEGLI OCCHI, MERCE!

Begli occhi, mercè!
Beautiful eyes, thanks!

Già sull'indiche maremme
Now on-the-deep-blue coastal-swamps

non ti chiamo a scior le vele.
not you do-I-call to loosen the sails.

Al suo duolo un cor fedele
For-[the] its pain a heart faithful

non desia premio di gemme.
(does) not desire (a) reward of gems.

Begli occhi, mercè!
Beautiful eyes, (accept my) thanks!

Tenaglia   E QUANDO VE N'ANDATE

E quando ve n'andate,
And when [yourselves] from here-do-you-go,
(And when will you leave,)

speranze adulatrici alla buon'ora?
hopes flattering,   at-the good-hour?
                         (in good time?)

Non v'accorgete ancora che m'annoiate?
Not [yourselves]–do-you-perceive yet that me-you-annoy?
(Don't you see that you annoy me?)

E quando ve n'andate?
And when will you leave?

Io più fiato in sen non ho, da nudrir vostro desire;
I more breath in bosom (do) not have to nourish your desire;

risolvetevi a partire, ch'io per voi morir non vò.
resolve-yourselves to depart, for I for you die (do) not want.
                         (for I do not want to die for you.)

Qual capriccio vi mandò a turbar la pace mia?
What caprice you sent to disturb [the] peace my?
(What caprice sent you to disturb my peace?)

Voi siete Arghi e pur la via
You are Arguses and nevertheless the way

di partir non ritrovate.
to depart not do-you-find.

E quando ve n'andate?
And when will you leave?

A pentir dunque s'avrà
To repent then [itself]-will-have

la mia fè che'l cor v'apria?
[the] my faith which-the heart to-you-opened?
(Will my faith, which opened my heart to you, have to repent?)

Deh prendendo un dolce addio date a me la libertà.
Then taking a sweet farewell give to me [the] liberty.

Io da voi non bramo già un partir senza ritorno,
I from you (do) not desire now a departure without return,

anzi, a far novo soggiorno
instead, to make (a) new sojourn

gradirò che ritorniate,
I-will-enjoy that you-should-return,

ma quando ve n'andate?
but when will you leave?

Tenaglia   QUANDO SARA QUEL DI

Quando sarà quel dì ch'io mi veggia da te
When will-be that day that-I myself may-see by you

favorito d'un sì?
favored by-a "yes"?

Cara bocca, dillo tu se a'caratteri di rose
Dear mouth, say-it [you] if in-letters of rose
                (say it, if in pink letters)

che sul labbro amor ti pose,
which on-the lip love to-you placed,
(which love has placed upon your lips,)

mi fai legger; servitù.
me you-make read; slavery.
(you make me read: slavery.)

Conto l'ore ad una ad una
I-count the-hours [at] one by one

come fosser anni interi:
as-if they-were years entire;

ma nel colmo dei pensieri
but in-the height of-[the] (my) thoughts

trovo scarsa la fortuna.
I-find scarce [the] fortune.

E se viver si può più,
And if live one can [more] (longer),

cara bocca, dillo tu.
dear mouth, say-it [you].

La mia fede m'assicura
[The] my faith me-assures

che parlar sempre di no quella donna mai non può
that [to]-speak always [of] no that woman [never] not can
(that woman cannot forever say no)

che fè bella la natura.
whom made beautiful [the] nature.
(whom nature made beautiful.)

462

Ricercate, o mie speranze,
Seek-out, O my hopes,

l'adirato mio tesor!
[the]-angry my treasure!

E se pur lo trovarete,
And if then him you-shall-find,

mentre un bacio gli darete,
while a kiss to-him you-will-give,

cangierà tosto il rigor.
he-will-change quickly [the] (his) severity.

Tu lo sai quanto t'amai.
You [it] know how-much you-I-loved,

tu lo sai, lo sai, crudel!
you it know, it you-know, cruel-one!

Io non bramo altra mercè,
I (do) not desire other compensation,

ma ricordati di me,
but remember-[yourself of] me,

e poi sprezza un infedel!
and then despise an unfaithful-one!

Ah, non lasciarmi, no, bell'idol mio,
Ah, (do) not leave-me, no, beautiful-idol mine,

di chi mi fiderò se tu m'inganni?
[of] whom [myself] will-I-trust if you me-deceive?

Di vita mancherei nel dirti addio:
[Of] life I-would-lack in-[the] saying-to-you goodbye:

che viver non potrei fra tanti affanni.
for live not I-could among so-many anxieties.

Dirò che fida sei
I-shall-say that faithful you-are;

su la mia fè riposa.
upon [the] my faith rest.
(rest upon my faith.)

Sarò per te pietosa,
I-shall-be for you merciful,

per me crudel sarò.
for me cruel I-shall-be.

Sapranno i labbri miei
Will-know-how [the] lips my

scoprirgli il tuo desio:
to-reveal-to-him [the] your longing:

ma la mia pena, o Dio
but [the] my suffering, O God,

come nasconderò?
how shall-I-conceal?

Dovrei, dovrei, ma no,
I-ought, I-ought, but no,

l'amor o Dio, la fè,
[the]-(my)-love, O God, [the] (my) pledge,

ah, che parlar non so,
ah, [that] to-speak not I-know-how,

spiegalo tu per me.
explain-it [you] for me.

Traetta   MA CHE VI COSTA

Ma che vi costa, signor tutore,
But what to-you does-it-cost, mister tutor,

un pochettino di far l'amore?
a little-bit to make [the]-love?

Tantin, tantino, venite quà.
Very-little, very-little, come here.

O Betta, diglielo, Sandra mia, pregalo.
O Betta, tell-him-[it], Sandra mine, ask-him-[it].

Ma che cos'è? Non c'è per me
But what [thing]-is-it? [Not] there-is for me

nè cortesia nè carità!
neither courtesy nor charity!

Traetta   OMBRA CARA, AMOROSA

Ombra cara, amorosa, ah perchè mai
Shade dear, loving, ah, why [ever]

tu corri al tuo riposo ed io qui resto?
(do) you hasten to-[the] your rest, and I here remain?

Tu tranquilla godrai
You tranquil, will-be-happy

nelle sedi beate ove non giunge
in-the places blessed where [not] comes

nè sdegno, nè dolor,
neither wrath, nor sorrow,

dove ricopre ogni cura mortale eterno obblio,
where covers every care mortal eternal oblivion;
(where eternal oblivion covers every mortal care;)

nè più rammenterai
nor longer will-you-remember

fra gli amplessi paterni il pianto mio,
in the embraces paternal [the] weeping my,

nè questo di dolor soggiorno infesto.
nor this of sorrow dwelling-place troublesome.

Io resto sempre a piangere dove mi guida ognor
I remain always to weep where me guides forever

d'uno in un altro orror la cruda sorte.
from-one to another horror [the] cruel fate.

E a terminar le lagrime, pietosa al mio dolor,
And to end the tears, merciful to my sorrow,

ahi, che non giunge ancor per me la morte.
alas, [that] not arrives yet for me [the] death.

469

Veracini   MECO VERRAI SU QUELLA
                            (Rosalinda)

Meco verrai su quella amena collinetta,
With-me you-will-come upon that pleasant little-hill,

libera pastorella l'agnelle a pascolar.
free shepherdess, the-lambs to pasture.

Smorzar la sete in sponda
To-quench [the] (our) thirst at (the) bank

potrem del ruscelletto,
we-shall-be-able of-the brooklet,

senza temer che l'onda,
without fearing that the-[wave] (water),

può il labbro avvelenar.
can the lip poison.

Verdi   CELESTE AIDA
                           (Aida)

Recit.:
Se quel guerrier io fossi!
If that warrior I were-to-be!

Se il mio sogno si avverasse!
If [the] my dream itself confirmed!
(If my dream were to come true!)

Un esercito di prodi
An army of brave-men

da me guidato... e la vittoria...
by me led... and [the] victory...

e il plauso di Menfi tutta!
and the acclaim of Memphis all!

E a te, mia dolce Aida, tornar
And to you, my sweet Aida, to-return

di lauri cinto...
[of] (with) laurels girded...

Dirti: per te ho pugnato,
To-say-to-you: for you I-have fought,

per te ho vinto!
for you I-have won!

Aria:
Celeste Aida, forma divina,
Heavenly Aida, form divine,

mistico serto di luce e fior
mystic garland of light and flower(s),

del mio pensiero tu sei regina,
of-[the] my thought(s) you are queen,

tu di mia vita sei lo splendor.
you of my life are the splendor.

Il tuo bel ciel vorrei ridarti,
[The] your beautiful sky I-would-like to-give-you-back, (and)

le dolci brezze del patrio suol;
the sweet breezes of-[the] (your) native soil;

un regal serto sul crin posarti,
a regal crown on-the hair place-to-you,
(set a royal crown on your locks,)

ergerti un trono vicino al sol.
raise-(for)-you a throne near [to]-the sun.

Verdi   O PATRIA MIA
                      (Aida)

Recit. :
Qui Radames verrà!
Here Radames will-come!

Che vorrà dirmi? Io tremo!
What will-he-wish to-say-to-me? I tremble!

Ah! se tu vieni a recarmi,
Ah, if you come to bring-me,

o crudel, l'ultimo addio
O cruel-one, the-last farewell,

del Nilo i cupi vortici
of-the Nile the dark whirlpools

mi daran tomba...e pace forse...
to-me will-give (a) tomb... and peace perhaps...

E pace forse e oblio.
And peace perhaps and oblivion.

Aria:
Oh, patria mia, mai più,
Oh, fatherland my, never more,

mai più ti rivedrò!
never more you will-I-see-again!

O cieli azzurri, o dolci aure native,
O skies azure, O sweet breezes native,

dove sereno il mio mattin brillò...
where serene [the] my morning shone...
(where the morning of my life shone serenely...)

O verdi colli...o profumate rive...
O green hills...O perfumed shores...

O patria mia, mai più, ti rivedrò!
O fatherland my, never more, you will-I-see-again!

No...no...mai più, mai più!
No...no...never more, never more!

473

O fresche valli, o queto asil beato
O fresh valleys, O quiet refuge blessed

che un dî promesso dell'amor mi fu...
that one day promised by-[the]-love to-me was...

Or che d'amore il sogno è dileguato...
Now that of-love the dream [is] (has) disappeared...

O patria mia, non ti vedrò mai più!
O fatherland my, not you will-I-see ever again!

Verdi   RITORNA VINCITOR
                               (Aida)

Ritorna vincitor!
Return (as) conqueror!

E dal mio labbro uscì l'empia parola!
And from-[the] my lip(s) escaped the-impious word!

Vincitor del padre mio...
Conqueror of-[the] father my...

Di lui che impugna l'armi per me...
Of him who takes-up [the] arms for me...

Per ridonarmi una patria, una reggia
To give-back-to-me a fatherland, a royal-palace

e il nome illustre che qui
and the name illustrious that here

celar m'è forza!
to-conceal to-me-is necessary!
(I am forced to conceal!)

Vincitor dei miei fratelli...
Conqueror of-[the] my brothers...

Ond'io lo vegga, tinto del sangue amato
So-that-I him see, stained with-the blood beloved,

trionfar nel plauso dell' Egizie coorti!
triumph in-the cheers of-the Egyptian cohorts!

E dietro il carro, un re...mio padre...di catene avvinto!
And behind the chariot, a king...my father...with chains bound!

L'insana parola, O Numi, sperdete!
The-insane word, O Gods, obliterate!

Al seno d'un padre la figlia rendete;
To-the bosom of-a father the daughter return;

struggete, struggete le squadre dei nostri oppressor!
destroy, destroy the troops of-[the] our oppressors!

475

Ah! sventurata! Che dissi? E l'amor mio?
Ah, unfortunate-one! What have-I-said? And [the]-love my?
                              (And   my love?)

Dunque scordar poss'io questo fervido amore
Then to-forget can-I this ardent love

che, oppressa e schiava,
that, oppressed and (a) slave,

come raggio di sol qui mi beava?
like (a) ray of (the) sun here me blessed?

Imprecherò la morte a Radames...
Shall-I-invoke (the) death to Radames...

A lui ch'amo pur tanto!
To him whom-I-love, however, so-much!

Ah! non fu in terra mai
Ah, not was on earth ever

da più crudeli angoscie un core affranto!
by more cruel anguish[es] a heart broken!

I sacri nomi di padre...d'amante
The sacred names of father...of-lover

nè profferir poss'io, nè ricordar...
neither to-utter can-I, nor remember...

Per l'un... per l'altro... confusa...
For the-one...for the-other...confused...

tremante...io piangere vorrei... Vorrei pregar.
trembling...I to-weep would-like...I-would-like to-pray.

Ma la mia prece in bestemmia
But [the] my prayer into blasphemy

si muta... delitto è il pianto a me...
itself changes...crime is the weeping to me...
                  (My tears are a crime,)

476

Colpa il sospir...in notte cupa la mente è perduta...
Sin the sigh...   in night deep the mind is lost...
(To sigh is a sin,)

E nell' ansia crudel vorrei morir.
And in-[the] anxiety cruel I-would-like to-die.

Numi, pietà del mio soffrir!
Gods, (have) pity on-[the] my suffering!

Speme non v'ha pel mio dolor...
Hope not there-has for-[the] my anguish...
(There is no hope for my anguish)

Amor fatal, tremendo amor, spezzami il cor, fammi morir!
Love fatal, terrible love, break-to-me the heart, make-me die!
                                        (break my heart into pieces!)

Numi, pietà del mio soffrir!
Gods, (have) pity on-[the] my suffering!

Verdi   ERI TU
                        (Un ballo in maschera)

Recit.:
Alzati! là tuo figlio
Lift yourself! There your son
(Get up!)

a te concedo riveder.
[to] you I-permit to-see-again.
(I permit you to see again.)

Nell'ombra e nel silenzio,
In-the-darkness and in-[the] silence,

là il tuo rossore e l'onta mia nascondi.
there [the] your blushing and [the]-shame my hide.
(there hide your blushes and my shame.)

Non è su lei, nel suo fragile petto
Not it-is on her, in-[the] her fragile breast
(It is not on her delicate breast)

che colpir degg'io. Altro, ben altro sangue
that strike must-I. Other, indeed, other blood
(that I must strike.)

a terger dessi l'offesa. Il sangue tuo!
to wipe-away (there) must-be the-injury. [The] blood your!
(must wipe away the injury--your blood!)

E lo trarrà il pugnale dallo sleal tuo core:
And it will-draw the dagger from-[the] disloyal your heart:
(And the dagger will draw the blood from your traitorous
     heart:)

delle lagrime mie vendicator!
of-[the] tears my avenger!
(the avenger of my tears!)

Aria:
Eri tu che macchiavi quell'anima,
It-was you that stained that-soul,

la delizia dell' anima mia:
the delight of-[the] soul my:

                        478

che m'affidi e d'un tratto esecrabile
whom [myself]-I-trusted, and with-one stroke abominable,

l'universo avveleni per me! Traditor!
the-universe poison for me! Traitor!
(you poison the universe for me!)

Che compensi in tal guisa
Who rewards in such (a) manner

dell'amico tuo primo la fè!
of-[the]-friend your foremost the faith!
(the faith of your foremost friend!)

O dolcezze perdute!
O sweetness[es] lost!

O memorie d'un amplesso che l'essere india,
O memories of-an embrace that the-being deifies
(that deifies the being)

quando Amelia sì bella, sì candida,
when Amelia, so beautiful, so pure,

sul mio seno brillava d'amor!
on-[the] my breast shone [of] (with)-love!

E finita.. non siede che l'odio
It-is finished...not remains [that] (but) [the]-hate
(there remains only hate)

e la morte nel vedovo cor!
and [the] death in-the widowed heart!

Verdi   RE DELL'ABISSO
                          (Un ballo in maschera)

Re dell'abisso, affrettati;
King of-the-abyss, hasten-[yourself];

precipita per l'etra,
plunge through the-ether,

Senza librar la folgore il tetto mio penetra.
Without freeing the thunderbolt [the] roof my penetrate.
(Come down through my roof without loosing your thunder-
     bolts.)

Omai tre volte l'upupa dall'alto sospirò;
Now three times the-lapwing from-the-height sighed;
(Three times the owl has hooted from on high;)

la salamandra ignivora tre volte sibilò,
the salamander fire-eating three times hissed,

e delle tombe il gemito tre volte a me parlò.
and from-the tomb the moaning three times to me spoke.

E lui! ne' palpiti come risento adesso
It-is he! In-the palpitations how I-feel-again now
            (Passionately once again I feel)

la voluttà riardere del suo tremendo amplesso!
the delight burn of-[the] his tremendous embrace!
(the thrill of his tremendous embrace burn me!)

La face del futuro nella sinistra egli ha.
The torch of-the future in-the left-hand he has.

M'arrise al mio scongiuro,
To-me-he-favored to-[the] my entreaty,
(He smiled at my entreaty,)

rifolgorar la fa:
to-flash-again it he-makes:
(he makes it flash again:)

nulla, più nulla ascondersi al guardo mio potrà!
nothing, more nothing hide-itself to-[the] gaze my can!
(nothing, no, nothing is hidden from my gaze!)

480

Verdi   SAPER VORRESTE
                               (Un ballo in maschera)

Saper vorreste di che si veste,
To-know you-would-like of what himself he-dresses,
(You would like to know how he is dressed,)

quando l'è cosa ch'ei vuol nascosa.
when it-is (a) thing that-he wishes hidden.

Oscar lo sa, ma nol dirà, tra, la, la, etc.
Oscar it knows, but not-[it] he-will-say, tra, la, la, etc.

Pieno d'amor mi balza il cor,
Full of-love to-me beats the heart,
(Full of love, my heart beats,)

ma pur discreto serba il segreto.
but yet discreetly it-keeps the secret.

Nol rapirà grado o beltà, tra, la, la, etc.
Not-it will-snatch-away rank or beauty, tra, la, la, etc.
(Neither rank nor beauty can make me tell.)

Ben io lo so ma nol dirò, tra, la, la, etc.
Well I it know, but not-it I-will-tell, tra, la, la, etc.
(Although I know very well, I won't tell.)

Verdi VOLTA LA TERREA FRONTE ALLE STELLE
(Un ballo in maschera)

Volta la terrea fronte alle stelle,
She-turns the earthy forehead to-the stars,
(She turns her dark brow to the stars,)

come sfavilla la sua pupilla,
how shines [the] her eye,
(how her eyes shine,)

quando alle belle il fin predice
when to-the beautiful-ones the end she-predicts,

mesto o felice..dei loro amor!
sad or happy, of-[the] their loves!

E con Lucifero d'accordo ognor!
She-is with Lucifer in-accord always!

Chi la profetica sua gonna afferra,
Who the prophetic her gown grasps,
(He who touches the gown of the prophetess,)

o passi'l mare, voli alla guerra,
or crosses-he-the sea, flies to-[the] war,
(whether he crosses the sea or flies off to war,)

le sue vicende soavi, amare, da questa
[the] his affairs, sweet, bitter, from this-one
(his fortune, sweet or bitter, from her)

apprende nel dubbio cor.
he-learns in-the doubting heart.
(he will learn.)

Verdi   ELLA GIAMMAI M'AMO
                              (Don Carlo)

Ella giammai m'amò! no, quel cor chiuso è a me,
She never me-loved! No, that heart closed is to me;

amor per me non ha. Io la rivedo ancor
love for me not she-has. I her see-again yet
(she has no love for me.   I can still see her)

contemplar triste in volto il mio crin bianco
contemplating, sad [in] (of) face, [the] my hair white

il dì che qui di Francia venne.
the day that here from France she-came.

No, amor per me non ha.
No, love for me not she-has.

Ove son? Quei doppier presso a finir!
Where am-I? Those candlesticks are-near to going-out!

L'aurora imbianca il mio veron! Già spunta il dì!
The-dawn whitens [the] my balcony! Already breaks the day!

Passar veggo i miei giorni lenti!
Pass I-see [the] my days slow(ly)!
(My days pass slowly!)

Il sonno, o Dio! sparì dai miei occhi languenti!
[The] sleep, O God, vanished from-[the] my eyes languid!

Dormirò sol nel manto mio regal
I-will-sleep only in-[the] mantle my royal

quando la mia giornata è giunta a sera,
when [the] my day [is] (has) arrived [to] (at) evening,

dormirò sotto la volta nera, là,
I-will-sleep under the vault black, there,

nell'avello dell'Escurial.
in-the-tomb of-the-Escorial.

Se il serto regal a me desse il poter
If (only) the crown royal to me gave the power

                              483

di leggere nei cor che Dio può sol veder!
to read in-[the] hearts what God can only see!

Se dorme il prence, veglia il traditore;
If sleeps the prince, is-awake the traitor;

il serto perde il re, il consorte l'onore!
the crown loses the king, the consort the-honor!
(the king loses his crown, the husband his honor!)

Verdi   O DON FATALE
                                   (Don Carlo)

O don fatale, o don crudel
O gift fatal, O gift cruel,

che in suo furor mi fece il cielo!
that in its fury to-me made the heaven!
(that heaven made me in its spite!)

Tu che ci fai si vane, altere,
You that us makes so vain, proud,

ti maledico o mia beltà!
you I-curse, O my beauty!

Versar sol posso il pianto,
Pour only can-I the tears,
(I can only weep,)

speme non ho, soffrir dovrò!
hope not I-have, to-suffer I-must!

Il mio delitto è orribil tanto
[The] my crime is horrible so-much
(My crime is so horrible)

che cancellar mai nol potrò!
that to-wipe-out never not-it can-I!

O mia Regina, io t'immolai
O my Queen, I you-sacrificed

al folle error di questo cor.
to-the mad mistake of this heart.

Solo in un chiostro al mondo ormai
Alone in a cloister, [to]-(from)-the world henceforth

dovrò celar il mio dolor! Ohimè!
must-I conceal [the] my grief! Alas!

Oh ciel! E Carlo?
Oh, heaven! And Carlo?

A morte domani, gran Dio! a morte andar vedrò!
To death tomorrow, great God, to death to-go I-shall-see!
(Great God, tomorrow I shall see him go to his death!)

Ah! un dì mi resta la speme m'arride,
Ah, one day to-me remains, [the] hope me-favors,

sia benedetto il ciel! Lo salverò! Ah! Sì!
be blessed [the] heaven! Him I-shall-save! Ah, yes!

Verdi   PER ME GIUNTO
                               (Don Carlo)

Recit. :
Son io, mio Carlo. Uscir tu dei da quest'orrendo avel.
Am I, my Carlo. Leave you must [from] this-horrible tomb.
(It-is I.)

Felice ancor io son se abbracciarti poss'io! Io ti salvai!
Happy still I am if to-embrace-you I-can! I you saved!
(I am happy that I can still embrace you. I saved your life!)

Convien qui dirci addio. O mio Carlo!
It-suits here to-tell-each-other goodbye. O my Carlo!
(It is necessary for us to say goodbye.)

Aria:
Per me giunto è il dì supremo,
For me arrived is the day final,

no, mai più ci rivedrem;
no, never more each-other we-shall-see;

ci congiunga Iddio nel ciel,
us let-unite God in-[the] heaven,
(may God unite us in heaven,)

ei che premia i suoi fedel'.
He that rewards [the] his faithful-ones.

Sul tuo ciglio il pianto io miro;
[on]-(in)-[the] your eye(s) the tear(s) I behold;

lagrimar, lagrimar così perchè? No, fa cor,
to-weep, to-weep thus, why? No, [make] (take) heart,

l'estremo spiro lieta è a chi morrà per te.
the-last breath happy is to him-who will-die for you.

Ascolta, il tempo stringe.
Listen, the time presses.

Rivolta ho già su me la folgore tremenda!
Turned I-have already on myself the thunderbolt tremendous!
(The thunderbolt of the King's vengeance is turned on me!)

Tu più non sei oggi il rival del Re;
You longer not are today the rival of-the King;

487

il fiero agitator delle Fiandre son io!
the fierce agitator of-[the] Flanders am I!

i fogli tuoi, trovati in mio poter,
[the] papers your, found in my [power] (hands),

della ribellion testimoni son chiari,
of-the rebellion testimonies are clear,
(are clear testimony of the rebellion,)

e questo capo al certo a prezzo è messo già.
and this head to-the certain to price is placed already.
(and there is certainly a price on my head.)

No, ti serba alla Fiandra,
No, yourself keep to-[the] Flanders,
(No, live for Flanders,)

ti serba alla grand'opra,
yourself keep [to]-(for)-the great-work,

tu la dovrai compire...
you it must complete...

Un nuovo secol d'or rinascer tu farai;
A new age of-gold to-be-born you will-make;

regnare tu dovevi, ed io morir per te.
to-reign you had-to, and I to-die for you.

Per me la vendetta del Re tardare non potea!
For me the vengeance of-the King to-wait not was-able!

O Carlo, ascolta, la madre t'aspetta
O Carlo, listen, [the] (your) mother you-awaits

a San Giusto doman; tutto ella sa...
at San Giusto tomorrow; everything she knows...

Ah! la terra mi manca!
Ah, the earth from-me slips-away!

Io morrò, ma lieto in core,
I will-die, but happy in (my) heart,

che potei serbar alla Spagna un salvatore!
that I-was-able to-preserve [to]-(for)-[the] Spain a savior!

Di me non ti scordar! Ah! la terra mi manca!
Of me not you forget! Ah, the earth from-me slips-away!
(Do not forget me!)

la mano a me...Ah! salva la Fiandra! Carlo, addio, ah!
the hand to me...Ah, save [the] Flanders! Carlo, goodbye,
    ah!
(give me your hand...)

Verdi   ERNANI, INVOLAMI
                         (Ernani)

Recit.:
Surta è la notte, e Silva non ritorna!
Risen is the night, and Silva (does) not return!

Ah, non tornasse ei più!
Ah, not would-return he more!
    (would that he returned no more!)

Questo odiato veglio, che quale immondo spettro
This hated old-one, that like (a) filthy spectre

ognor m'insegue, col favellar d'amore,
always me-follows, with-the speaking of-love,

più sempre Ernani mi configge in core.
more always Ernani to-me nails in heart.
(presses Ernani ever more deeply into my heart.)

Aria:
Ernani! Ernani, involami all'abborrito amplesso.
Ernani! Ernani, steal-me from-the-abhorred embrace.

Fuggiamo, se teco vivere mi sia d'amor concesso,
Let-us-fly, if with-you to-live to-me be by-love allowed,

per antri e lande inospite
through caves and lands inhospitable

ti seguirà il mio piè.
you will-follow [the] my foot(steps).
(my footsteps will follow you.)

Un Eden di delizia saran quegli antri a me.
An Eden of delight will-be those caves to me.

Verdi
INFELICE! E TUO CREDEVI
(Ernani)

Recit.:
Che mai vegg'io!
What ever see-I!

Nel penetral più sacro di mia magione,
In-the innermost-part most sacred of my mansion,

presso a lei che sposa esser dovrà d'un Silva,
near to her who bride to-be must of-a Silva,
(near her who is to be the bride of a Silva,)

due seduttori io scorgo?
two seducers I discover?

Entrate, olà, miei fidi cavalieri.
Enter, ho-there, my faithful knights.

Sia ognun testimon del disonore,
Let-be everyone (a) witness of-the dishonor,

dell'onta che si reca al suo signore.
of-the-shame that itself brings to-[the] his lord.
(to the shame brought upon his lord.)

Aria:
Infelice! e tuo credevi
Unhappy-one! and your (love) you-believed (to be)

si bel giglio, immacolato!
such (a) beautiful lily, immaculate!

Del tuo crine fra le nevi, piomba invece il disonor.
Of-[the] your hair among the snows, falls instead the
    dishonor.
(Instead, dishonor falls upon your white head.)

Ah, perchè l'etade in seno, giovin core m'ha serbato!
Ah, why the-age in breast, young heart to-me-has kept!
(Ah, why has age kept a young heart in my breast?)

Mi dovean gli anni almeno
To-me should-have the years-at-least
(The years should have at least)

491

far di gelo ancora il cor.
to-make of ice again the heart.
(made my heart of ice also.)

Verdi   DAL LABBRO IL CANTO ESTASIATO VOLA
(Falstaff)

Dal labbro il canto estasiato vola
From-[the] (my) lip(s) the song ecstatic flies

pei silenzi notturni e va lontano
through-the silence[s] nocturnal and goes afar

e alfin ritrova un altro labbro umano
and finally meets-again [an]other lip(s) human

che gli risponde colla sua parola.
that them answer with-[the] its word.
(that answer with their voice.)

Allor la nota che non è più sola
Then the note that not is any-longer alone

vibra di gioia in un accordo arcano
trembles [of] (with) joy in an accord secret

e innamorando l'aer antelucano con altra voce
and lovingly the-air before-daybreak with another voice
(and lovingly filling the skies before dawn with another voice)

al suo fonte rivola.
to-[the] its source flies-back.

Quivi ripiglia suon,
There it-takes-back (the) sound,

ma la sua cura tende sempre
but [the] its treatment is-directed always

ad unir chi lo disuna.
to unite those-whom it separates.

Così baciai la disiata bocca!
Thus I-kissed the longed-for mouth!

Bocca baciata non perde ventura.
(A) mouth kissed not loses prospect.
(A mouth that is kissed does not lose its prospects.)

493

Nanetta: Anzi rinnova come fa la luna.
            Rather it-renews as does the moon.
            (Rather it revives just as the moon does.)

Ma il canto muor nel bacio che lo tocca.
But the song dies in-the kiss that it touches.
                           (that touches it.)

Verdi   E SOGNO? O REALTA?
                         (Falstaff)

E sogno? o realtà?
Is-it (a) dream? Or reality?

Due rami enormi crescon sulla mia testa.
Two branches enormous grow on-[the] my head.
(Two enormous horns are growing on my forehead.)

E un sogno? Mastro Ford! Dormi?
Is-it a dream? Master Ford! Are-you-sleeping?

Svegliati! Su! Ti desta! Tua moglie sgarra
Wake-yourself! Up! Yourself rouse! Your wife errs
                            (Your wife is straying)

e mette in mal'assetto l'onor tuo,
and puts in bad-order [the]-honor your,
                    (your honor,)

la tua casa, ed il tuo letto!
[the] your house, and [the] your bed!

L'ora è fissata, tramato l'inganno;
The-hour is fixed, plotted (is) the-deceit;

sei gabbato e truffato! E poi diranno
you-are cheated and swindled! And yet they-will-say

che un marito geloso è un insensato!
that a husband jealous is a foolish-one!

Già dietro a me nomi d'infame conio
Already behind [to] me names of-scandalous joke

fischian passando;
they-whistle passing;
(Already behind my back I'm being called scandalous names;)

mormora lo scherno. O matrimonio: Inferno!
is-murmuring [the] scorn. O matrimony: Hell!

Donna: Demonio! Nella lor moglie abbian fede i babbei!
Woman: Demon! In-[the] their wives let-have faith [the] fools!
                 (Let fools trust their wives!)

Verdi E SOGNO? O REALTA? (continued)

Affiderei la mia birra a un Tedesco,
I-would-trust [the] my beer to a German,

tutto il mio desco a un Olandese lurco,
all [the] my dining-table to a Hollander greedy,

la mia bottiglia d'acquavite a un Turco,
[the] my bottle of-brandy to a Turk,

non mia moglie a sè stessa. O laida sorte!
not my wife to herself. O ugly fate!

Quella brutta parola in cor mi torna: Le corna! Bue!
That ugly word in heart to me turns: The horns!   Ox!
              (turns in my heart:)

Capron! Le fusa torte! Ah! le corna!
Goat! The spindles twisted! Ah, the horns!
    (Cuckold!)

Ma non mi sfuggirai: No!
But not from-me will-you-escape! No!

Sozzo, reo, dannato epicureo!
Filthy, iniquitous, damned sensualist!

Prima li accoppio e poi li colgo.
First them I-couple and then them I-catch.
(First I'll get them together and then catch them in the act!)

Io scoppio! Vendicherò l'affronto!
I am-exploding! I-will-avenge the-insult!

Laudata sempre sia nel fondo del mio cor
Praised forever be in-the bottom of-[the] my heart

la gelosia.
[the] jealousy.
(Let jealousy be praised forever from the bottom of my
    heart.)

496

Verdi   L'ONORE! LADRI!
                             (Falstaff)

Recit.:
Ehi! paggio! Andate a impendervi
Hey, page! Go [to] hang-yourselves

ma non più a me!
but not longer [to] (on) me!

Due lettere, prendi, per due signore.
Two letters, take, for two ladies.

Consegna tosto, corri,
Deliver (them) quickly, run,

via lesto, va! Lesto, va!
away (with you, be) quick, go! (Be) quick, go!

Aria:
L'onore! ladri: Voi state ligi all'onor vostro, voi!
[The]-honor! Thieves! You are loyal to-[the]-honor your, you!

Cloache d'ignominia, quando, non sempre
Sewers of-dishonor, when, not always

noi possiam star ligi al nostro.
we can be loyal to-[the] ours.

Io stesso, sì, io, io, devo talor
I myself, yes, I, I must sometimes

da un lato porre il timor di Dio,
[from] (to) one side put the fear of God,

e, per necessità, sviar l'onore,
and, by necessity, put-out-of-the-way [the]-honor,

usare stratagemmi ed equivoci,
to-use stratagems and double-dealings,

destreggiar, bordeggiare.
to-use-skill, to-ply-to-windward.

E voi, coi vostri cenci
And you, with-[the] your rags

497

e coll' occhiata torta da gattopardo
and with-[the] (your) glance twisted like (a) lynx,

e i fetidi sghignazzi avete a scorta!
and [the] (your) filthy guffaws you-have as escort!

Il vostro Onor! Che onore? Che onore!
[The] your honor! what honor? What honor!

Che onore! Che ciancia! Che baja!
What honor! What humbug! What (a) joke!

Può l'onor riempirvi la pancia? No.
Can [the]-honor fill-up-you the belly? No.
                (fill your belly?)

Può l'onor rimettervi uno stinco? Non può.
Can [the]-honor put-back a shinbone? Not it-can.
                (mend a broken shinbone?)

Nè un piede? No. Nè un dito? No. Nè un capello? No.
Nor a foot? No. Nor a finger? No. Nor a hair? No.

L'onor non è chirirgo. Ch'è dunque?
[The]-honor not is (a) surgeon.   What-is-it then?

Una parola. Che c'è in questa parola?
A word. What there-is in this word?

C'e dell' aria che vola. Bel costrutto!
There-is of-the air that flies. Fine construction!
(There is some air that floats away.)

L'onore lo può sentir chi è morto? No.
[The]-honor it can feel he-who is dead? No.
(Can he who is dead feel honor?)

Vive sol coi vivi? Neppure:
Lives-it only with-the living? Not even (that):

perchè a torto lo gonfian le lusinghiere,
because wrongfully it puffs-up the flatteries,
                (flattery puffs it up,)

lo corrompe l'orgoglio, l'ammorban le calunnie;
it infects [the]-pride, it-sicken [the] slanders;
(pride infects it, slander sickens it;)

e per me non ne voglio, no!
and for me not of-it I-wish, no!
(and I want none of it, no!)

Ma, per tornare a voi, furfanti,
But, to return to you, rascals,

ho atteso troppo e vi discaccio.
I-have expected too-much and you I-dismiss.

Ola! Lesti! Al galoppo!
Ho, there! (Be) quick! [to]-(at)-the gallop!

Il capestro assai bene vi sta. Lesti!
The halter very well you fits. (Be) quick!

Al galoppo! Ladri! Via di quà!
[To]-(at)-the gallop! Thieves! Away from here!

Verdi MADRE, PIETOSA VERGINE
(La Forza del destino)

Recit. :
Son giunta! Grazie, O Dio! Estremo asil quest'è per me!
I-am arrived! Thanks, O God! Final refuge this-is for me!
(I have arrived!)

Son giunta! Io tremo!
I-am arrived! I tremble!
(I have arrived!)

La mia orrenda storia è nota in quell'albergo.
[The] my horrible story is known in that-inn,

e mio fratel narrolla!
and my (own) brother told-it!

Se scoperta m'avesse! Cielo!
If discovered me-he-had! Heaven(s)!
(If he had found me out!)

Ei disse naviga vers'occaso don Alvaro!
He said sails toward-west Don Alvaro!
(He said Don Alvaro was sailing for the west!)

Ne morto cadde quella notte in cui io,
Nor dead did-he-fall that night in which I,

io del sangue di mio padre intrisa,
I with-the blood of my father soaked,

l'ho seguito, e il perdei!
him-I-have followed, and him I-lost!

Ed or mi lascia, mi fugge!
And now me he-leaves, me he-flees from!

Ah, ohimè, non reggo a tant'ambascia!
Ah, alas, not (can) I-bear [to] so-much grief!

Aria:
Madre, Madre, pietosa Vergine,
Mother, Mother, compassionate Virgin,

perdona al mio peccato,
pardon [to] my sin,

500

m'aita quell'ingrato dal core a cancellar.
me-help that-ungrateful-one from-the heart to erase.
(help me to purge that ungrateful one from my heart.)

In queste solitudini espierò l'errore.
In these solitudes I-will-expiate the-guilt.
(In this solitude I will atone for my guilt.)

Pietà di me, pietà, Signor, deh! non m'abbandonar.
Pity [of] me, pity, Lord; ah, (do) not me-abandon.

Pietà, pietà di me, Signore.
Pity, pity [of] me, Lord.

Ah, que' sublimi cantici, dell'organo i concenti,
Ah, what sublime singing, of-the organ the harmonies,

che come incenso ascendono a Dio sui firmamenti,
that like incense ascend to God [on]-(in)-the firmament[s].

inspirano a quest'alma fede, conforto e calma!
they-inspire to this-soul faith, comfort and calm!

Al santo asilo accorrasi;
To-the holy refuge I-hasten-[myself];

e l'oserò a quest'ora?
and it-will-I-dare at this-hour?

Alcun potria sorprendermi!
Someone will-be-able to-surprise-me!

O misera Leonora, tremi?
O miserable Leonora, do-you-tremble?

Il pio frate accoglierti, no, non recuserà, no.
The pious brother welcomes-you, no, not will-he-refuse, no.

Non mi lasciar, pietà, Signor!
(Do) not me leave; pity, Lord!

Deh, non m'abbandonar, pietà di me, Signor.
Ah, (do) not me-abandon; pity [of] me, Lord.

Verdi   O TU CHE IN SENO AGLI ANGELI
                               (La forza del destino)

O tu che in seno agli angeli,
O you, that in (the) bosom of-the angels,

eternamente pura salisti
eternally pure, ascended,

bella incolume dalla mortal jattura,
beautiful (and) safe from-[the] mortal disgrace,

non iscordar di volger lo sguardo a me tapino,
(do) not forget to turn the glance to me, wretched-one,
(do not forget to look down upon me--wretched one,)

che senza nome ed esule, in odio del destin,
who, without (a) name and (an) exile in hate of-the destiny,
                              (hated by fate,)

chiedo anelando, ahi, misero,
I-beg, desiring-eagerly, alas, miserable-one,

la morte d'incontrar.
[the] death to-encounter.

Leonora mia, soccorrimi, pietà del mio penar,
Leonora mine, help-me, pity [to-the] my suffering,

soccorrimi, pietà di me!
help-me, pity [to] me!

                              502

Verdi   PACE, PACE
                         (La Forza del Destino)

Pace, mio Dio! Cruda sventura m'astringe,
Peace, my God! Cruel misfortune me-constrains,

ahimè, a languir; come il dì primo da tanti anni
alas, to languish; like the day first since so-many years
                        (as it has from the first day, so many years
                        ago,)

dura profondo il mio soffrir. Pace, mio Dio!
lasts profound [the] my suffering. Peace, my God!
(my suffering continues.)

L'amai, gli è ver! Ma di beltà e valore
Him-I-loved, it is true. But with good-looks and valor

cotanto Iddio l'ornò, che l'amo ancor,
to-such-an extent God him-endowed, that him-I-love still,

ne togliermi dal core l'immagin sua saprò.
nor to-tear-to-me from-the heart the-image his will-I-know-how.
(nor will I know how to tear his image from my heart.)

Fatalità! Un delitto disgiunti n'ha quaggiù!
Fatal-destiny! A crime separated us-has here-below!
                        (A crime has separated us here below!)

Alvaro, io t'amo e su nel ciel è scritto:
Alvaro, I-you-love, and up in-[the] heaven it-is written:

non ti vedrò mai più! Oh Dio, fa ch'io muoia;
[not] you will-I-see never again! O God, make that-I die;

che la calma può darmi morte sol.
that the calm can give-me death alone.
(since death alone can give me peace.)

Invan la pace qui sperò quest'alma
In-vain [the] peace here hoped this-soul,
(In vain here this soul hoped for peace,)

in preda a tanto duol, in mezzo a tanto duol.
[in] prey to so-much affliction, in (the) midst of so-much
        grief.

Misero pane...a prolungarmi vieni
Miserable bread...to prolong-to-me you-come
                     (you come to prolong)

la sconsolata vita. Ma chi giunge?
[the] (my) disconsolate life.   But who approaches?

Chi profanare ardisce il sacro loco? Maledizione!
Who to-profane dares the sacred place?   (A) curse (upon you!)

Verdi COME DAL CIEL PRECIPITA
(Macbeth)

Recit. :
Studia il passo, o mio figlio.
Study the step, O my son.
(Watch your step)

Usciam da queste tenebre.
Let-us-leave [from] this darkness.

Un senso ignoto nascer mi sento in petto
A sense unknown to-be-born to-me I-feel in (my) breast
(A strange premonition is growing in my breast)

pien di tristo presagio e di sospetto.
full of sad omen and of suspicion.

Aria:
Come dal ciel precipita l'ombra
How from-the sky falls-headlong the-shadow

più sempre oscura!
more always dark!

In notte ugual trafissero Duncano, il mio signor.
[In] (on a) night similar they-stabbed Duncan, [the] my lord.

Mille affannose imagini m'annunciano sventura,
(A) thousand troublesome pictures to-me-announce misfortune.

e il mio pensiero ingombrano
and [the] my thought(s) they-occupy

di larve e di terror.
with ghosts and with terror.

Ohimè! Fuggi, mio figlio! o tradimento!
Alas! Flee, my son! O treason!

Verdi   AVE MARIA
                         (Otello)

Ave Maria, piena di grazia, eletta
Hail, Mary, full of grace, chosen

fra le spose e le vergini sei tu,
among [the] brides and [the] virgins are you,

sia benedetto il frutto, o benedetta,
be blessed the fruit, o blessed-one,

di tue materne viscere Gesu.
of your maternal womb, Jesus.

Prega per chi adorando a te si prostra,
Pray for her-who, adoring, to you herself prostrates,

prega pel peccator, per l'innocente,
pray for-the sinner, for the-innocent,

e pel debole oppresso e pel possente,
and for-the weak, oppressed, and for-the powerful-one,

misero anch'esso, tua pietà dimostra.
wretched also-he, your pity display.
(who is wretched, also show pity.)

Prega per chi sotto l'oltraggio
Pray for him-who under [the]-outrage

piega la fronte e sotto la malvagia sorte;
bends the forehead [and] under [the] wicked destiny;

per noi tu prega sempre e nell' ora della morte nostra,
for us [you] pray always, and in-the hour of-[the] death our,

prega per noi. Ave Maria...
pray for us. Hail, Mary...

nell'ora della morte. Ave!... Amen!
in-the hour of-[the] death. Hail!... Amen!

Verdi   SALCE! SALCE! (WILLOW SONG)
                         (Otello)

Son mesta tanto. Mia madre aveva una povera ancella
I-am sad, so-much. My mother had a poor maidservant,

innamorata e bella; era il suo nome Barbara.
in-love and beautiful; was [the] her name Barbara.

Amava un uom che poi l'abbandonò.
She-loved a man who later her-abandoned.

Cantava una canzone: la canzon del Salce.
She-used-to-sing a song: the song of-the willow.

Mi disciogli le chiome...
To-me loosen the hair...
(Undo my hair...)

Io questa sera ho la memoria piena di quella cantilena:
I this evening have the memory full of that sad-music:
(This evening my memory is filled with that sad song:)

"Piangea, cantando nell' erma landa, piangea la mesta.
"She wept, singing in-the lonely land, wept she sadly.
                    (on the lonely heath,)

O Salce! Sedea chinando sul sen la testa!
O Willow! She-sat, inclining on-the breast the head!
                    (her head on her breast!)

O Salce! Cantiamo! il Salce funebre
O Willow! let-us-sing! the willow funereal
                    (the weeping willow)

sarà la mia ghirlanda."
will-be [the] my garland."

Affrettati: fra poco giunge Otello...
Hurry-[yourself]: shortly comes Otello...

"Scorreano i rivi fra le zolle in fior,
"Glided the brooks among the clods in flower,
                    (flowering fields,)

gemea quel core affranto, e dalle ciglia le sgorgava
moaned that heart broken, and from-the eyelids to-her flowed
(Her broken heart moaned, and from her eyes flowed)

507

l'amara onda del pianto. Salce! Cantiamo!
the-bitter wave of-[the] weeping. Willow! Let-us-sing!

Il Salce funebre sara la mia ghirlanda.
The willow funereal will-be [the] my garland.
   (weeping willow)

Scendean gli augelli a vol dai rami cupi
Came-down the birds in flight from-the branches dark

verso quel dolce canto. E gli occhi suoi piangean tanto,
toward that sweet song. And [the] eyes her wept so-much,
           (And her eyes wept so much)

da impietosir le rupi."
to move-to-pity the stones."
(that they would have moved the stones to pity.")

Riponi quest'annello. Povera Barbara!
Put-away this-ring. Poor Barbara!

Solea la storia con questo semplice suono finir:
She-was-accustomed the story with this simple tune to-end:

"Egli era nato per la sua gloria, io per amar..."
"He was born for [the] his glory, I [for] to-love..."

Ascolta. Odo un lamento. Taci. Chi batte a quella porta?
Listen. I-hear a moan. Be-silent. Who knocks at that door?

"Io per amarlo e per morir...Cantiamo! Salce!"
"I [for] to-love-him and [for] to-die...Let-us-sing! Willow!"

Emilia, addio. Come m'ardon le ciglia!
Emilia, goodbye. How to-me-burn the eyelids!
      (How my eyes burn!)

E presagio di pianto. Buona notte. Ah! Emilia, addio!
It-is (a) presentiment of weeping. Good night. Ah, Emilia,
   goodbye!

Verdi   VANNE; LA TUA META GIA VEDO (CREDO)
                        (Otello)

Vanne; la tua meta già vedo.
Go; [the] your goal already I-see.

Ti spinge il tuo dimone, e il tuo dimon son io,
You spurs-on [the] your demon, and [the] your demon am I,
(Your demon spurs you on,)

e me trascina il mio, nel quale io credo
and me drives [the] mine, in-[the] which I believe,
(and mine drives me, the one that I believe in,)

inesorato Iddio!
(an) inexorable God!

Credo in un Dio crudel che m'ha creato
I-believe in a God cruel that me-has created
                        (that has created me)

simile a sè, a che nell' ira io nomo.
like [to] himself, and whom in-[the] (my) wrath I name.

Dalla viltà d'un germe o d'un atomo vile son nato.
From-the vileness of-a germ or of-an atom vile am-I born.
                        (vile was I born.)

Son scellerato perchè son uomo;
I-am wicked because I-am (a) man;

e sento il fango originario in me.
and I-feel the mud native in myself.

Si! Questa è la mia fè!
Yes, this is [the] my faith (creed)!

Credo con fermo cuor, siccome crede
I-believe with (a) firm heart, just-as believes

la vedovella al tempio,
the widow at-the temple,
                        (in church,)

che il mal ch'io penso e che da me procede
that the evil that-I think and that from me comes,

per   mio destino adempio.
by my destiny I-fulfill.

Credo che il giusto è un istrion beffardo
I-believe that the just-man is an actor jesting

e nel viso e nel cuor
and in-the face and in-the heart,
(both with his face and with his heart,)

che tutto è in lui bugiardo;
that all is in him false;

lagrima, bacio, guardo, sacrificio ed onor.
tear(s), kiss(es), glance(s), sacrifice and honor.

e credo l'uom gioco d'iniqua sorte
and I-believe [the]-man (to be the) jest of wicked fate,

dal germe della culla al verme dell'avel.
from-the germ of-the cradle to-the worm of-the-grave.

Vien dopo tanta irrision la Morte.
Comes after so-much derision [the] death.

E poi? La Morte è il Nulla,
And then? [The] death is [the] nothing,

è vecchia fola il Ciel.
is old idle-story [the] heaven.
(Heaven is an old idle story.)

Verdi   CARO NOME
                         (Rigoletto)

Recit.:
Gualtier Maldè! Nome di lui sì amato,
Gualtier Maldè! Name of him so beloved,

ti scolpisci nel core innamorato!
yourself engrave in-the heart loving!
(your name is engraved on my loving heart!)

Aria:
Caro nome che il mio cor festi primo palpitar,
Dear name that [the] my heart made first to-beat,
(Dear name that first made my heart beat,)

le delizie dell'amor mi dêi sempre rammentar!
the delights of-[the]-love to-me you-must always remind!
(you must always remind me of the delights of love!)

Col pensier il mio desir a te sempre volerà,
With-the thought [the] my desire to you always will-fly,
(In my thoughts my desire will always fly to you,)

e fin l'ultimo sospir, caro nome, tuo sarà.
and even [the]-(my)-last sigh, dear name, yours will-be.

Il mio desir a te ognora volerà,
[The] my desire to you always will-fly,

fin l'ultimo sospiro tuo sarà. Gualtier Maldè!
even the-last sigh yours will-be. Gualtier Maldè!

Verdi   CORTIGIANI, VIL RAZZA DANNATA
                         (Rigoletto)

Recit.:
Si, la mia figlia... d'una tal vittoria...
Yes, [the] my daughter...of-a such victory...
                    (at such a victory...)

che?... adesso non ridete? Ella è là... La vogl'io...
what?...now not you-laugh? She is there..Her want-I...

la renderete!
her you-will-give-back!

Aria:
Cortigiani, vil razza dannata,
Courtiers, vile race damned,

per qual prezzo vendeste il mio bene?
for what price you-sold [the] my happiness?

A voi nulla per l'oro sconviene!
To you nothing for [the]-money is-improper!
(There is nothing you would not do for money!)

Ma mia figlia è impagabil tesor.
But my daughter is (a) priceless treasure.

La rendete... o, se pur disarmata,
Her give-back...or, if yet disarmed,
                    (even if unarmed,)

questa man per voi fora cruenta;
this hand for you will-be bloody;

nulla in terra più l'uomo paventa,
nothing on earth any-longer the-man fears,

se dei figli difende l'onor.
if of-[the] (his) children he-defends the-honor.

Quella porta, assassini,
That door, assassins,

m'aprite, la porta m'aprite!
to-me-open, the door to-me open!

                    512

Ah! voi tutti...a me contro...venite! Tutti contro me! Ah!
Ah, you all... to me against...come! All against me! Ah!
    (against me)

Ebben, piango...Marullo...signore...
Very-well, I-weep...Marullo...my-lord...

tu ch'hai l'alma gentil come il core,
you that-have the-soul gentle as the heart,

dimmi tu dove l'hanno nascosta?
tell-me you where her-they-have hidden?

E là? non è vero? Tu taci ohimè!
She-is there? not it-is true? You are-silent! Alas!
    (Is it not so?)

Miei signori...perdono, pietate...
My lords... forgive, have-pity...

Al vegliardo la figlia ridate...
To-the old-man the daughter give-back...

Ridonarla a voi nulla ora costa,
To-give-her-back [to] you nothing now costs,
(Now it costs you nothing to give her back,)

tutto al mondo è tal figlia per me!
all in-the world is such daughter for me!
(She is all the world to me.)

Signori, perdon, perdono, pietà!
Lords, pardon, pardon, pity!

Ridate a me la figlia;
Give-back to me [the] (my) daughter;

pietà, signori, pietà!
pity, lords, pity!

513

Verdi   LA DONNA E MOBILE
                          (Rigoletto)

La donna è mobile qual pium al vento,
[The] woman is fickle; like (a) feather [to]-(in)-the wind,

muta d'accento e di pensiero.
she-changes [of]-(her)-words and [of] thought(s).

Sempre un amabile leggiadro viso,
Always a lovable, pretty face,

in pianto o in riso, è menzognero.
in weeping or in laughter, she is lying.

E sempre misero chi a lei s'affida,
He-is always wretched who to her himself-entrusts,

chi le confida malcauto il core!
who (to) her entrusts heedlessly the heart!
(who recklessly entrusts her with his heart!)

Pur mai non sentesi felice appieno
Yet never (does he) [not] feel-himself happy completely

chi su quel seno non liba amore!
who on that breast (does) not drink love!

514

Verdi　　　　　　　　　　PARI SIAMO
　　　　　　　　　　　　(Rigoletto)

Pari siamo...
Equal we-are...

Io la lingua, egli ha il pugnale;
I the tongue, he has the dagger;
(I have my tongue for a weapon, he has his dagger;)

l'uomo son io che ride, ei quel che spegne!
the-man am I that laughs, he that who kills!
　　　　　　　　　　　　(he the one who kills!)

Quel vecchio maledivami! O uomini!... o natura!
That old-man cursed-me! O mankind! o nature!

Vil scellerato mi faceste voi!
Vile rascal me made you!
　　　　　　(you have made me!)

Oh rabbia! esser difforme! Oh rabbia! esser buffone!
Oh, fury, to-be deformed! Oh, fury, to-be (a) buffoon!

Non dover, non poter altro che ridere!
Not allowed, not able (to do) other than laugh!

Il retaggio d'ogni uom m'è tolto:
The heritage of-every man from-me-is taken away:

il pianto...Questo padrone mio,
[the] weeping...This master (of) mine,

giovin, giocondo, sì possente, bello
young, gay, so powerful, handsome,

sonnecchiando mi dice: fa ch'io rida, buffone...
dozing, to-me says: make that-I laugh, buffoon...

forzarmi deggio e farlo! Oh dannazione!
to-force-myself must-I and do-it! Oh, damnation!

Odio a voi, cortigiani schernitori!...
Hatred to you, courtiers scornful!...

Se iniquo son, per cagion vostra è solo.
If wicked I-am, for cause yours is alone.
               (you alone are the cause.)

Ma in altr'uomo qui mi cangio!
But into another-man here myself I-change!

Quel vecchio maledivami!
That old-man cursed-me!

Tal pensiero perchè conturba ognor la mente mia?
Such-a thought why troubles always [the] mind my?
(Why does such a thought keep troubling my mind?)

Mi coglierà sventura? Ah no! E follia!
Me will-strike misfortune? Ah, no. It-is folly!
(Will misfortune strike me?)

Quanta in mordervi ho gioia!
How-much in biting-you I-have joy!
(How much pleasure I have in biting you!)

Verdi   PARMI VEDER LE LAGRIME
                         (Rigoletto)

Recit.:
Ella mi fu rapita!
She from-me was snatched-away!

E quando, o ciel? Ne' brevi istanti,
And when, o heaven? In-the brief moments,

prima che il mio presagio interno
before [the] my foreboding inner

sull'orma corsa ancora mi spingesse!
on-the-footstep taken again me spurred-on!
(spurred me on to run and retrace my footsteps!)

Schiuso era l'uscio!...E la magion deserta!
Open was-the-door!...And the house deserted!

E dove ora sarà quel'angiol caro?
And where now will-be that-angel dear?

Colei che prima potè in questo core
She that first could in this heart

destar la fiamma di costanti affetti?
kindle the flame of constant affection[s]?

Colei sì pura, al cui modesto guardo
She, so pure, [to-the] (by) whose modest glance

quasi spinto a virtù talor mi credo!
almost impelled to virtue sometimes myself I-believe!
(I believe myself almost impelled toward virtue!)

Ella mi fu rapita! E chi l'ardiva?
She from-me was snatched-away! And who-it-dared?
                         (And who dared to do it?)

Ma ne avrò vendetta;
But [of-it] I-will-have revenge;

lo chiede il pianto della mia diletta.
it demands the weeping of-[the] my beloved.
(the weeping of my beloved demands it.)

517

Aria:
Parmi veder le lagrime
It-seems-to-me (that I) see the tears

scorrenti da quel ciglio,
flowing from that eye,
          (her eyes,)

quando fra il dubbio e l'ansia
when between [the] doubt and [the]-anguish

del subito periglio,
of-the sudden danger,

dell'amor nostro memore,
of-the-love our remembering,
(recalling our love,)

il suo Gualtier chiamò.
(for) [the] her Gualtier she-called.

Ned ei potea soccorrerti, cara fanciulla amata;
Nor he could help-you, dear child beloved;
(Nor could he help you,)

ei che vorria dell'anima
he who would-like of-the-soul
              (with all his soul)

farti quaggiù beata;
to-make-you on-this-earth happy;

ei che le sfere agl'angeli per te non invidiò.
he who the spheres to-the-angels for you not envied.
(he, who because of you, did not envy the angels their
    heavenly spheres.)

Verdi   QUESTA O QUELLA
                     (Rigoletto)

Questa o quella per me pari sono
This-one or that-one for me (the) same are

a quant'altre d'intorno mi vedo.
[to] as-many-others around me I-see.

Del mio core l'impero non cedo
Of-[the] my heart the-power not I-yield

meglio ad una che ad altra beltà.
better to one than to another beauty.

La costoro avvenenza è qual dono
[The] their grace is like (a) gift

di che il fato ne infiora la vita;
with which [the] fate [of-it] beautifies [the] life;

s'oggi questa mi torna gradita,
if-today this-one to-me becomes pleasing,

forse un'altra doman lo sarà.
perhaps another tomorrow it will-be.

La costanza, tiranna del core,
[The] constancy, tyrant of-the heart,

detestiamo qual morbo crudele,
let-us-detest like (a) disease cruel,

sol chi vuole si serbi fedele;
(let) only those-who wish [themselves] keep faithful;
                              (remain faithful;)

non v'ha amor, se non v'è libertà.
not there-[have]-(is) love, if not there-is liberty.
(there is no love without freedom,)

De' mariti il geloso furore,
Of-[the] husbands the jealous fury,

degli amanti le smanie derido;
of-[the] lovers the frenzy I-deride;

519

anco d'argo i cent'occhi disfido
even of-Argus the hundred-eyes I-defy

se mi punge una qualche beltà.
if me entices [a] some beauty.
(if some beauty entices me.)

Verdi   TUTTE LE FESTE
                               (Rigoletto)

Tutte le feste al tempio mentre pregava Iddio,
All the holy-days at-the church while I-prayed (to) God,

bello e fatale un giovane
handsome and irresistible, a young-man

offriasi al guardo mio...
presented-himself to-[the] gaze my...

Se i labbri nostri tacquero,
If [the] lips our were-silent,

dagl' occhi il cor parlò.
from-the eyes the heart spoke.
(our hearts spoke through our eyes.)

Furtivo fra le tenebre sol ieri a me giungeva...
Furtively among the shadows only yesterday to me he-came...

Sono studente, povero, commosso mi diceva,
I-am (a) student, poor, with-emotion to-me he-said,

e con ardente palpito amor mi protestò.
and with ardent palpitation love to-me he-declared.
                (impulsiveness)

Partì... Il mio core aprivasi a speme più gradita,
He-left...[The] my heart opened itself to hope most welcome.

quando improvvisi apparvero color che m'han rapita,
when suddenly appeared those who me-have abducted,

e a forza qui m'addussero nell'ansia più crudel.
and with force here me-brought in-[the] anxiety most cruel.

521

Verdi IL LACERATO SPIRITO
(Simon Boccanegra)

Recit.:
A te l'estremo addio, palagio altero,
To you the-last farewell, palace proud,

freddo sepolcro dell'angiolo mio!
cold sepulchre of-[the]-angel my!

Nè a proteggerti valsi!
Nor to protect-you was-I-able!

Oh maledetto! Oh vile seduttore!
O cursed-man! O vile seducer!

E tu Vergin, soffristi rapita a lei la verginal corona?
And you, Virgin, suffered ravished to her the virginal crown?
(And you, Blessed Virgin, suffered her virtue to be ravished?)

Ma che dissi! Deliro! Ah, mi perdona!
But what do-I-say! I-rave! Ah, me forgive!

Aria:
Il lacerato spirito del mesto genitore
The torn spirit of-the sad father

era serbato a strazio d'infamia e di dolore.
was preserved [to] (for the) torment of-infamy and of sorrow.

Il serto a lei de' martiri pietoso il cielo die;
The crown to her-of-[the] martyrs mercifully [the] heaven
        gave;

resa al fulgor degli angeli,
restored to-the splendor of-the angels,

prega, Maria, per me.
pray, Mary, for me.

522

Verdi   ADDIO, DEL PASSATO
                         (La Traviata)

Addio, del passato bei sogni ridenti
Goodbye, of-the past beautiful dreams smiling,
        (beautiful, smiling dreams of the past,)

le rose del volto già sono pallenti;
the roses [of-the] (in my) face already are pale;

l'amore d'Alfredo perfino mi manca,
the-love of-Alfredo also to-me is-lacking,
(I am without Alfredo's love also,)

conforto sostegno dell'anima stanca...
(the) comfort, support of-the-soul weary...
                    (of my weary soul...)

Ah! della traviata sorridi al desio,
Ah, of-the lost-one smile at-the wish,
(Ah, smile upon the wish of the lost one,)

a lei, deh perdona, tu accoglila, o Dio!
to her, ah, give-pardon, [you] receive-her, O God!

Ah! tutto... or tutto finì.
Ah! All... now all is-finished.

Le gioie, i dolori tra poco avran fine;
The joys, the sorrows soon will-have (an) end;

la tomba ai mortali di tutto è confine.
the tomb to-[the] mortals of everything is (the) end.

Non lagrima o fiore avrà la mia fossa!
Not (a) tear or flower will-have [the] my grave!
(No tear or flower will my grave have!)

Non croce col nome
Not (a) cross with-the name (on it)

che copra quest'ossa!
that may-cover these-bones!

Ah! della traviata sorridi al desio,
Ah, of-the lost-one smile at-the wish,
(Ah, smile upon the wish of the lost one,)

a lei, deh perdona, tu accoglila, o Dio!
to her, ah, give-pardon, [you] receive-her, O God!

Ah! tutto... or tutto finì.
Ah! All... now all is-finished.

Verdi AH FORS'E LUI... SEMPRE LIBERA
(La Traviata)

Recit. :
E strano... in core scolpiti ho quegli accenti!
It's strange--in heart carved I-have those words!
(I have those words carved in my heart!)

Saria per me sventura un serio amore?
Would-be for me misfortune a serious love?
(Would a serious love be a misfortune for me?)

Che risolvi o turbata anima mia?
What are-you-resolving, O disturbed spirit my?
(O my anguished spirit?)

Null'uomo ancor t'accendeva...Oh gioia ch'io non conobbi,
No-man yet you-aroused...O joy that-I not knew,
(No man aroused you before...O joy, that I did not know,)

esser amata amando! E sdegnarla poss'io
to-be loved loving! And to-spurn-it can-I
(what it was to love and be loved! And can I spurn this)

per l'aride follie del viver mio?
for the-barren follies of-[the] life my?

Aria:
Ah fors'è lui che l'anima solinga ne' tumulti
Ah, perhaps-is he that the-spirit alone in-the tumults
(Ah, perhaps it is he whom my spirit, alone amid tumults)

godea sovente pingere de' suoi colori occulti...
enjoyed often to-paint with its colors mysterious...

Lui, che modesto e vigile all'egre soglie ascese,
He, who, modest and vigilant, to-the-ill thresholds ascended,
(came to my sickroom door,)

e nuova febbre accese destandomi all' amor.
and (a) new fever kindled, waking-me to-[the] love.

A quell'amor, quell'amor ch'è palpito
To that-love, that-love which-is (the) pulse

dell'universo, dell'universo intero,
of-the-universe, of-the universe entire,

525

misterioso, altero, croce e delizia al cor.
mysterious, haughty, cross and delight to-the heart.

A me, fanciulla, un candido e trepido desire
To me, (as a) girl, an ingenuous and trembling desire

quest'effigiò dolcissimo Signor dell' avvenire,
this-depicted sweetest Lord of-the future,
(depicted him the lord of my future,)

quando ne' cieli il raggio di sua beltà vedea,
when in-the skies the ray of his beauty I-saw,

e tutta me pascea di quel divino error.
and wholly itself I-fed on that divine mistake.

Sentia che amore è palpito dell' universo intero,
I-felt that love is (the) pulse of the universe entire,

misterioso, altero, croce e delizia al cor.
mysterious, haughty, cross and delight to-the heart.

Recit.:
Follie!...Delirio vano è questo!
Follies!...Delirium vain is this!

Povera donna, sola, abbandonata in questo popoloso deserto
Poor woman, alone, abandoned in this populous desert

che appellano Parigi, che spero or più?
that they-call Paris, what I-hope now more?
                    (what more can I hope for now?)

Che far degg'io? Gioire!
What to-do must-I? Enjoy!
(What must I do? Enjoy myself!)

Di voluttà ne' vortici perir! Gioir!
Of pleasure in-the whirlpools to-perish! Enjoy!
(Perish in the whirlpools of pleasure! Enjoy myself!)

Aria:
Sempre libera degg'io folleggiare di gioia in gioia,
Always free must-I act-foolishly from joy to joy,
                    (flit giddily from joy to joy,)

vo' che scorra il viver mio
I-wish that may-glide [the] life my
(I want my life to glide)

pe' sentieri del piacer.
along the paths of-[the] pleasure.

Nasca il giorno, o il giorno muoia,
Is-born the day, or the day dies,
(Whether the day is born or dying.)

sempre lieta ne' ritrovi,
always merry [in-the] (at) parties,

a diletti sempre nuovi dee volar il mio pensier.
to delights always new must fly [the] my thought.

DE' MIEI BOLLENTI SPIRITI
(La Traviata)

Recit. :
Lunge da lei per me non v'ha diletto!
Far from her for me not there-has delight!
(Away from her there is no joy for me!)

Volaron già tre lune dacchè la mia Violetta
Have-flown already three months since [the] my Violetta

agi per me lasciò, dovizie, amori
comforts for me left, wealth, loves
(abandoned comfort, wealth, and love for me)

e le pompose feste, ov' agli omaggi avvezza,
and the ostentatious feasts, where to-the homage[s]
    accustomed,
(and showy parties, where, accustomed to admiration,)

vedea schiavo ciascun di sua bellezza...
she-saw slave everyone of her beauty...
(she saw every man enslaved by her beauty...)

Ed or contenta in questa ameni luoghi
And now, content in these agreeable [places] (surroundings),

tutto scorda per me.
everything she-forgets for me.

Qui presso a lei io rinascer mi sento,
Here near [to] her I born-again myself feel,
                (I feel reborn,)

e dal soffio d'amor rigenerato
and by-the breath of-love regenerated,

scordo ne' gaudi suoi tutto il passato.
I-forget in-[the] joys its all the past.
(I forget all the past in the joys of love.)

Aria:
De' miei bollenti spiriti il giovanile ardore
Of-[the] my bubbling spirits the youthful ardor
(The youthful ardor of my bubbling spirits)

ella temprò col placido sorriso dell'amor!
she tempered with-the calm smile of-[the]-love!

Dal dì che disse:
From-the day that she-said:

"Vivere io voglio a te fedel,"
"To-live I wish to you faithful,"
("I want to live faithful to you,")

dell'universo immemore io vivo quasi in ciel.
of-the-universe unmindful I live as-if in heaven.

Verdi   DI PROVENZA IL MAR, IL SUOL
                         (La Traviata)

Di Provenza il mar, il suol,
Of Provence the sea, the soil,

chi dal cor ti cancellò?
who from-the heart to-you erased?
(Who has erased the sea and soil of Provence from your
    heart?)

Al natio fulgente sol qual destino ti furò ?
To-(from)-the native brilliant sun what destiny you stole?
(What destiny stole you from your native, brilliant sun?)

Oh rammenta pur nel duol
Oh, remember even in-[the] sadness

ch'ivi gioia a te brillò,
that-there joy to you shone,
(that joy glowed for you there,)

e che pace colà sol su te splendere ancor può...
and that peace there only on you shine still can...
(only there can peace still shine on you...)

Dio mi guidò! Ah il tuo vecchio genitor
God me guided! Ah, [the] your old father,
(God guided me!)

tu non sai quanto soffrì!
you (do) not know how-much he-suffered!

Te lontano di squallor
You (being) far-away, with wretchedness

il suo tetto si coprì...
[the] his roof [itself] (was) covered...

Ma se alfin ti trovo ancor, se in me speme non fallì,
But if at-last you I-find still, if in me hope (did) not fail,

se la voce dell' onor
if the voice of-[the] honor

in te appien non ammutì, Dio m'esaudì.
in you completely not-has-become mute, God to-me-gave-ear.
                                    (God listened to me.)

                         530

Verdi   OH MIO RIMORSO!
                          (La Traviata)

Oh mio rimorso! oh infamia!
Oh, my remorse! Oh, shame!

Io vissi in tale errore!
I lived in such error!

Ma il turpe sonno a frangere
But the shameful slumber to break-off

il ver mi balenò!
the truth to-me flashed!
(but the truth flashed to me to break off my shameful slumber!)

Per poco in seno acquetati,
For a-little-while in (my) breast be-silent,

o grido dell' onore;
O cry of-[the] honor;

m'avrai securo vindice;
but-you-will-have certain vengeance;

quest'onta laverò.
this-disgrace I-will-wash-away.

Oh mio rossor! oh infamia!
Oh, my [blushing] (embarrassment)! oh, shame!

ah sì, quest'onta laverò;
ah, yes, this-disgrace I-will-wash-away!

AH! CHE LA MORTE OGNORA
(Il Trovatore)

Ah! che la morte ognora è tarda nel venir,
Ah, [that the] death always is slow in-[the] coming,

a chi desia morir! Addio, Leonora, addio!
to him-who desires to-die! Goodbye, Leonora, goodbye!

Sconto col sangue mio l'amor che posi in te!
I-pay with-[the] blood my the-love that I-placed in you!
(I am paying for the love I gave you with my blood!)

Non ti scordar di me, Leonora!
(Do) not [yourself] forget [of] me, Leonora!

Addio, Leonora, addio!
Goodbye, Leonora, goodbye!

Verdi   AH SI, BEN MIO
                              (Il Trovatore)

Recit. :
Amor, sublime amore, in tale istante
Love, sublime love, in such (a) moment (as this),

ti favelli al core.
to-you may-it-speak to-the heart.
(may it speak to your heart.)

Aria:
Ah sì, ben mio, coll'essere
Ah, yes, beloved mine, with-[the]-(all my)-being

io tuo, tu mia consorte,
I (am) yours, (and) you (are) my consort,

avrò più l'alma intrepida,
I-will-have more the-spirit fearless,

il braccio avrò più forte.
the arm I-will-have more strong.
(my arm will be stronger.)

Ma pur, se nella pagina de' miei destini è scritto
But yet, if in-the page of-[the] my destinies is written

ch'io resti fra le vittime,
that-I should-remain among the victims,

dal ferro ostil trafitto,
by-the weapon hostile pierced,
(pierced by the foe's weapon,)

fra quegli estremi aneliti a te il pensier verrà,
among those last breaths to you the thought will-come,

e solo in ciel precederti la morte a me parrà.
and only into heaven to-precede-you [the] death to me will-
    seem.

                              533

Verdi   IL BALEN DEL SUO SORRISO
                         (Il Trovatore)

Recit. :
Tutto è deserto; ne per l'aure ancora
All is deserted; nor through the-air[s] yet

suona l'usato carme. In tempo io giungo!..
sounds the-usual strain. In time I come!...

Ferrando: Ardita opra, o signore, imprendi.
          Bold work, o sir, you-undertake.

Ardita, e qual furente amore ed irritato orgoglio
Bold, and what furious love and provoked pride
(Bold indeed; it is what both furious love and provoked pride)

chiesero a me.
demanded [to] (of) me.

Spento il rival, caduto ogni ostacol sembrava
Dead [the] (my) rival, fallen every obstacle, it-seemed,

a' miei desiri; novello e più possente
to-[the] my desires; (a) new and more powerful (obstacle)

ella ne appresta...l'altare...
she of-them prepares...the-altar...
(to my desires she prepares--the altar.)

Ah no! Non fia d'altri Leonora! Leonora è mia!
Ah, no! Not shall-be of-another Leonora! Leonora is mine!
       (Leonora will not belong to another!)

Aria:
Il balen del suo sorriso d'una stella vince il raggio;
The flash of-[the] her smile of-a star conquers the ray;
                      (is brighter than a star's ray;)

il fulgor del suo bel viso
the splendor of-[the] her beautiful face

novo infonde a me coraggio.
new instills to me courage.
(instills new courage in me.)

                         534

Ah! l'amor ond'ardo
Ah, (let) the-love with-which I-burn

le favelli in mio favor,
to-her speak in my favor,

sperda il sole d'un suo sguardo
(let)-disperse the sun of-[a] her glance
(let the sun of her glance disperse)

la tempesta del mio cor.
the tempest [of-the] (in) my heart.

Verdi   D'AMOR SULL'ALI ROSEE
                          (Il Trovatore)

Recit.:
Timor di me? Sicura, presta è la mia difesa.
Fear [of] (for) me? Sure, ready is [the] my defense.

In quest'oscura notte ravvolta, presso a te son io,
In this-dark night wrapped, near to you am I,

e tu nol sai! Gemente aura, che intorno spiri,
and you not-it know! Moaning breeze, that around blows,
(and you do not know it!)   (that blows all about,)

deh, pietosa gli arreca i miei sospiri.
ah, mercifully to-him bring [the] my sighs.

Aria:
D'amor sull'ali rosee vanne, sospir dolente,
Of-love on-the-wings rosy go, sigh mournful,
(Mournful sigh, go on the rosy wings of love,)

del prigioniero misero conforta l'egra mente
of-the prisoner wretched comfort the-ailing spirit
(comfort the ailing spirit of the wretched prisoner,)

com'aura di speranza aleggia in quella stanza,
like-(a)-breath of hope flutter into that room,

lo desta alle memorie, ai sogni dell'amor!
him wake to-the memories, to-the dreams of-[the]-love!

Ma, deh, non dirgli improvvido
But, ah, (do) not tell-him imprudently

le pene del mio cor!
the sufferings of-[the] my heart!

Verdi   DESERTO SULLA TERRA
                               (Il Trovatore)

Deserto sulla terra, col rio destino in guerra,
Lonely on-the earth, with-[the] evil destiny [in] (at) war,

è sola speme un cor,
is (the) only hope one heart,
(his only hope is in one heart,)

un cor al Trovator!
a heart [to]-(for)-the Troubadour!

Ma s'ei quel cor possiede,
But if-he that heart possesses,

bello di casta fede,
beautiful [of] (with) chaste faith,

è d'ogni re maggior... maggior il Trovator!
is than-every king greater... greater the Troubadour!
(the Troubadour is greater than any king!)

Verdi   DI QUELLA PIRA
                         (Il Trovatore)

Di quella pira l'orrendo foco
Of that pyre the-horrible fire
(The horrible fire of that pyre)

tutte le fibre m'arse, avvampò!
all the fibers to-me-burned, enflamed!
(burned and enflamed all the fibers of my being!)

Empi, spegnetela,
Inhuman-ones, extinguish-it,

o ch'io fra poco col sangue vostro la spegnerò!
or that-I shortly with-[the] blood your it will-put-out!
(or shortly I will put it out with your blood!)

Era già figlio prima d'amarti;
I-was already (her) son before ⌊of⌋-loving you;

non può frenarmi il tuo martir...
not can restrain-me [the] your suffering...
(your suffering cannot restrain me...)

Madre infelice, corro a salvarti,
Mother unhappy, I-run to save-you,

o teco almeno corro a morir!
or with-you at-least I-run to die!

538

Verdi   STRIDE LA VAMPA!
                               (Il Trovatore)

Stride la vampa! La folla indomita
Shrieks the blaze! The crowd, unrestrained,
(The blaze crackles!)

corre a quel foco, lieta in sembianza!
runs to that fire, happy in appearance!
                    (their faces happy!)

Urli di gioia intorno echeggiano;
Howls of joy around echo;
                    (echo all around;)

cinta di sgherri donna s'avanza;
surrounded [of] (by) cutthroats (the) woman comes-forward;

sinistra splende sui volti orribili la tetra fiamma
sinister shines on-the faces horrible the dull flame

che s'alza, che s'alza al ciel!
that itself-raises, that itself-raises to-the sky!
(that rises to the sky!)

Stride la vampa! Giunge la vittima nero vestita,
Shrieks the blaze! Comes the victim, black dressed,
(The blaze crackles!)

discinta e scalza,
ungirded and barefoot,

grido feroce di morte levasi;
(a) shriek ferocious of death raises-itself;
(a death shriek rises;)

l'eco il ripete di balza in balza.
the-echo it repeats from cliff [in] (to) cliff.
(the echo repeats it)

539

Verdi   TACEA LA NOTTE PLACIDA
                               Il Trovatore)

Tacea la notte placida
Was-silent the night placid
(The placid night was silent)

e bella in ciel sereno;
and beautiful in (the) sky serene;

la luna il viso argenteo mostrava lieto e pieno...
the moon [the] (his) face silvery showed happy and full...

quando suonar per l'aere, infino allor sì muto,
when sounding through the-air, until then so quiet,

dolci s'udiro e flebili
sweet [themselves]-were-heard and mournful

gli accordi d'un liuto, e versi melanconici
the harmonies of-a lute, and verses melancholy

un trovator cantò. Versi di prece, ed umile,
a troubadour sang. Verses of supplication, and humble,

qual d'uom che prega Iddio:
like (those) of-(a)-man that prays (to) God:

in quella ripeteasi un nome, il nome mio!
in that repeated-itself a name, [the] name my!
(in those verses a name was repeated, my name!)

Corsi al veron sollecita... egli era desso!
I-ran to-the terrace quickly... he it-was [himself]!

Gioia provai che agl'angeli
Joy I-experienced that [to]-the-angels

solo è provar concesso!
only is-to-experience granted!
(only are allowed to experience!)

Al core, al guardo estatico
To-[the] (my) heart, to-[the] (my) glance ecstatic

540

la terra un ciel sembrò!
the earth a heaven seemed!
(earth seemed like heaven!)

Di tale amor, che dirsi mal può dalla parola,
Of such love, that to-speak-itself poorly can from-the word,
(By such a love, that words can hardly tell,)

d'amor, che intendo io sola, il cor s'innebriò.
of-love, that know I only, the heart itself-intoxicated.
(by a love that only I know, my heart was intoxicated.)

Il mio destino compiersi non può che a lui dappresso...
[The] my destiny fulfill-itself not can but to him close-to...
(My destiny can be fulfilled only when I am near him...)

S'io non vivrò per esso, per esso morirò, ah sì.
If-I not will-live for him, for him I-will-die, ah, yes.
(If I cannot live for him.)

Fa così lodoletta che fuggì
Does thus (the) lark that fled

da crudel empio augel che l'ingannò.
from-(the) cruel wicked bird which [it-deceived].
(deceived it.)

Tutta sa di quel fier la crudeltà,
All it-knows of that fierce-one the cruelty,

ma non può non seguir quell'infedel,
but not she-can not follow that-unfaithful-one,
(she cannot stop following that unfaithful one,)

cui fedel un tempo amò.
whom faithful(ly) one time she-loved.

Sentirsi dire dal caro bene:
to-hear-to-oneself say by-the dear treasure:
(To hear one's sweet treasure say:)

ho cinto il core d'altre catene,
I-have bound [the] (my) heart with-other chains,

questo è un martire, questo è un dolore
this is a martyrdom, this is a sorrow

che un'alma fida soffrir non può.
which a-soul faithful endure not can.

Se la mia fede così l'affanna,
If [the] my faith thus her-afflicts,

perchè, tiranna, m'innamorò?
why, tyrannical-woman, me-inflamed-with-love?
(why did the tyrannical woman awaken my love?)

Si bella mercede all'opra m'invita.
So beautiful (a) reward to-the-work me-invites.

Mio bene, mia vita, fedel ti sarò
My treasure, my life, faithful to-you I-shall-be,

e i lacci del core,
and the bonds of-the heart,

o dolce mio amore, mai sciolglier saprò.
O sweet my love, never to-undo will-I-know-how.

Teco, sî, vengo anch'io
You-with, yes, come also-I
(With you, I, too, will come)

e meco viene Amor
and me-with comes love;
    (with-me)

non paventar, cor mio.
(do) not fear, heart my.

Vedovella afflitta e sola
Little-widow, grieving and alone,

ch'io passeggio in veste nera,
whom-I pass-[by] in clothing black,

oramai vicino è l'anno
at-length near(ly-over) is the-year (of mourning).

Mentre vado per le strade
While I-go through the streets

con modeste e basse ciglia
with modest and lowered eye-lashes,

sento dir: "Povera figlia!
I-hear say: "Poor [daughter] (woman)!

che gran danno, che peccato
what (a) great [loss] (shame), what (a) pity

che non abbia un uomo allato!"
that not she-has a man at-(her)-side!"

Ma frattanto il tempo vola;
But meanwhile the time flies;

passa il dì, torna la sera
passes the day, returns the evening,

e nessun rifa il mio danno.
and no-one repairs [the] my loss.

Un certo non so che
A certain [not-I-know what] (something)

mi giunge e passa il cor,
me reaches and passes-through [the] (my) heart,

e pur dolor non è.
and yet pain not it-is.

Se questo fosse amor?
If this were love?
(Could this be love?)

Nel suo vorace ardor
In-[the] its voracious ardor

già posi incauta il piè.
already I-have-placed reckless(ly) [the] (my) foot.

Filli, di gioia vuoi farmi morir
Phyllis, with joy you-want to-make-me die

ed io di pena mi sento languir.
and I with suffering myself feel languish.

Donar mi vuoi un ben che non puoi
To-give to-me you-want a treasure which not you can
(You want to give me a treasure which you cannot give)

e ch'io non posso già mai conseguir.
and which-I not can [already] never acquire.
(and which I can never make mine.)

Vivaldi　　　　　　　　INGRATA, SI MI SVENA
　　　　　　　　　　　　(Ingrata Lidia)

Ingrata, sì mi svena,
Ungrateful-one, yes, to-me open-the-veins,
(Yes, ungrateful one, cut open my veins,)

lacera sì quel core in cui lo stral d'amore
lacerate [yes] that heart in which the arrow of-love

la tua vezzosa e bella immagine scolpì.
[the] your charming and beautiful image has-carved.
(has carved your charming and beautiful image.)

O di tua man mi svena
Either with your hand to-me open-the-veins
                    (open my veins)

o con un guardo il mio morir consola,
or with a glance [the] my death console,
                    (console my death,)

po'alma senza pena
then-(the)-soul without suffering

con tal mercede, ai rai del di s'invola.
with such (a) reward, from-the rays of-[the] day departs.
                    (departs from the light of day.)

Piango, gemo, sospiro e peno,
I-weep, I-moan, I-sigh, and I-suffer,

e* la piaga rinchiusa è nel cor.
and the wound enclosed is in-[the] (my) heart.

Solo chiedo per pace del seno
Only I-ask, for peace [of-the] (in my) bosom,

che m'uccida più fiero dolor.
that me-may-kill (a) more fierce pain.
(that a more fierce pain may kill me.)

*Some texts have: o la piaga
                  oh, the wound

Pur ch'à te grata sia la mia morte,
Provided that-to you welcome would-be [the] my death,

anco tacendo godrò morir,
[yet remaining-silent] (in silence) I-shall-be-happy to-die,

se non può farsi miglior mia sorte
if not can make-itself better my fate
(if my fate cannot be better)

che per quei lumi fedel languir.
than for those [lights] (eyes) faithful(ly) to-languish.

Se cerca, se dice:
If she-seeks, if she-says:

l'amico dov'è?
[the-friend] (my beloved) where-is-he?

L'amico infelice, rispondi, morì!
[The]-(my)-lover unfortunate, reply, he-died!

Ah, no! Sì gran duolo non darle per me!
Ah, no! Such great sorrow (do) not give-her for me!

Rispondi, ma solo: piangendo partì!
Reply, but only: weeping he-left!

Che abisso di pene
What (an) abyss of suffering[s]

lasciare il suo bene,
to-leave [the] one's treasure,

lasciarlo per sempre, lasciarlo così!
to-leave-it for ever, to-leave-it thus!

Vivaldi　　　　　　　VIENI, VIENI, O MIO DILETTO

Vieni, vieni, o mio diletto,
Come, come, O my beloved,

che il mio core,* tutto affetto,
for [the] my heart, all affection,

già t'aspetta e ognor ti chiama.
already you-awaits and always you calls.
(awaits you and always calls for you.)

　*Some texts have: è tutto affetto,
　　　　　　　　　　is all affection,

Index of Titles and First Lines

558